This needs to
be skimmed
Early in course,
then studied diligently

Note in section of person that
Biblical types of person that
the psychological or real
centered are always done
by Fosdick!

**BETHEL SEMINARY WEST
LIBRARY**
6116 Arosa Street
San Diego, CA 92115-3902

D1097993

Meaning of Preaching II - 1, 2.

Hermeneutics - 3, 10 (p 237-248)

Remainder w. Sermon itself...

A QUEST FOR
REFORMATION IN PREACHING

A Quest For Reformation in Preaching

by H. C. BROWN, JR.

WORD BOOKS, Publishers
Waco, Texas—London, England

Copyright © 1968
WORD BOOKS, WACO, TEXAS
All Rights Reserved

Library of Congress Catalog Card Number: 67-26938

Grateful acknowledgment is made to the following for permission to use copyright material:

THE DIVISION OF CHRISTIAN EDUCATION OF THE NATIONAL COUNCIL OF THE CHURCHES OF CHRIST
Quotations from The Revised Standard Version of the Bible, copyright © 1946 and 1952.

CAMBRIDGE UNIVERSITY PRESS
Quotations from *The New English Bible, New Testament,* © The Delegates of the Oxford University Press and the Syndics of the Cambridge University Press, 1961. Used by permission.

HARPER AND ROW PUBLISHERS, INC.
Selections from *Riverside Sermons* by Harry Emerson Fosdick. Copyright © 1958.

HARPER AND ROW PUBLISHERS, INC.
Selections from *The Waiting Father* by Helmut Thielicke. Copyright © 1959, John W. Doberstein.

HARPER AND ROW PUBLISHERS, INC.
Selections from *Deliverance to the Captives* by Karl Barth. Copyright © 1961, Student Christian Movement Press.

HARPER AND ROW PUBLISHERS, INC.
Selections from *Favorite Sermons of John A. Broadus,* V. L. Stanfield, Copyright © 1959.

FLEMING H. REVELL COMPANY
Selections from *The Westminster Pulpit* by G. Campbell Morgan.

WILLIAM B. EERDMANS PUBLISHING COMPANY
Selections from *Studies in the Sermon on the Mount,* Vol. 21, by D. Martyn Lloyd Jones. Used by permission.

BROADMAN PRESS
Selections from *Southwestern Sermons* and *More Southern Baptist Preaching,* edited by H. C. Brown, Jr.

Printed in U.S.A.

Dedication

to
G. EARL GUINN
and
H. H. HOBBS

Preface

Nothing is so powerful as an idea whose time has come!
And the time has come for reformation in preaching!
The state of preaching in the last one-third of the twentieth century cries out for reformation. Not novel change or superficial innovation but genuine transforming reformation is needed today in preaching. The conditions demanding reformation in preaching are analyzed in chapters one and two.

How can reformation come to preaching? Reformation can come to preaching through the will of God, through the spiritual fitness of ministers, through the spiritual hunger of God's people, and through the homiletical or preaching fitness of the men in the ministry. All four of these are indispensable for a complete and soul-satisfying reformation. The first three, although of utmost importance, are beyond the scope of this volume. The fourth, homiletical fitness, embraces five convictions which, if understood and practiced by preachers, will aid the quest for reformation of preaching.

First, homiletical fitness which will assist the reformation of preaching may be achieved by a correct understanding of the true scope of preaching. For centuries homiletics or preaching has been viewed by most ministers as a one-dimensional discipline, i.e., as a discipline of rhetoric. True homiletics involves much more than rhetoric in that it consists of the correct use of Biblical content, hermeneutical principles, theological perspectives, psychological orientation, rhetorical rules and oratorical principles. When preachers see the magnificent scope of the craft of their calling, they will pursue the task of preaching with renewed dedication and zeal. The true sixfold scope of preaching is set out in chapter two.

Second, homiletical fitness which will assist the reformation of preaching may be obtained by an understanding of the true nature of the text of the sermon as the fabric of the sermon. False views of Scripture as text exist by the score. When preachers recover an understanding and practice of Scripture as text—as the fabric of the sermon —and when they learn to manage that text in a number of complex sermonic situations, they will assist the reformation of preaching. The correct management of Scripture for sermonic use is set out in chapter three.

Third, homiletical fitness which will assist the reformation of preaching may be achieved by a correct understanding and use of the functional elements of preaching. These functional elements of preaching— explanation, application, and argument—provide the preacher with superb instruments for securing strong content in his sermons. The functional elements of preaching are defined in chapter four.

Fourth, homiletical fitness which will assist the reformation of preaching may be secured by a correct understanding of the authentic nature of a sermon. For centuries, ministers have viewed sermons in terms of form—as expository, textual, and topical sermons—and have thereby severely limited the discipline of preaching. Authentic sermons must be understood in terms of authority, purpose, and form. The true nature of a sermon is set out in brief terms in chapter two and is further defined and illustrated in chapters five through nine. Moreover, the sermons used in chapters five through nine to illustrate authentic sermons are analyzed according to their uses of the three functional elements of preaching.

Fifth, homiletical fitness which will assist the reformation of preaching may be obtained by a correct use of practical procedures for the preparation of authentic Biblical sermons. These practical procedures involve the correct use of the basic sermon items prepared in a correct chronological order. A true chronology for the preparation of Biblical sermons is set out in chapter ten.

The understanding of, belief in, and practice of the sixfold scope of preaching, the text as the fabric of the sermon, the three functional elements of preaching, the three-dimensional nature of authentic Biblical sermons, and the correct chronology for the preparation of Biblical sermons will enable a minister to be homiletically competent and to engage in a genuine quest for reformation in preaching.

And the time has come for reformation in preaching!

Acknowledgments

Sincere appreciation is expressed to Dr. Robert E. Naylor, President of Southwestern Baptist Theological Seminary, and to Dr. Jesse J. Northcutt, Dean of the School of Theology of Southwestern Seminary, for granting to me a leave in the fall of 1964 and the summer of 1965 during which time a considerable part of this book was prepared.

Moreover, gratitude is expressed to my colleagues of the faculty— C. W. Brister, Carl Clark, Gordon Clinard, Milton Ferguson, Virtus Gideon, Curtis Vaughan, and Yandall Woodfin—for proofreading assistance, discerning suggestions, and stimulating dialogue.

To those graduate students in preaching seminars during the years of 1962-67, I extend my most sincere appreciation. Many hours of creative research and stimulating dialogue with these dedicated and earnest students of preaching did much to shape the views presented in this book.

Without adequate secretarial help this book would have been seriously delayed. Therefore, I wish to thank Mrs. Barron Harris, secretary during the fall of 1964, Mrs. Lynda Leech, secretary during the 1965-66 school year, and Mrs. Sue Ramey, secretary during the summer of 1965, for effective secretarial assistance.

Contents

Part II

Part I
THE NEED FOR REFORMATION IN PREACHING

Chapter 1

THE POVERTY OF PREACHING CONTENT

A poignant phrase rang around the world in the late 1930's and early 1940's: "Too little and too late!"

It described the paucity of the free world's courage, creative leadership, combat men, and materials. The phrase briefly and graphically depicted the free world's shortage of those things needed for victory in the fight against tyranny.

In Czechoslovakia and Austria in 1938 it was "too little and too late!"

In Poland in 1939 it was "too little and too late!"

In France, Belgium, and Holland in 1940 it was "too little and too late!"

At Pearl Harbor on December 7, 1941, it was "too little and too late!"

In the Philippines in the spring of 1942 it was "too little and too late!"

William S. White captured in graphic words one sad result of the free world's "too little and too late" stance when he wrote *They Were Expendable* in the midst of World War II. This dramatic story of the motor torpedo fleet in the Philippines recounted the incredibly brave fight waged by the PT men and boats against the might of the Japanese Navy. In the end, Bataan and Corregidor fell; MacArthur retreated to Australia; and the men and boats of the tiny fleet "were expendable!"

"Too little and too late!"

Is not this phrase descriptive of preaching content in the late twentieth century? Is not today's pulpit characterized by a pathetic poverty of content? Is this phrase not descriptive of those things needed for spiritual victories in preaching? Yes. Without a doubt modern preaching presents a clear and tragic picture of "too little!" Only God knows if it is yet too late!

Why should this condition exist now? Are we living in another Dark Age? Are there world conditions which have poisoned the minds of the modern ministry so that contemporary preachers can only produce inferior content? The last two questions must be answered negatively. There is nothing inherently wrong with the modern world which has not been wrong with it before. In similar periods in the past, strong preachers have risen to the occasion to proclaim rich content for their poverty-stricken hour. What, then, is wrong now? Why do we have so much poor preaching from Protestant pulpits?

The reason is that Protestant ministers hold inadequate and inferior concepts about the ministry in general and preaching in particular. These inadequate and inferior concepts make impossible the task of creative preaching. Men holding such views have been presenting cheap and shoddy content to starving congregations! For as long as preachers hold to these distortions about the ministry and preaching they will continue to produce sermons deficient in content.

DISTORTED ATTITUDES TOWARD THE MINISTRY

What, then, are the distorted attitudes which many Protestant ministers hold about the ministry?

The Pulpit Coach

There is first of all the pulpit coach. These ministers are the Knute Rocknes and Amos Alonzo Staggs of the pulpit. Their creed is action. Their motto is phrased in English which matches their preaching content: "Them preachers who ain't meeting ain't doin' nothin' much!" Their patron saint is the comedian who said, "The government builds roads and church folks wear them out going to meetings!"

In his weekly bulletin, one pulpit coach complained about, yet gloried in, his restless round of activities:

> When I am late for a dinner engagement my wife raises an eyebrow and sternly demands, "Why are you late this time?" So, in order to defend myself, last week I kept a careful record of my activities: I put in 95 hours work, spoke 16 times, attended 8 banquets and luncheons, visited 67 people in hospitals and homes, counseled with 27 other people, met with 7 committees, wrote 7 letters of recommendation for preachers seeking better places of

service, calmed 9 angry church members, held 96 telephone conversations, and in between times drank 37 cups of coffee and 3 Cokes![1]

This is the pulpit coach in action.

In this true to life yet all but unbelievable report of one pastor's work week, no mention is made in the record of Bible study, reading, prayer, or sermon preparation. Activities! Activities are all one can see splashed across the face of this church bulletin report of the pulpit coach.

The pulpit coach calls for total commitment from his people, but he himself does not give it. He spends one to two hours on a sermon, preaches for thirty minutes to one thousand people—using five hundred hours of his people's time—and loudly calls for total commitment from the people. Total commitment from the people, but not from the preacher! What kind of mentality is it which will allow an otherwise alert and spiritual man to exchange two hours for five hundred and to believe that he can demand unconditional dedication without also giving it? It is the mentality which sees self as the pulpit coach! The coach plans, directs, and exhorts, but he himself never enters the arena of conflict. For football and baseball this arrangement works well, but not for the ministry.

Pierce Harris described this modern minister in these terms:

> The modern preacher has to make as many visits as a country doctor, shake as many hands as a politician, prepare as many briefs as a lawyer, see as many people as a specialist. He has to be as good an executive as the president of a university, and as good a financier as a bank president, and in the midst of it all, he has to be so good a diplomat that he could umpire a baseball game between the Knights of Columbus and the Ku Klux Klan.[2]

The pulpit coach!

The Gospel Falsifier

There is in the second place the gospel falsifier. The willful heretic who corrupts the Christian gospel is an almost nonexistent character, but the man who through ignorance, carelessness, or confusion preaches a distorted and perverted gospel is readily found in the evangelical pulpits of our land. A young minister prepared an evangelistic or gospel sermon which he called "The Four Greatest Sins!" The sermon set out these sins as the dance hall, the beer halls, the roadhouse, and the honky-tonk! When it was suggested to the young preacher that these

---

[1]A paraphrase of one paragraph from a local church bulletin.
[2]Used by permission of Pierce Harris. From an article in *The Atlanta Journal.*

items were not four separate things but several variations of the same thing, that they were not the greatest sins, and that they certainly did not present the gospel, he was indignant. His first remark addressed to the one with whom he was talking was, "What's the matter with you? Aren't you opposed to whiskey?" The type of mind which insists on calling anything and everything gospel content is rather closed in its approach to Biblical evidence. This is the type of mind which produces the gospel falsifier.

The gospel is not just any truth. It is not even just any truth with which one agrees. Neither is it truth loudly proclaimed, nor even "hell-fire-and-brimstone" truth dogmatically uttered from the pulpit. And finally, gospel truth is not even just any Biblical truth.

What, then, is gospel truth? God, through Paul, said, "It was God's good pleasure through the foolishness of the preaching to save them that believe" (1 Cor. 1:21b, ASV). The Apostle Paul did not proclaim that preaching saved those who believed, but he said that *the thing preached* saved them. *The thing preached* was the *kerygma*—the gospel. 1 Corinthians 1:21b means, "it was God's good pleasure through the foolishness of kerygmatic preaching, gospel preaching, to save them that believe."

The New Testament makes a distinction between *kerygma*, the gospel which saves, and *didache*, the teaching which edifies. At times the kerygmatic content was preached to Christians for their comfort and strength as well as to motivate for service. When gospel content was preached to Christians, it became *didache*. However, it was the good news about salvation through the Lord Jesus Christ, when proclaimed to non-Christians, which was called gospel. It is this *kerygma* or gospel which, when preached, becomes the kerygmatic act.

The gospel falsifier ignores an abundance of Biblical data and sets forth week by week personal doctrine which he calls gospel preaching.

The gospel falsifier!

The Clown Prince of the Pulpit

There is in the third place the clown prince of the pulpit. The idols of this man are the current television, stage, movie, and radio comedians. His motto, borrowed from show business, is "Leave 'em laughing!"

Though the clown prince of the pulpit knows that humor is a delightful speech procedure to be dispensed as seasoning is for food, he is so addicted to the laughter and applause of the people that he constantly overuses it. Rather than sprinkling a little salt on steak, he sprinkles hamburger meat on blocks of salt. He has misused a powerful tool to such an extent that it has become a junior-sized monster in his hands.

Everything in a sermon is viewed as a means for bringing a smile to a tired face or a chuckle to a depressed parishioner. The minister, burdened himself by the crushing problems of the atomic-hydrogen-space age, seeks to alleviate gloom among his people by his preaching. He knows the load of care resting upon his congregation and notices that they enjoy a delightfully humorous story. Therefore, he turns from prophetic preaching to entertaining preaching. He becomes a clown prince by slow degrees. The change from prophet to clown prince is so gradual that the minister is not aware that he now models his messages after nightclub comics rather than after the crucified and resurrected Lord.

In a central Texas resort city, a depressed woman attended services her first Sunday in town in the hope that she would receive spiritual strength to aid in the fight to recover her health. On the Sunday morning of her visit, the preacher chose to entertain the audience for twenty-five minutes. He then attempted to preach for about five minutes. The lady returned to her hotel room, threw herself across the bed, wept copiously, and thought seriously about suicide. Ill in body and mind, she had desperately sought spiritual sustenance and had been given a comic performance. What a tragic way for that preacher to have spent his time before God and the people!

The clown prince of the pulpit!

The Madison Avenue Con Artist

There is in the fourth place the Madison Avenue con artist. The idols of this man are the public relations expert and the Hollywood press agent. His technique is to be as flashy as possible, but he attempts never to administer fatal shock. His strong ministerial virtue, he thinks, is his flair for flashy sermon titles. He attempts to use attractive and appealing titles, but these usually degenerate to trite, vulgar, suggestive, and sensational names. He argues that people "do come out" to hear him, and he claims that the end justifies the means. He has used the technique for so long that his "taste buds" are destroyed, and he can no longer separate the fresh and interesting title from the cheap and sensational one.

Observe the Madison Avenue con artist's approach by noting his use of sensational titles. He preaches on the triumphal entry of Christ into Jerusalem and focuses attention on the little donkey on which Christ rode. He calls his sermon "The Lowly Jackass!" What an incredible perspective! The Son of God, the Lord of all creation, was soon to be crucified, and this preacher talks about a donkey. The preacher was attempting to say that as that little donkey served Christ, so should the congregation. This is a simple and harmless comparison if it is left as a simple comparison. But what kind of mentality does it take to transfer the focus from Jesus Christ to the donkey and to preach about "The Lowly Jackass!"

Again, observe the Madison Avenue con artist as he attempts to speak teen talk and calls his sermon on the cross "Dead Man on a Stick!" A cheap use of words, is it not? Moreover, this attitude leads even to the use of old and ancient titles which have been "knocking about" for decades and in some cases for centuries. An audience will surely cringe when told that they are about to hear another sermon on "Seven Ducks in a Muddy Pond," or "The Heavyweight Champion Who Lost His Title," or "The Preacher Who Lost His Head at a Dance," or "Beds Too Short and Covers Too Narrow!" Thousands of these cheap and sensational titles exist and do constant sermonic harm to Protestant congregations.

The Madison Avenue con artist!

The Psychological Pump-Primer

The idols of this man are the latest "fad-leaders" in psychologically oriented sermons. This pious piddling pulpiteer peddles psychological pep pills for pale and puny people. He does so in the hope that his folks will every day in every way be better and better. He sincerely hopes that his sermons, filled with psychiatric jargon, will scare away the upcoming "blue Monday," tension headaches, acid indigestion, family quarrels, and feeble Friday.

Inevitably the psychological pump-primer treats symptoms rather than causes. He tries to administer comfort when forgiveness is the need of sinful hearts. He attempts to inspire and to uplift with encouraging words, but the man mired in sin is so heavily laden that he cannot respond. The cheap use of psychological truth will always be insufficient. When the body is tortured by cancer, psychological pep talks have about as much effect as two aspirin and a soda pop.

The psychological pump-primer!

Not only do numbers of modern ministers despise and depreciate the preaching role in the ministry, they disdain the discipline of homiletics. Therefore, one must ask if poor preaching mechanics, or poor preaching tools, can contribute to poor preaching content. They can contribute, they have contributed, they do contribute, and they will continue to contribute to poor preaching content unless authentic reformation comes to preaching. That there are an abundance of poor preaching procedures—homiletic tools—in use in the Protestant pulpits of America is known to most observers of the current pulpit.

Why should this condition exist? Are there no effective tools available for the modern preacher? Are there homiletical secrets which only selected men can know and utilize to produce quality sermons? Are there clues shut up to one nation, or to one denomination, or to men of one theological persuasion, or to one particular century? All three questions must be answered negatively. It is true that the pulpit of Germany in the sixteenth century ranks high in the history of preaching. Likewise, the great French Catholic preachers in the seventeenth century, the British preachers in the seventeenth and nineteenth centuries, and the strong American preachers of the nineteenth century rank with the great proclaimers of the ages. These nations and periods embraced several denominations, numerous theological viewpoints, and, of course, four nations and three centuries.

There are probably no great homiletical secrets, or clues, or formulas lost in the archives of Germany, France, England, America, or any other nation, which would reform preaching were they brought to light. The histories of preaching in these nations are known in considerable detail. *The scarcity of effective preaching procedures—tools for sermonic craftsmanship—exists because preachers have not availed themselves of the known resources of the craft of preaching. Each generation and each man in his generation must exert himself in order to fashion and use for himself the proved creative rules and principles of preaching. No man can be given a ready-made homiletical tool chest any more than he can be given a ready-made predigested theological system. Preaching procedures are poor in the main because preachers simply have not taken the time and energy to master them.*

That such a condition prevails taxes one's mind to believe. Yet the facts are that the condition does exist to a serious degree.

DISTORTED ATTITUDES TOWARD HOMILETICS

Early and Easy Success in Preaching

Many preachers are poor sermonic craftsmen because of early and easy success in preaching. The people who fill the pews of Protestant churches tend to be gracious, gentle, and kind to young ministers. Many, in fact, go so far as to praise to the skies the early efforts of young preachers. If these young men have even an average amount of platform presence and oratorical skill—and most of them do—they are compared favorably with Spurgeon, Beecher, Wesley, and even Luther and Calvin. Tragically, many of these young ministers fail to recognize these generous and gracious remarks for what they are—sincere efforts to encourage and to build confidence for a hard and unknown future.

When a young man accepts these compliments as proof that he does not need to study how to preach—and countless numbers do—the only result can be that another minister has entered his work with a deep indifference to the craft of his calling. Another preacher enters the ministry seriously handicapped. He will suffer this self-imposed handicap until he experiences a genuine homiletical reformation. Apart from a complete reformation of attitude and practice, this minister will almost surely never learn to preach. He will never learn to preach because he will never believe that he needs to *learn* to preach.

A False Conception of God's Call and Gifts

Again, many preachers are poor sermonic craftsmen because of a misunderstanding of God's call and gifts. It is not a joke, although usually treated as one, that preachers actually believe that God instantaneously will inspire their hearts and fill their mouths with powerful words for the preaching hour. Preachers believe that God does this as a matter of obligation since he was the moving force in their call. Though this misconception is based on faulty Biblical interpretation, the view that God will provide all words for preaching has been preached and repeated so often that with some men it has taken on the force of divine law. When a young preacher begins his preaching ministry with this particular theological persuasion, he not only believes that homiletics is worthless, he also believes that the study of homiletics constitutes a lack of faith and is an affront to the God who called him. This man will never learn to preach because he believes that God will preach through him.

A Simple Lack of Knowledge

Many preachers are poor sermonic craftsmen because of a lack of knowledge. One would believe that all men could see the relationship between the tools of a trade and the successful practice of that trade. Such an obvious connection, however, between homiletics and successful preaching has escaped notice by many Protestant preachers. These preachers show this lack of knowledge by using trite and crude jokes about sermons being "three points and a poem," and by casting aspersions upon homiletics in numerous ways. Loud and vociferous "amens" can be elicited from assemblies and conventions by the pulpit orator who ridicules and makes light of the craft of preaching.

While it is true that some systems of homiletics are rather superficial and shallow and should be recognized as such, a distinction should be made between such systems and the good ones which work. All homiletical rules, principles, and systems are not on the same quality level. The same thing may be said, of course, for systems of theology.

An intelligent minister is able to discern easily that a carpenter can take his tools and build dog houses for canines, or palaces for kings, or that he can construct cribs for corn, or castles for crowned queens. A preacher can see the varied results of carpentry with the greatest of ease. Yet because of a gap in knowledge, an intellectual deficiency of some sort, about the connection between the use of creative homiletic tools and the construction of effective sermons, some preachers fail to understand the need for sermonic tools. A man with this attitude will never learn to preach because he doesn't know that homiletics is worthwhile and that it can be learned.

Personal Laziness

Many preachers are poor sermonic craftsmen because of personal laziness. Frankly, the task of sitting at a desk, of reading technical volumes, of wrestling with the true meaning of a Scripture verse, of finding the eternal truth of Scripture, and of writing sermon manuscripts constitutes hard, tedious, and difficult work. Some men, therefore, say that this type of labor does not appeal to them. This is very likely true. Hard work seldom appeals to certain men. It is more enjoyable to visit the saints, to comfort the afflicted, and even to afflict the comfortable than it is to perform difficult mental labor.

However hard the task may be, if the task is essential it must be done. And preaching is a work which must be done by ministers. Most ministers, however, could reduce the work load in sermon preparation considerably if they would but learn to prepare sermons correctly. In the meantime, while engaged in the work of studying homiletics, the preacher should pursue the task of sermon preparation to the best of his ability. How sad it sounds to hear a minister complain that sermon preparation is hard! How pathetically similar his excuse is to those given to him when he exhorts his people to serve God! Laziness, whether found in pew or pulpit, is a most unattractive trait. The lazy preacher will never learn to preach because he is lazy.

A Disdain for the Mechanical

Many preachers are poor sermonic craftsmen because of a disdain for the mechanical. Can spiritual things be analyzed, dissected, understood, arranged, polished, and preached? Can people actually hear God speak through sermonic processes? The answers ought to be obvious because both are affirmative. Yet, so many preachers claim that mechanical studies destroy spiritual issues that one must be alert to keep from being taken in by the criticism. Of course, God can speak through a sermon—through preaching! And of course, spiritual truth can be analyzed, dissected, understood, arranged, polished, and preached!

All that the preacher who disdains mechanics has to do is to read the Old Testament, the New Testament, Christian history, the history of preaching, or the creative preachers of this hour, and he will see evidence that God has continued, is continuing, and will continue to speak through men who dare to structure spiritual sustenance for the souls of saints and sinners. There is no irreparable breach between the spiritual and mechanical in homiletics.

It is true, however, that a great host of Protestant preachers are simply indifferent to the challenge of learning the tools of their trade, homiletics. When one compares this ministerial attitude to that of professional athletes, the minister comes off a poor second. Professional football, basketball, and baseball players work diligently for years mastering plays, principles, and procedures of their chosen sport in order to star or even to make the team. A professional golfer will hit practice shots by the thousands so that in tournament play, on a given shot, he can say to himself, "I have successfully executed this shot thousands of times and I can do it again!" Wherefore, he proceeds to hit it again successfully.

During the 1940's a seriousness of purpose that resulted in hard dedicated practicing came into professional sports in America. All athletes who desired to succeed had to measure up to the new standards. An occasional playboy still makes good in professional sports, but he is the exception. By and large, the stars of all major professional sports are those men and women who pay the stern price in discipline and dedication in order to be skilled in the tools of their profession.

Again, compare the indifferent attitude of the preacher toward homiletics with the possible indifference of a surgeon toward surgical skills or a pilot toward flying skills. How many would risk serious surgery at the hands of a doctor known to depreciate the correct use of proper instruments and techniques in the operating room? No one! Or, how many people would risk a flight with a pilot known to disregard basic rules of flying because he was too indifferent to master them? Again, no one! Or, more to the point, can any one really imagine that a surgeon or a pilot would be amiss in mastering the skills of his work? Not really. It is incredible that indifference should exist in the ministry concerning homiletics, but it does. The indifferent minister will never learn to preach because he will never really try to learn.

When Adolf Hitler stood at the English Channel in June, 1940, he vowed to walk the streets of London in a matter of weeks. The British Empire stood tottering on the verge of imminent collapse. Only the incomparable courage and staunch defiance of Winston Churchill and the British people saved England and the free world. These noble people recognized the need of their hour, and they met that need.

Today the status of preaching in regard to content is just as serious as was the plight of England in June, 1940. May God grant us the wisdom and courage to do for our hour what Churchill and England did for theirs!

> God of grace and God of glory,
> On Thy people pour Thy power;
> Crown Thine ancient church's story,
> Bring her bud to glorious flower.
> Grant us wisdom, Grant us courage,
> For the facing of this hour.
>
> For the facing of this hour.
> Set our feet on lofty places;
> Gird our lives that they may be
> Armored with all Christ-like graces
> In the fight to set men free.
> Grant us wisdom, Grant us courage,
> That we fail not man nor Thee!
> That we fail not man nor Thee![3]

---

[3]Used by permission of Harry Emerson Fosdick.

Chapter 2

THE PROBLEMS OF PREACHING PRINCIPLES

Modern homiletics has failed to clarify two basic questions: the first, "What is preaching?" and the second, "What is a sermon?" Do not miss the meaning of the first sentence. It does not state that modern homiletics has failed to *define* these two important questions. It says that however modern homiletics has defined "preaching" and "sermons," modern homiletics has failed to clarify these two fundamental ideas.

Historically, homileticians have, at various times, focused attention on three areas of study: form, content, and style. The Protestant preacher reads one homiletic volume whose emphasis seems to be: "Master mechanical methods, and you will have the meat of homiletics!" He reads a second book and perceives that the author believes in content as the important factor. And he reads another volume and understands that it is neither form nor content but style which must be mastered. This problem reminds the preacher of a person shopping for food and trying to decide what to buy according to packaging, contents, or cost, but not for all three in the same product. But when one makes a purchase he does get all three, does he not? And in preaching, form, content, and style are all necessary and important, are they not?

The possibility is very real that this divided emphasis in homiletics has caused the failures in communications concerning the basic principles of preaching. Because a little of everything has been emphasized, not many things specifically have been made clear. As a consequence, the ministry has suffered because of confusion concerning the fundamental principles of preaching.

THE PROBLEM OF THE SCOPE OF PREACHING

Preachers and homileticians have been satisfied, it seems, to allow preaching to limp along as a one-dimensional discipline. Many definitions of preaching have, in fact, focused attention on the one dimension of rhetoric or form. When preachers have discussed preaching, the discussions inevitably have taken the turn of emphasizing sermon points. When laymen have heard countless times the refrain from pulpits of "first," "second," and third," they have concluded that these carefully enumerated points were the important elements of the message. While homileticians, writers, and ministers have not deliberately distorted the definition of preaching, they have nonetheless presented a view of preaching which has been corrupted and largely one-dimensional. Whatever homileticians, teachers, writers, and ministers have intended to say preaching was and is, the message which has been communicated is that "preaching is the correct use of form for proclamation." The accent has fallen loud and clear on the view that rhetoric or form is the chief element in preaching.

Preaching never has been, is not now, and never will be a one-dimensional emphasis on rhetoric or form. Actually, preaching cannot be limited to one facet or dimension no matter how it may be abused and corrupted. By the nature of its birth and Biblical life, by the nature of the demands placed upon it, preaching must always be multidimensional. It can be mutilated so that the picture is lost, but it must be multidimensional because of its birth and nature.

God spoke to prophets and apostles, caused them to know and understand His message, moved them to preach that message to Israel and to the young church, and caused them to record that message for future use. A vast amount of Scripture, both in the Old Testament and in the New Testament, was first presented in oratorical sermonic form, and it must therefore be understood in such terms. The minister's task in preaching is to take up God's revealed written word and explain and apply it to God's people.

The demands made upon preaching force one to ask: "How could such a task be limited to the correct use of rhetoric?" "How could the proper principles of grammar in sermons exhaust the meaning of preaching?" It is incredible that any minister, teacher, writer, or layman has ever conceived of preaching in merely rhetorical or formal terms. It is absolutely incredible!

If preaching never has been, is not, and never can be a discipline with one facet, what are its facets or true dimensions? The answer constitutes the first great principle of preaching. *Preaching is the use of the Bible for sermons which are hermeneutically accurate, theologically oriented, psychologically directed, rhetorically structured, and orally communicated to the audience by a God-called minister led by the Holy Spirit.* Preaching cannot be understood by any definition which fails to include all six enumerated facets and disciplines. Reformation in preaching will be aided immeasurably when writers, teachers, and ministers correctly identify that the content of preaching is the *Bible,* that the chief tool of preaching is *hermeneutics* or the study of principles of interpretation, that the perspective of preaching is *theology,* that the approach of preaching is *audience psychology,* that the structure of preaching is *rhetoric,* and that the expression of preaching is *oratory* or oral speech. Moreover, this process involves a God-called minister who follows the promptings of the Holy Spirit. Preaching is nothing less than all these disciplines correlated and subjugated to the minister's use in sermon preparation. A professor in a university or seminary may be able to isolate himself with one of these six great disciplines as an area of interest and study, but a preacher can never do so. A preacher must unify, master, and utilize all six disciplines both at his desk and in his pulpit. Moreover, he may also freely use the disciplines of history, science, literature, philosophy, ethics, archaeology, and others as he brings illumination and insight to his sermons. All the theological disciplines stand available to serve the man who understands preaching, and who dares to speak for God. Until ministers learn to understand preaching in terms of its Biblical origin and to understand the vast demands made upon it by its true nature, they will be willing for it to limp along as a one-dimensional discipline. But when preachers do grasp the meaning of the Biblical origin of preaching and the nature of the vast demands placed upon it by its nature, they will be caught up in the reformation of preaching. The hour has come for reformation in preaching!

THE PROBLEM OF THE NATURE OF AUTHENTIC SERMONS

Modern homileticians have not only failed to define the scope of preaching correctly, but they have also failed to clarify the meaning of a sermon or sermons. For most of the history of homiletics, ministers have attempted to define sermons in some such terms as expository, textual, and topical. Vast confusion has surrounded these three ancient terms and others in common use until they now mean all things to all ministers. In seeking reformation in preaching, the true nature of sermons, the second great principle of preaching, should be spelled out. *A careful study of published messages reveals that authentic sermons must be described by no less than three categories: authority, purpose, and form. These three are the indispensable elements in an authentic definition of sermons because authority is the ultimate question in religion, because purpose or intention must be known about a text before that Scripture can be understood, and because without form there is no communication.*

How, then, are authority, purpose, and form related to authentic sermons? What is the nature of authority, purpose, and form as they reveal the character of authentic sermons?

Authorative Biblical Content

Authentic sermons contain authoritative Biblical content. Since the basic question in homiletics, as well as in theology, Biblical studies, philosophy, and ethics, is the question of authority, one must look to the principles of authority to supply the first portion of a systematic threefold pattern which will adequately describe authentic Biblical sermons.[1]

General principles of authority. Authority is that which guides or controls. Specifically, authority is the person, law, custom, principle, institution, or instrument which has the right or ability to guide and control others.

Authority should be distinguished from force. Force and authority, though often united in a pattern of harmony, are not always unified. The state or government, by law, has authority as well as force to command that the authority be obeyed. The state has authority and force to collect taxes, to raise an army, and to control criminals. On the other hand, an army general with great authority may be deposed by junior officers because they hold the allegiance of the men in the ranks. The general, then, has authority but no actual force or power.

Six major categories of authority are usually recognized.[2] Imperial authority is the power to rule, to reign, to control, and to direct. Imperial power belongs to kings, queens, generals, principals, and presidents and is obtained by inheritance, election, force, custom, or tradition. Delegated authority—an extension of imperial authority— belongs to army officers of the lower rank, to policemen, to school teachers, and to committees. Stipulative authority is the authority set out by definite agreement or by stipulation. Civic, social, and religious

---

[1]See Herbert H. Farmer, "The Bible: Its Significance and Authority," *The Interpreter's Bible* (New York: Abingdon-Cokesbury Press, 1952), I, 3-31; Bernard Ramm, *The Pattern of Religious Authority* (Grand Rapids: Wm. B. Eerdman Publishing Co., 1959); and P. T. Forsyth, *The Principles of Authority* (2d ed.; London: Independent Press, Ltd., 1952).

[2]Ramm, *op, cit.,* pp. 10-13.

organizations set out constitutions and bylaws and agree or stipulate that these are binding or authoritative for their organizations. Veracious authority, the authority of truth, belongs to knowledgeable men, truthful books, and valid principles. These either directly possess truth or are qualified in leading others to the discovery of truth. Functional authority, a subdivision of veracious authority, is also called substitutional authority. In the classroom young pupils, while in the process of seeking truth, learn to accept the authority of the teacher. The authority of custom belongs to certain customs, ideas, procedures, and principles which have been acquired over a period of time through general popular acceptance or approval. Often the origin as well as the original meaning of the custom has been lost.

Only in the presence of true authority can there be true freedom. The absence of authority in the state produces tyranny while the absence of authority in education produces ignorance through a lack of learning. The absence of authority in personal conduct produces disgusting and revolting license. The absence of true authority in religion produces unbridled subjectivism on the one hand and authoritarianism, unlawful uses of authority, on the other. Authority obviously commends itself to sensible men.

The acceptance of authority and the grounds for authority must not be confused. Imperial authority and veracious authority exist whether or not a particular person accepts them. It is true, however, that for any authority to be beneficial for a particular person, that person must personally accept the authority. The criminal in the alley does not void the true authority of the policeman on the corner because he rebels against police authority. The policeman on the corner, rather than being a help and blessing to the criminal, uses his authority, augmented with force, for the apprehension and incarceration of the criminal.

General principles of religious authority. The basic questions concerning religious authority are "How is religious authority determined?" "By whom or by what is religious authority determined?" The answers given are many: by God, the Roman Catholic Church, tradition, the councils and creeds of Christianity, the Bible, the state, man's best judgment and clearest reasoning, congregational action, personal experience, or by some combination of these.

The creative genius of the mind of Augustine wrestled with this problem as with others. Step by step and line by line Augustine was led by the momentum of his own inward experience and thought to see that *revelation* and *authority* were correlates. The answer to his question, How does God express His authority?, is precisely this: *By divine self-revelation.*[3]

This authority principle of God in sacrificial self-revelation evidences five merits:[4] (1) Subjectivism is avoided because data about God originates with God, and obviously, therefore, outside of man with his finite intellect. (2) Authoritarianism is avoided because this self-revelation is a revelation of grace and truth. (3) Exclusive reliance on a written authority is avoided because God's revelation is recognized as broader than and older than just written authority. There have been two periods of sacred history during which the basic authority could not possibly have been a written authority: the period of beginning from Adam to Moses; and the period of the early days of Christianity when the remembered oral words and the remembered deeds of Jesus, before they were written down, controlled the young faith. Even though the young church had the Old Testament, it was controlled by the words and deeds of Jesus. (4) The finite's sitting in the place of the infinite is avoided because this authority is grounded in God's self-disclosure. Tillich's view of the Protestant principle supports this view:

> The Protestant principle contains the divine and human protest against any absolute claim made for a relative reality, even if this claim is made by a Protestant church. The Protestant principle is the judge of every religious and cultural reality, including the religion and culture which calls itself Protestant. . . . It is the guardian against all the attempts of the finite and conditional in thinking and acting. It is the prophetic judgment against religious pride, ecclesiastical arrogance, and secular self-sufficiency and their destructive consequences.[5]

The subjective principles of liberals, the authoritarian principles of the Roman Catholics, and the dogmatic principles of extreme fundamentalism are three examples of how men allow the finite to sit in the place of the infinite. (5) The impersonal acting as authority is avoided because divine self-revelation is personal authority. The final authority resides in God Himself.

Authority, therefore, resides in God who revealed Himself in a personal sacrificial self-disclosure. How, then, is this authority related to man?

God chose to delegate His authority. It is only through this delegation of God's authority that Christians have been able to know Him,

---

[3]*Ibid.*, p. 19.
[4]*Ibid.*, pp. 21-26.
[5]Paul Tillich, *The Protestant Era* (Chicago: University of Chicago Press, 1948), p. 163.

to have authoritative data for witnessing, and to have the guidance of the Holy Spirit in understanding and explaining Scripture. Revelation did not come to nations or even to the nation Israel. Revelation did not come to the church. Revelation came to selected persons, and they in turn conveyed the revelation to Israel and to the church and ultimately put the revelation into writing.

Because the prophet spoke the revealed word, he spoke with authority. Let no one assume that the prophet possessed authority in himself or in his words and deeds. Only to the degree that he spoke the revealed word did he possess authority. To disobey the prophet when he spoke the revealed word was to disobey God. Simon Peter interpreted this when he said, "For it was not through any human whim that men prophesied of old; men they were, but impelled by the Holy Spirit, they spoke the words of God" (II Peter 1:21, NEB). Peter declared, therefore, that the real authority for those who heard the prophets was the Holy Spirit speaking God's revealed words.

As God used prophets for the production of the Old Testament, likewise He used the apostles and their associates for the writing of the New Testament. In order that His words and deeds be remembered and recorded after His ascension, Jesus called the apostles and delegated His authority to them. The only authority which Peter, James, and John, along with the other apostles, possessed was a delegated authority —a delegated authority specifically for the purpose of witnessing to Jesus Christ. Christ did not empower them with authority as individuals in their own rights, nor did He give them power and authority to transmit their office to future generations. They had authority only as true witnesses of Jesus Christ. Their main function was to convey revelation about Jesus.

The work of the apostles first found expression in oral testimony and later in written form. The written form, the New Testament, carried the same authentic apostolic authority which had been delegated to them by Jesus Christ their Lord. There was no decay of authority from the apostles to the Bible. The New Testament carried the same authority for the early churches as did the authority of the apostles. The Holy Spirit who inspired the prophets and guided the writing of the Old Testament is the same Spirit who inspired the apostles and guided the writing of the New Testament. Furthermore, it is the Holy Spirit who guides Christians as they read Scripture and witnesses in their hearts in order that they may see the truth of God in the Bible.

The result of such delegation of God's authority is that in the Bible we have God's authentic message.

> The necessity for authoritative writings of some sort is implicit in the idea of a historic revelation and redemption; without such writings the historic

events, along with their crucial significance for men, would have been lost in
alien systems of thought, or in embroidered legends, or in theosophical and
mystical speculations, if indeed the knowledge of them had not faded away
altogether into oblivion, their memory and influence gradually dissipated and
dissolved into the unregenerate life of mankind.[6]

The church has always accepted the Bible as God's delegated veracious authority because it understands the absolute necessity for the
Bible.

> From the earliest period of the history the Christian church has regarded
> the Scriptures as being in some sense the special revelation of God, and
> therefore as being in some sense the final standard or norm of Christian
> truth.[7]

Norms or standards may be understood in two ways: (1) as an extrinsic standard such as a yardstick which may measure with a specific
degree of accuracy, and (2) as an intrinsic standard such as the living
principle of growth in an organism or the living spirit of a nation or
people. The intrinsic standard, though less mechanical than the extrinsic,
is nonetheless valid and real.

> The normative relation of the Bible to the faith and life of the church is
> clearly of the intrinsic kind. It is, we must insist, not the less a true norm
> for being intrinsic, indeed, it is not the less a final norm, in the sense that no
> question of faith or conduct can be deemed to be rightly determined which
> is not thought out with the Bible, as it were, being present throughout the
> discussion and taking a dominant and authoritative part in it. . . . If it is
> true that we cannot rightly apprehend the essentials of the Christian faith
> and life without using the Bible as an authoritative source and norm, it is
> equally true that we cannot apprehend the Bible as such a source and norm,
> still less rightly use it, apart from a living participation in the church's faith
> and life.[8]

Since the supreme revelation of God is Jesus Christ and the Scripture
is the document of revelation, how are these two to be related? Is their
authority contradictory or supplementary? It is Farmer's view that the
Bible is essential to the normative relationship of the living Christ to
the church.

> If . . . we so understand God's saving work through Christ that *it requires
> as an indispensable element in it the encounter, continually re-enacted, with
> the concrete individuality of the historic Savior,* then we can see at once why
> the biblical documents become an indispensable factor in Christ's living

---

[6]Farmer, *op. cit.*, p. 23.
[7]*Ibid.*, p. 3.
[8]*Ibid.*, pp. 4-5.

relationship to the church. For without the Bible such encounter could not take place.[9]

Revelation implies the need for a written revelation. The written revelation, the Bible, is an absolutely essential part of the process of revelation itself, for it is in the written revelation that we find the historic Christ. Without the historic Christ there is no witness to God in self-disclosure.

> The Spirit takes of the things of Christ and shows them to us, and the fruits of the Spirit are the virtues of Christ. But this means that there has to be a Christ—a historic Christ—for the Spirit to show us; and that in turn means that there has to be a historical record.[10]

In conclusion, our religious authority is God in personal self-disclosure. From the fact of God in self-disclosure comes religious authority in a multidimensional form which includes Jesus Christ, the living revealed personal Word of God, who is the supreme revelation of God; the Holy Spirit, who inspired the prophets and apostles so that they received God's true revelation and so that they remembered and recorded all that we need to know about God; and the Bible, which, inspired by the Holy Spirit, is God's document of revelation and which witnesses supremely to Jesus Christ.

Relationship of Biblical authority and preaching. Since the only authentic document for authoritative content about God in personal revelation is the Bible, the task of the preacher is to use the Bible correctly in sermon preparation and delivery. To the degree that the minister trusts the Bible to be accurate and authentic, to the degree that he listens to the Holy Spirit while engaged in interpreting the Bible, to the degree that God's self-revelation is "built" into the sermon, and to the degree that the minister preaches his "Biblical sermon" under the leadership of the Holy Spirit, the message is authentic and authoritative.

The authority of the prophets and apostles resided in their fidelity in witnessing to God's revelation and especially to Jesus Christ. The preacher will preach authoritative content only when he emulates the prophets and apostles by witnessing to God's personal self-revelation. Biblical authority and preaching should be correlates. Preaching should be an extension of God's revelation from the Bible to the sermon to the people. When this ideal is achieved, the minister preaches with authentic Biblical authority.

---

[9]*Ibid.*, p. 14.
[10]*Ibid.*, p. 15.

Types of Biblical sermons as to authority. Because of the complicated nature of true homiletics, short and simple terms for authentic Biblical sermons are unsatisfactory. If short terms such as "expository," "textual," and "topical" were exact, they would be invaluable. The pattern of terms for authentic Biblical sermons according to authority consists of five categories and several subcategories.

The *direct* Biblical sermon uses Scripture in the message with the same sense as it has in the text. The sermon employs the natural and logical meaning of the text in a direct, straightforward fashion. Only by moving exactly and correctly from the grammatical-historical "then" to the relevant "now" can a sermon be a direct Biblical sermon. The text and sermon are parallel, harmonious, and correlate. The sermon says the same thing as its text.

Men have preached direct Biblical sermons, though not by this name, from the beginning of Christianity. The term "direct" has been selected because it presents fewer problems and answers more questions than any one of a dozen or more terms with which experiments have been conducted.

Four subclasses of the direct Biblical sermon have been identified: (1) the direct Biblical sermon using commands and imperatives of the Bible; (2) the direct Biblical sermon using affirmations of Scripture; (3) the direct Biblical sermon using negatives and "thou shalt nots" of Scripture; (4) the direct Biblical sermon using eternal truths of Scripture. The fourth is broad and complex and presents problems in interpretation. These four classes are discussed and illustrated in chapter five.

The *indirect* Biblical sermon uses Scripture in the message in an indirect way or with a variation from the sense of the text. The indirect Biblical sermon departs from the true meaning of the text with a slight variation from the central idea of the passage. In one sense the indirect Biblical sermon moves at a tangent from the central idea of the text. It does so by adding selected ideas to the central idea of the text.

The indirect Biblical sermon, though not by this name, has also been preached from the beginning of Christianity. Three subclasses of the indirect Biblical sermon have been found and identified: (1) the indirect Biblical sermon which supplements the Biblical idea by completing a Scriptural implication; (2) the indirect Biblical sermon which particularizes a statement of general truth or a general idea; (3) the indirect Biblical sermon which compares and contrasts the Biblical idea with a supplied idea (the sermon supplies physical terms for spiritual ideas or vice versa). These three classes of the indirect Biblical sermon are discussed and illustrated in chapter six.

The *casual* Biblical sermon uses Scripture in the message in a free and loose way in regard to the true sense of the text. This sermon should, but usually does not, begin with the historical meaning of the text before it proceeds to develop the message in a free and casual way. Two broad subclasses of the casual Biblical sermon have been identified: (1) the casual Biblical sermon which uses a rhetorical suggestion from Scripture; and (2) the casual Biblical sermon which uses an essay with a text. These are discussed and illustrated in chapter six.

The *combination* Biblical sermon uses the above three types of sermons in an infinite number of ways. Moreover, the combination Biblical sermon, unfortunately, also uses corrupted Biblical patterns. Since there is an indefinite number of combinations, a few selected illustrations in chapter six demonstrate both the correct and incorrect uses of the combination Biblical sermon.

The *corrupted* Biblical sermon does not use but rather abuses the Bible. An inexhaustible number of ways have been devised for twisting, abusing, and corrupting texts. Several of the more prominent types are described in chapter six.

Authoritative Biblical Purpose

The definition of purpose. The second major category for authentic Biblical sermons is authoritative Biblical purpose. Purpose in preaching may be used to refer either to the purpose or intention of the Biblical writer for the text or to the preacher's objective or purpose for the sermon. The Biblical sermon utilizes the same purpose, intention, or objective as the Biblical passage.

Types of purpose. Six broad categories of purpose, both in Scripture and sermons, are (1) that men know Jesus Christ and obtain life eternal, the evangelistic or kerygmatic goal; (2) that Christians grow in knowledge of God, the doctrinal, factual, and teaching objective; (3) that Christians grow in fellowship with the Lord, the devotional purpose; (4) that Christians develop in effective service for God, the actional or consecrative goal; (5) that Christians grow in grace and strength, the supportive, pastoral, or enheartening purpose; and (6) that Christians develop in Christlike conduct, the ethical or moral goal. The last five goals when seen as a whole constitute the edification aspect for the elect of God.

In seeking to understand the true and natural meaning of a text, the minister will also seek to determine the purpose or intention which the Biblical writer had for the passage. Whether the text seeks to speak to a man about salvation through Jesus Christ or whether the text seeks to speak to one about growth in edification the purpose is a matter of utmost importance in sermon preparation. If the minister, through ignorance or carelessness, mixes these fundamental purposes, he will prepare a confusing sermon. Moreover, the Holy Spirit witnesses through Scripture according to the true meaning of Scripture.

Relationship of purpose, Scripture, and sermon. In Biblical study for sermon preparation the minister should discover, as far as he is able, the true, natural, and valid purpose or intention of Scripture. When this purpose has been discovered, it becomes part of the data for the sermon. When the Biblical purpose of a text does become an integral part of the minister's message, then Scripture purpose and sermon purpose are harmonious.

How does Biblical purpose relate to the five types of sermons as to authority? In the direct Biblical sermon, Biblical purpose and sermon purpose are equal. In the indirect Biblical sermon, Biblical purpose and sermon purpose should be, at the least, compatible and, at the best, equal. When the indirect Biblical sermon supplements the text, it can and should stay with the textual purpose. Unfortunately, many sermons of this type do not do so. Obviously, if the indirect Biblical sermon adds to or supplements the text and also departs from the purpose of the text, then the sermon is weaker and less authoritative. In the casual Biblical sermon, the sermon usually disregards the natural meaning and purpose of the text. For this additional reason, the casual Biblical sermon is weak in Biblical authority. In the combination Biblical sermon, the infinite variations demand that each sermon be examined in its own right. Some combination sermons develop the Biblical purpose and some do not. The sermon is a better sermon whenever it does unfold the Scriptural purpose. In the corrupted Biblical sermon the meaning and purpose of the text are usually twisted or corrupted in some fashion.

Types of Biblical sermons as to purpose. The types of Biblical sermons as to purpose are six: (1) the evangelistic, (2) the doctrinal, (3) the devotional, (4) the actional, (5) the supportive, and (6) the ethical or moral. These are illustrated in chapters seven and eight.

Acceptable Biblical Form

Nature of form. All concrete things have form. One cannot think with any accuracy about "dogness" or "houseness" or "flowerness" or "peopleness." Even if the nondefinitive terms "dog," "house," "flower," or "people" be spoken or written about, the hearer or reader will supply concrete form and substance.

Form is the shape, order, plan, and structure conveyed to us as we read about, listen to, examine, or see objects. Philosophers discuss form endlessly, but here the only need is a simple one: to find a way to describe the form of sermons prepared, preached, heard, or read.

Types of preaching form. Two broad and unlimited subclasses of form have come to preachers out of several thousand years of preaching by prophets, apostles, missionaries, priests, preachers, and laymen. From the Hebrews, Greeks, and Romans have come the essential elements of form which shape modern American preaching.

The *homily*, or the simple form, comes to us from the Near Eastern world. Primarily the Hebrews, as prophets and apostles, through the Old and New Testaments, have shaped our concepts of the homily. The homily was simple and informal. The prophets, Jesus, and the apostles, as natives of the Near Eastern world, used the homily as the normal pattern in their preaching.

The *rhetorical* or structural or organized form comes to us largely from Greece and Rome. The rhetorical form uses unity, emphasis, and coherence and makes use of the best contemporary literary devices. The rhetorical form makes use of outlining and functional development. Functional development is the developing or unfolding or elaborating process of filling out and completing the outline. The basic functional literary devices are explanation, argument (logic and reasoning), and application.

The relationship of Scripture, form, and preaching. Scriptural form has been described as simple and informal. The form of the literary materials in the Bible and the form of the homily are one form. There are variations, to be sure, but Biblical form and the homily sermon form are correlates.

Countless problems have resulted in preaching because the scholastics of the Middle Ages, and their modern descendants (whether so called or not) have organized sermons into smooth, balanced, unified, orderly, and coherent patterns without adequate regard for the true nature of their Biblical content. The modern scholastic often outlines a sermon after the following pattern (some teachers and books even instruct young men to organize their messages in some such pattern):

Introduction (with all necessary items)
Body
   I. _____
      1. _____
         (1) _____
         (2) _____
         (3) _____

2. _____
    (1) _____
    (2) _____
    (3) _____
3. _____
    (1) _____
    (2) _____
    (3) _____
II. _____
1. _____
    (1) _____
    (2) _____
    (3) _____
2. _____
    (1) _____
    (2) _____
    (3) _____
3. _____
    (1) _____
    (2) _____
    (3) _____
III. _____
1. _____
    (1) _____
    (2) _____
    (3) _____
2. _____
    (1) _____
    (2) _____
    (3) _____
3. _____
    (1) _____
    (2) _____
    (3) _____
Conclusion

If there is a text in the Bible written like this illustrative outline, it has remained well concealed. When a preacher takes a great Scriptural truth and forces and stuffs the Biblical truth into a rigid and mechanical pattern like the outline above, he abuses and corrupts that Scripture. The prophets and apostles did not think or write in such mechanical, balanced, orderly ways.

It is the minister's task to find the natural meaning of a passage of Scripture and to find the simplest and most clear-cut method for organizing and preaching that text. The minister's task is complicated by the fact that his Biblical data come largely, if not exclusively, in simple patterns while he himself has been trained to think, to prepare, and to deliver in rhetorical patterns. Modern life is organized and arranged by unity, order, and purpose.

How may the minister combine the two types of form? Ministers have found their answer in a pleasing blend of the Biblical and Greco-Roman forms. Discerning preachers have discovered that occasionally Hebrew form will reveal a simple pattern which, if left simple, matches Greco-Roman form and is still Biblical. It appears thus:

> Introduction
> Body
> I. From Scripture
> II. From Scripture
> Conclusion

This outline shows the simplest rhetorical pattern possible to write, and it can be Biblical at the same time.

Moreover, ministers have discovered that there are Scriptures (Paul's more than those of other Biblical writers) which naturally contain more detail than other passages and which may be shown with more structure.

> Introduction
> Body
> I. From Scripture
>   1. From Scripture
>   2. From Scripture
>   3. From Scripture
> II. From Scripture
>   1. From Scripture
>   2. From Scripture
> Conclusion

There is no rigid mechanical structure in the last outline because Paul wrote the passage this way. Very likely Paul wrote his text in a simple and informal way, and it is a pleasing coincidence that his words may be organized and outlined in accordance with rhetorical rules of unity, order, and coherence.

Again, pulpit masters have found that when natural rhetorical order is not clearly shown in a text, they may use a simple rhetorical pattern without doing violence to the text. When the pattern becomes extended as in the outline on pages 39-40, Scripture is inevitably twisted. However, the great preachers have found that a preacher does not need to extend an outline to the limits shown on pages 39-40. One may take a text with no recognizable structure and use a simple outline without violence. The following simple structures have been encountered count-less times in published messages. They may be both Biblical in content and rhetorical in form.

      Introduction
      Body
   I. _____
  II. _____
      Conclusion

or like this:

      Introduction
      Body
    I. _____
   II. _____
  III. _____
   IV. _____
      Conclusion

or again as this one:

   I. _____
      Introduction
      Body
      1. _____
      2. _____
  II. _____
      1. _____
      2. _____
      Conclusion

By taking the natural, though unplanned, rhetorical patterns of Scripture and by using a simple and acceptable outline, preachers have been able to produce authentic Biblical sermons. They have been able to preach authoritative content with the same purpose as the text and in a form compatible and acceptable to the Bible and to modern rhetoric. Procedures for filling out these simple patterns are discussed and illustrated in chapter nine.

Authentic Biblical sermons must be understood in the light of Biblical authority, Biblical purpose, and creative form. Authentic Biblical sermons need this new threefold approach in order to explain all valid data. Authentic Biblical sermons according to authority, purpose, and form are explained and illustrated in chapters five through nine.

Through the understanding and use of authentic Biblical sermons, the minister will take part in a genuine reformation of preaching. And the time has come for a true reformation of preaching! Who dares to participate?

Part II

THE WAY TO REFORMATION
IN PREACHING

Chapter 3

THE MANAGEMENT OF SCRIPTURE

The reformation of preaching depends upon the proper handling and management of Scripture in various sermonic areas. Biblical authority and purpose can be either undergirded or voided by the way the minister decides to use the Bible in a number of complex sermon situations. Foundational to this discussion is the fact that Scripture may be used sermonically as text, context, support, and illustration. The complex sermon situations evolve from these foundational uses of Scripture.

First, Scripture may be used as text. The word *text* comes from a Latin term *textus* meaning "fabric," which in turn comes from *texere* meaning "to weave." Thus *textus* is the "fabric of one's weaving." In relation to preaching, text came to be used as the fabric of Scripture which served as the basic component of the sermon. In the sermon the text is the Word of God woven into a sermon. In essence a sermon is composed of text from the Bible plus explanation, argument, and application from the preacher. Scripture has as its basic function in preaching, then, the task of being text or fabric for sermons. Thus, when Scripture is used properly as text, the minister has the possibility of preaching with authentic Biblical authority. Reformation in preaching is dependent upon ministers who preach sermons with authentic Biblical authority.

Since there is only one divinely revealed source for sermons—the Scriptures—one would suppose that teachers and writers in homiletics would labor tirelessly and endlessly to make clear that the Scripture is supposed to be the fabric for sermons. Furthermore, one would suppose that every preacher would know this fact beyond any question of doubt. This, however, is open to question. Virtually every book on homiletics does discuss the use of Scriptures as texts for sermons, but even so there is not much evidence that such discussions have made any substantially unified impressions on the minds of preachers. Effort may have been expended to teach the true nature of a text, but success has been slow in appearing.

Preachers refer to the Scripture for the sermon as the *text*, and by this they mean a large variety of things: (1) The Scripture text is the starting point for the sermon idea. (2) The Scripture text is the "nail" from which the preacher hangs his thoughts. (3) The Scripture text is the "springboard" for the sermon. (4) The Scripture text is the foundation for the sermon. (5) The Scripture text is the general guide for sermon preparation. (6) The Scripture text is the Bible passage announced and read in connection with a sermon. (7) The Scripture text is the composite use of several passages from different books of the Bible. (8) The Scripture text is a long passage of Scripture. (9) The Scripture text is the basis for the sermon title and key points. (10) The Scripture text is the oft-repeated Biblical phrase or Biblical allusion in the sermon. (11) The Scripture text is the general truth used in the sermon which touches upon the broad principles of Christianity. Such diversity of thought graphically demonstrates the widespread confusion ministers have about the original concept of *text* which affirms that the Scripture is the fabric of the sermon. The eleven definitions of text cited above are usually false, although some of them on occasion are true and accurate. It is time for ministers to return to the original concept of text: fabric for the sermon.

Second, Scripture may be used as context. Context means "with the text." Thus, context means Scriptural matter which, in some manner, goes with the text or fabric of the sermon. Many texts, if not all texts, demand that the context be known and understood in order that the text be treated properly. There are three dimensions of context, and the minister will investigate and use one or all as his original text demands.

The immediate context of Scripture involves the remainder of the sentence (if a word, phrase, or clause be used), the remainder of the verse (if less than a verse be used), the remainder of the paragraph (if less than a paragraph be used), and the surrounding paragraphs (if as much as a full paragraph be used). Depending on the nature of the text, at times two, three, and even four of these make up the immediate context.

There is a larger context in addition to the immediate context. The larger context is present at the same time as the immediate context and involves the remainder of the Biblical chapter, the remainder of the section of the book, and the remainder of the book. The larger context simply involves all the remainder of the material, in addition to the text, in a particular book of the Bible.

In addition to the immediate and larger context, there is a total context which involves the balance of the Old or the New Testament and the balance of the Bible. The total context is present at the same time as the larger and immediate context.

Third, Scripture may be used as support or as cross-reference. Scripture, in addition to being used as text and context, may be used as support for the text. To support the text with other Scriptures means to use additional passages which present essentially the same truth as the basic text. These supportive Scriptures could become part of the basic text in that they mean the same thing as that original text. However, preachers do not intend, as a rule, for the extra passages to become text, but rather use them believing that the weight of the second, third, and fourth passages will convince and convict. This valid desire to convince and convict normally motivates a minister to use Scripture as support of a text idea which is already distinctly clear. When presented in moderation, this use of Scripture may be pleasing and valuable.

Problems arise, however, in the use of Scripture as support. For one thing, since the original text is true, the minister does not actually need the second, third, and fourth passages to prove it. Again, the presentation of a great number of passages tends to confuse the audience. A clear and concise presentation and explanation of one passage, normally, carries more weight. Furthermore, when the minister uses extra passages for support, he is in danger of using them without careful study. When he merely thrusts Scripture into the sermon for support, but does not exegete it properly, he is in danger of corrupting Scripture and of proof-texting his sermon without regard to the meaning of Scripture.

In spite of these problems, however, the minister may well use Scripture as support. He must be careful to see that he understands each additional passage and to be sure that each additional passage teaches the same as the text. With those two safeguards in mind the minister should feel no hesitancy in using supporting Scripture.

Fourth, Scripture may be used as illustration. Scripture may be used as an illustration of the original text. While Scripture as support and Scripture as illustration are often confused, there is a slight difference between them. In using Scripture as illustration, the preacher will normally present an additional passage about a person or even biography or narration in order to throw light upon or to illuminate the basic text which may not be as clear as the minister desires. To use additional Scriptures as illustrations means "to cast added light" upon difficult thoughts, ideas, points, or the basic text itself. However, when Scripture is used as support, the minister normally selects a passage which explains or affirms something in the same manner as the text. While this slight distinction is discernible, most preachers do not make it. Normally, nothing crucial is involved in confusing the two, but if the preacher can identify which one he is using, he adds concreteness to his sermonic work.

On the basis of these four foundational sermonic uses of Scripture, what are the complex areas which evolve? Four may be' enumerated: (1) there is an adequate source for the sermon idea; (2) there is an adequate quantity of Scripture for the sermon; (3) there is an adequate locale or grounding for the Scriptural data; and (4) there is an accurate interpretation of Scripture.

AN ADEQUATE SOURCE FOR THE SERMON IDEA

When the preacher secures Biblical authority in preaching, the source of the sermon idea becomes important to him. The sermon may originate in any one of five broad areas: the Bible, the congregation's need, a planned program of preaching, the preacher's vast personal contacts and resources, and flashes of inspiration. The last four are usually non-Biblical, though not necessarily so.

Through Scripture

The best source for the origin of the sermon idea is the Bible. This does not say that the sermon idea *must* begin in Scripture, but it does say that the most logical point of departure for a sermon is the Bible. By beginning the sermon with Scripture the minister avoids two struggles: (1) the struggle to move from a non-Biblical idea to a compatible text, and (2) the struggle to keep the original non-Biblical idea from dominating, controlling, and leading astray the true idea of the text.

To begin the sermon with a text gives numerous advantages to the preacher: (1) time is saved in moving from idea to text; (2) confusion between sermon idea and text idea is saved in the attempt to correlate them; and (3) the resultant sermon is more likely to be Biblical.

Through Non-Biblical Sources

Freedom must be maintained in sermon preparation. In spite of the advantages of beginning with a text, some men find that their personalities and homiletic methods often lead them to begin with an observed need in the congregation or with a planned program of preaching or with some personal insight or conviction or with an almost indefinable flash of inspiration. What should a man do in sermon preparation when this type of problem is present? First, he would be wise to recognize the presence of the problem; second, he would be wise to demand that, regardless of the source of the idea, the sermon idea and a text be matched properly; and third, he would be wise to demand of himself that after matching the text and sermon idea he allow the text to control further sermon development. Apart from these basic safeguards, the preacher will probably not be able to prepare a Biblical sermon.

AN ADEQUATE QUANTITY OF SCRIPTURE

How Much Scripture *Must* One Use in Sermons?

Ministers honestly desire to know whether or not preaching tradition has reached a consensus concerning *how much* Scripture *must* be used to prepare a sermon. Preaching tradition, fortunately or unfortunately, has not arrived at one hard and fast answer. Rather, preaching experience indicates that there must be a rather flexible answer. The answer is that the quantity of Scripture used should be sufficient to establish an authoritative foundation for the sermon.

How Much Scripture *May* One Use in Sermons?

Perhaps this question may be answered more readily. But, again, the answer must be flexible. The preacher may use as much Scripture as he needs. Chalmer Faw has suggested that texts may be thought about and preached in eight variations as to length and/or amount: (1) the entire Bible, (2) the Old Testament, (3) the New Testament, (4) one book, e.g., Jonah or Philippians, (5) one great section of a book, e.g., Matthew 5-7, (6) one great paragraph, e.g., John 3:1-15, Ephesians 2:1-10, or Amos 5:21-24, (7) one great Biblical sentence, e.g., Psalm 1:1-2 or Psalm 23:1, and (8) the Biblical "atom," such as Luke 24:6a, "He . . . is risen."[1] To these eight may be added the chapter sermon,

---

[1]Chalmer E. Faw, *A Guide to Biblical Preaching* (Nashville: Broadman Press, 1962).

the verse sermon, and the Biblical sections such as Law, Prophets, and Gospels. With at least eleven variations open to a preacher as to length, he should have no difficulty in securing pleasing variety.

In order to have adequate homiletic form and arrangement, what are the guides concerning the proper amount of Scripture? The minister should be sure (1) that the complete idea of the text is included, (2) that the context is known and understood, and (3) that sufficient Scripture is included.

AN ADEQUATE LOCALE FOR SCRIPTURE

From how many locations in Scripture may the text come? This issue is similar to the issue concerning the quantity of Scripture, but it is different in that it struggles with whether to locate the text in one place, or several places, or in thematic ideas.

The One-Passage Sermon

The one-passage sermon utilizes one text in one location in Scripture. Normally this is the strongest, clearest, and best way to preach the Bible. From the standpoint of homiletic quality, the minister will discover that by taking one solid block of Scripture, studying it in context, and preparing and preaching his sermon from that one text, he will produce a stronger sermon. This will be true week by week. The one-passage message saves time in studying, presents more clarity in Biblical explanation, provides a better instrument for teaching people the context and connections of Scripture, is more readily available for use in a continuous treatment of the great books of the Bible, and carries more authority in that one segment of Scripture.

The Multi-Passage Sermon

The multiple-passage sermon utilizes portions of Scripture from two, three, or more places in the Bible. The multiple passage sermon makes use of such natural groups of Scripture as the three accounts of Demas, the parallel accounts of the four Gospels, Old Testament questions and New Testament answers, and questions by people and answers by Jesus. These groupings of texts follow some type of natural and logical textual arrangement. A common though inaccurate name for this sermon is the multiple-text sermon. The name "multiple-text" is inaccurate in that if two or more portions of Scripture be matched and used properly, then they are not a multiple-text sermon but a multiple-passage sermon.

By the basic definition of text, the amount and location of Scripture does not change the word "text" into a multiple concept. If two or more passages match, then they are one text, and, of course, they may come from two or more passages.

If the multiple-passage sermon be done properly, why cannot it be as strong and effective as a one-passage sermon? The crux of the issue is "if it be done properly." The multiple-passage sermon is extremely difficult to manage well, and the problems are numerous. If three passages are used, for example, these difficulties are encountered: (1) three passages require three times as much exegetical work and study as a one-passage sermon (most ministers do not have or will not find the extra time); (2) three passages are often difficult to blend into one harmonious homiletical and oratorical whole; and (3) normally, three passages do not give the people a solid block or explanation which they may take home but rather give to them three fragments which are more difficult to retain and remember.

There are advantages, however, to a correct and judicious use of the multiple-passage sermon. When exegetical and homiletical matters are properly managed, the multiple-passage sermon does afford a wider variety in themes treated, provides a larger exposure to personalities and issues of Scripture, and occasionally yields an exciting treatment of a great idea as in Fosdick's "The Power to See It Through."[2]

The Thematic Biblical Sermon

The thematic Biblical sermon makes use of a systematic treatment of a great Christian idea and selects passages of Scripture for the proper development of the idea. There are times when the multiple-passage sermon and the thematic Biblical sermon appear to be the same. As a rule, however, one may distinguish them by noting that an *idea*, such as faith or sin or regeneration, runs through the thematic Biblical sermons, while a Biblical connection, e.g., several passages on Paul, runs through the multiple-passage sermons. Nevertheless, there are sermons published which cannot be separated at this point. The preacher preparing his own sermon, however, should always know which route he follows: multiple-passage or thematic Biblical. The same difficulties as well as the same advantages accrue to the thematic Biblical sermon as to the multiple-passage sermon.

One of the more difficult questions in homiletics involves the proper identification of Biblical authority in a multiple-passage sermon, a thematic Biblical sermon, or a sermon which uses Scripture in addition

---

[2]This sermon is discussed in chapter six.

BETHEL SEMINARY WEST
LIBRARY
6116 Arosa Street
San Diego, CA 92115-3902

to text, as context, support, or illustration. Upon hearing a multiple-passage or thematic Biblical sermon which also generously utilizes supplementary Scriptures, a hearer tends at first to feel that the message has been saturated with Scripture and is automatically Biblically authoritative. Such may be the case, but such, however, is not automatically the case. The sermon may be Biblically authoritative provided that both text and supplementary passages are properly exegeted and presented. Direct Biblical authority is present in a sermon when both content and purpose of the entire sermon and of all Scriptures are harmonious and correlate. Moreover, the form of the sermon should be compatible with content and purpose so that both are clearly revealed rather than concealed by sermon form.

Since Scriptures may be used as text and context (as one-passage, multiple-passage, or thematic Biblical sermon), they should be used in the sermon with their natural and normal meaning. When this occurs, direct Biblical authority is present. Moreover, when Scripture is also used either as support or illustration or both, the preacher should also use the supplementary Scriptures with their natural and normal meaning. When this occurs, the supplementary Scriptures assist direct Biblical authority. Authority is influenced and colored but not fully determined by Scripture as support or illustration. Scripture as support or illustration adds to or clarifies the text and context. Since Scripture as support and Scripture as illustration both serve as supplements, they are not to be considered as primary determinants for authority.

When Scripture is used either as support or illustration or both, a minister is more likely to skip careful interpretation than if it is used as text or context. When careful exegetical work is eliminated, the minister will tend to misuse Scripture and the result is that supplementary Scriptures may confuse authority rather than assist it. It is to be remembered that Biblical authority comes to a sermon not by an avalanche of Biblical words, thoughts, and ideas, but by a correct presentation of the natural meaning and intention of Scripture of any proper length. Not volume of words but accuracy of explanation determines Biblical authority.

In those cases, however, when the preacher uses Scripture correctly either as support or illustration or both, extra Scriptures supplement the Biblical authority of the expounded text and context. Thus Scripture as support and Scripture as illustration join the text and sermon in being correlate.

AN ACCURATE INTERPRETATION OF SCRIPTURE

To secure Biblical authority in a sermon the preacher will discover the true meaning and use of his text. He will utilize the central idea of his text in a correct grammatical and historical way.

Discovering the "Then" of Scripture

Through the use of the critical method of Bible study the preacher will discover the original meaning of his text. Apart from the natural, grammatical, and historical meaning of a passage, the minister cannot preach authentic Biblical sermons. The historical meaning, the "then" of Scripture, serves as the only adequate basis for formulating the present tense application, the "now" of Scripture.

Discovering the "Now" of Scripture

Harry Emerson Fosdick convinced the great majority of preachers that there is more to the Bible than the stories of the Medes, the Persians, and the dwellers in Mesopotamia. There must be a present-tense message in Scripture which confronts each hearer as he listens. This present-tense message is the "now," the eternal reality of God's message. To be valid, this "now" must be based on the historical "then." Both are necessary for authentic Biblical preaching.

Using the Central Idea of the Text

The central idea of the text describes the true historical meaning of a passage. The affirmation of the sermon describes the central idea of the text as translated into a present-tense statement. This present-tense statement is the proposition. Three broad choices are open to each preacher as he decides how to use the central idea of the text and the proposition.

Using all of the central idea. If the minister has chosen Luke 15:1-32 as his text and has properly exegeted it, he will discover that the central idea of the text is "Jesus declared God's love for the lost." There are any number of ways to state the central idea of the text: "Jesus, in defending His interest in sinners, declared that God loved sinners." Or it may be stated, "Jesus, in explaining His association with publicans and siners, affirmed that God Himself loved publicans and sinners." However it is stated, the central idea of the text contains the wonderful and glad tidings that God loves sinners.

By translating this into a present-tense statement, an affirmation or proposition, the preacher declares to his people that "God loves sinners." Again, this may be written with numerous variations in style as long as God's love for the lost is emphasized. This redemptive truth applies now as well as it did then. It is an eternal truth.

The minister may desire to use the entire fifteenth chapter of Luke and may wish to preach on the whole concept of God's love for the lost. If he so desires, he may use the entire central idea of the text and preach on the entire chapter. This procedure, of course, may be used for texts both shorter and longer than Luke 15:1-32.

Using part of the central idea of the text. Because Luke 15:1-32 contains such a broad and majestic view of God's love for the lost, the preacher may decide to use only a part of this great chapter. He may select the parable of the lost sheep, the parable of the lost coin, the parable of the lost boy who left home, or the parable of the lost boy who stayed at home. If, for example, the preacher decides to use the parable of the lost boy who left home, he will reduce his text from Luke 15:1-32 to Luke 15:11-24. As he reduces his text to Luke 15:11-24 his immediate context then becomes Luke 15:1-10 and 25-32. The central idea for Luke 15:11-24 remains the same as for Luke 15:1-32 because Jesus told the same truth about God's love in four different ways.

If this line of development is pursued, the preacher will discover that he has five scenes or facets to the story of the son who left home: (1) his departure into sin, (2) his deception by sin, (3) his recognition of his tragic condition, (4) his return and confession to the loving father, and (5) his pardon and forgiveness by the loving father.

To carry the idea one step further, the preacher may, after study, decide that Luke 15:11-24 is too broad, and he may reduce his text to Luke 15:13-16, which shows the destructiveness of sin. In this case, the immediate context becomes Luke 15:11-12 and 17-32. The larger context becomes Luke 15:1-12, 17-32 as well as the remainder of the section, and the remainder of the book of Luke. The central idea of Luke 15:13-16 is that "sin brought the son to the pit of destruction." From this central idea of the text the preacher may say that "sin always destroys one in rebellion against God."

Using a secondary idea in relation to the central idea of the text. The preacher may use all of the central idea of the text or a major part of it. In addition to these primary uses of the central idea of the text he may select and use a secondary idea in the text. A secondary or minor idea in a passage is a sub-subfacet of the dominant truth or is a somewhat parenthetical expression or thought injected into the text by the original writer.

In using the fruits of interpretation, the minister, after he discovers the central idea of the text, will employ all the central idea, a valid part of it, or a minor or secondary thought in connection with it. The choice as to which of these to use remains the decision of the preacher.

Chapter 4

THE FUNCTIONAL ELEMENTS OF PREACHING

The reformation of preaching depends upon the proclamation of authentic Biblical content. One effective procedure for placing authentic Biblical content in sermons is through the use of the functional elements of preaching—explanation, application, and argument.

How can the preacher insure for himself the benefit of authentic Biblical content in his sermons? He may do this by remembering that a sermon outline never stands alone as a complete sermon. The outline must be filled out and developed before a complete sermon exists. The preacher cannot produce an adequate sermon merely by outlining the major thoughts and then dividing and redividing those thoughts. At some point the preacher must stop dividing and must begin to develop, to expand, and to fill out his structure. The preacher may fill out his sermon with the functional elements of preaching.

Homiletics, law, speech, and other disciplines each make distinctive uses of language to serve individual needs. In homiletics, the function of language in a sermon is to explain, to apply, and to reason (argue). Explanation, application, and argument, therefore, are the technical names for the functional uses of language in preaching. These three— explanation, application, and argumentation—are purposeful in nature in that they aid in accomplishing the goal or objective of the sermon.

Each sermon seeks to accomplish *one* goal or objective in the form of a specific objective. The specific objective is drawn from one of six major objectives which are derived from the basic spiritual needs of man and from Scripture. The six major objectives are: (1) the evangelistic, the need to be converted; (2) the doctrinal, the need to understand divine truth; (3) the ethical, the need to live in a

Christian relationship with other people; (4) the supportive, the need to share God's grace as the occasion demands; (5) the devotional, the need to love and worship God; and (6) the actional, the need to serve and to work for God. One of these six major objectives, or purposes, should be determined for a particular sermon by the nature of the text. The specific objective should grow out of the major objective and be consistent with the central idea of the text, thesis, major objective, title, the sermon proper, and the invitation.

The three functional elements are not completely separate and distinct from one another. Rather, they overlap, aid, and assist each other, and often appear to be one element and then appear to be another. The best way to learn to separate and to use these three elements is to read and to mark sermons paragraph by paragraph according to which elements have been used. After reading and marking twenty to twenty-five sermons, the preacher's skill in recognizing and using the functional elements will increase.

THE ELEMENT OF EXPLANATION

Explanation means to make plain, to make clear, to explain, to make understandable. It treats both Biblical and non-Biblical data in sermons. Explanation seeks to make clear those ideas or items which should be clarified.

Major Items Needing Explanation

In the well-prepared sermon, numerous items require explanation. It is the task of the minister both to recognize those items which may need explanation and to explain them. The major items and ideas in a sermon which may need explanation are: (1) words, phrases, clauses, sentences, and paragraphs of the text and/or the context; (2) the background of the text and/or context according to the particular Scripture used; (3) the central idea of the text and/or context; (4) the thesis for the sermon which is correctly related to the text and/or context, or the thesis for the sermon which departs in some measure from the text and/or context; (5) the purpose, both major and specific, for the sermon which is true to the text and/or context; or the purpose, major and specific, for the sermon which departs from the text and/or context; (6) the title of the sermon which is true to the text and/or context; or the title of the sermon which departs from the text and/or context; (7) the parts of the sermon—the introduction, body, conclusion, and invitation; (8) the significant points of the sermon—major points, subpoints, and sub-subpoints; (9) sentences and paragraphs of application; (10) sentences and paragraphs of argumentation; (11) illustrations of all types; and (12) any ideas. words, phrases, clauses, sentences, and paragraphs which are obscure or confusing.

Major Methods of Rhetoric for Accomplishing Explanation

The foregoing section has enumerated those items which may require explanation in a sermon. In contrast, this section sets forth the major rhetorical methods which help to explain.

Exposition. By exposition the minister is able to present truth, to present facts, and to explain by exposing details. Exposition presents truth, facts, and data of all types. Moreover, exposition makes assertions, sets out the fruit or results of exegetical work concerning words, phrases, clauses, sentences, and paragraphs from the text. Furthermore, exposition makes transitions by using sentences and paragraphs to move the sermon from idea to idea, from point to point, or from part to part. Exposition also reveals truth by sentences and paragraphs of a summary and concluding nature. Finally. one must remember that exposition may be used for both Biblical and non-Biblical materials. It is incorrect to think of exposition as a rhetorical method limited to Biblical data.

Division. To divide data means to separate the sermon materials into two or more points. The title of the sermon, as it contains the essence of the text, the central idea of the text, the thesis. and purpose, serves as the item to be divided. The title may be divided into two or more major or roman points. each major point in turn may be divided into two or more subpoints, and each subpoint may be divided into two or more sub-subpoints. Technically, the minister may continue to divide beyond the sub-subpoint level, but to do so is to load the sermon with excessive mechanical details. In most sermons the minister will find that the use of only major points or major points with subpoints will be sufficient.

Division is properly a way to explain. A minister, by pointing out, in sequence, the two or three or four normal parts of an idea, assists the audience to understand that idea. And understanding is the reason for explanation, is it not?

Narration. A third major method of explaining is to recite or to narrate the events or facts in a story. True narration has action, a character or characters, and setting. It is the record of events which succeed each other in sequence. Narration, the verbal expression of the action or encounter, appeals to the imagination and the emotions.

Narration serves the minister effectively by making possible the use of extended sections of Scripture. In preaching on the life of Moses, David, or Paul who would attempt to read all the important sections of Scripture relating to these three? One could consume the entire time of numerous sermons in reading the pertinent Scriptures. One may use narration to focus attention, in a terse way, on numerous events and long periods of time.

Description. Description tells how a thing looks, tastes, feels, smells, sounds, and acts. Thus it appeals to the senses and creates a vivid mental impression for the reader or hearer. Description, in contrast to narration, appeals to the intellect rather than to the emotions. Description aids the minister to explain so effectively that a listener will exclaim, "I see it now! I understand!"

Argument. Argument may be used to explain. When it is so used by definite plan, it is part of explanation.

Illustration. To illustrate means to make clear, to picture, and to throw light. The primary function of an illustration is to be a servant of the three functional elements. All data given here about illustrations under explanation also apply to the use of illustrations under application and argument. Therefore, the minister should use an illustration with a clear picture as to which functional element it serves.

In addition to knowing the correct purpose for an illustration, the preacher should treat the following aspects with special care: (1) the type of introduction employed, (2) the nature of the illustration, and (3) the source for the illustration. The first area involves style and appeal for the illustration, and the other two areas involve credibility for the illustration.

An illustration may be introduced in a formal and mechanical manner by saying, "Let me illustrate," or "Consider the following illustration." This formal, mechanical method of introduction for an illustration leaves much to be desired. Unless one has an overpowering reason to make the introduction intrude into the picture, the formal, mechanical introduction should not be used. Again, the minister may present his illustrations with direct and factual introductions. To use the direct, factual introduction is to give sufficient data so as to establish credibility for the illustration. This type of introduction majors on illustrating without talking about the process.

The nature of facts presented with the illustration will determine whether or not the illustration is accepted or rejected. An audience will accept almost any type of material for an illustration provided they know what type of material it is. In order to identify the nature of the illustrative material used, the preacher may ask himself a series of questions. First, is the illustration factual? Does it treat an actual event? Does the illustration deal with truth? Second, is the illustration a type of fiction created by one other than the preacher? Third, is the illustration the opinion of someone other than the minister? Fourth, is the illustration a personal creation of the preacher as a parable, supposition, or a hypothetical case? Fifth, is the illustration poetry or prose? There is an overlapping between question five and some of the first four, but question five is needed to identify some materials which do not fit the first four groups or which are not accurately described by them. By asking these questions the preacher can know whether or not the illustration will be credible to his audience. If the minister does not know the character or the basic nature of his illustrative data, how can he present it with any sense of certainty to the audience? It does make a difference whether an illustration is real or make-believe, truth or falsehood, opinion or fact, personal creation or quotation.

The source for the illustration is important to the preacher. Illustrations which have come from primary and reliable sources are far more pertinent than illustrations from secondary or tertiary sources of unknown reliability. The valid sources for effective illustrations are virtually limitless. Consider these among the most valuable: (1) the Bible; (2) all forms and types of history; (3) science, with legions of subdivisions; (4) literature in countless forms; (5) personal events and contacts of the preacher; (6) the arts; (7) sports; (8) the world of show business; (9) industry and management; (10) labor and farming; (11) law, government, nations, and wars; (12) theology, ethics, philosophy; (13) printed sermons; (14) devotional literature; (15) mathematics and statistics; (16) humor; and (17) personal observations of the preacher.

Beginning with the illustrative sermon of Karl Barth used in chapter five, the proper identification of illustrative data is shown. Moreover, for Barth's sermon, all three functional elements are marked and classified. In each case, the illustration is identified as to which functional element it serves, the type of introduction used for the illustration, the nature of the illustration, and the source for the illustration.

Secondary Methods of Rhetoric for Accomplishing Explanation

In addition to the six major methods of explaining, there are other methods, not as important or flexible as the major methods, which may be used for explanation. These secondary methods are usually used with the major methods of rhetoric for accomplishing explanation. When the preacher is able to do so, he should identify both the major and secondary methods. These secondary methods overlap at times, assist other secondary methods, and at times stand alone in paragraphs.

The chief secondary rhetorical methods for accomplishing explanation are: (1) comparison; (2) contrast; (3) comparison and contrast; (4) questions and answers; and (5) cross-references from Scripture. The cross-reference use of Scripture is the supportive use of Scripture. These extra Scripture passages mean essentially the same thing as the text or context for the sermon. They are brought into the message to support and undergird the original text of the sermon.

THE ELEMENT OF APPLICATION

The second major functional element in preaching is application. Application means to relate, to involve, to move to action. When the preacher uses application in a sermon, he speaks to the audience in such a way that they see how the sermon is appropriate, fitting, and suitable for them. Application means to show to the audience that they can use and put to a practical personal use the truth of the message. In applied science, rules and principles are used in order to accomplish tasks such as building bridges, sailing ships, and inventing and discovering miracle drugs. In preaching, application shows the hearer how he can solve problems, live a better life, please God, and perform other spiritual acts and duties. Application is the natural companion for explanation. As explanation presents the message of God's "then," so application presents the message of God's "now."

Application should be present in a sermon because many, if not most, of those in the audience lack the special spiritual, hermeneutical, homiletical, and mental skills necessary to apply the truth of the sermon to themselves. Moreover, many lack the will and desire to apply spiritual truth to sensitive areas of their lives. The preacher, as the minister of the soul, should assist all in his audience by using application.

A double bridge must be built and crossed by the preacher before he can use application with telling effect. The preacher must move his audience from the Biblical world to the modern world. He must also move his audience from the act of listening to a speaker to an act of personal participation with the preacher as he witnesses to God's self-disclosure in Jesus Christ. When these two bridges are successfully crossed, effective communication takes place between preacher and people.

Application may be used in the introduction, sermon body, conclusion, and invitation. It may be used in one, two, three, or all four of these. Contrary to older homiletical views which relegated application primarily to the conclusion, modern communication applies sermon data in all parts as the sermon moves along.

The Focus of Application

The preacher may bring application to a focus on a large number of persons and areas. Since this is true, the preacher should decide exactly who or what is to receive the thrust of application. The sermon application may focus on the universe, the world and space, the earth, Western civilization, the United States, the major geographical sections of this nation, the state in which the preacher is a minister, the city in which the sermon is being preached, the particular denomination and/or individual church, the officers and leaders of the church, the senior members, the adults, the young people, the teen-agers, children, babies, or all members. To whom is the material applied? There can be no effective application until the minister settles this issue.

The Language of Application

Application depends upon nouns and pronouns for its effectiveness. First person and second person pronouns make application direct and personal. One strong form of application is the second person application as when the minister says, "You need to do these four things!" There are times, however, when the application should be first person. The preacher should include himself in the application when it is appropriate to do so. Let him say, "We should grow in grace!" When the preacher can honestly include himself in application, he also confesses his common spiritual needs with his people.

Application may be made indefinite when discretion suggests something less than a frontal attack. The preacher may say, "the man guilty of adultery," or "the one who lies," or "the young person who cheats." Other indefinite words which may be used are: person, someone, people, others, a Christian, a church member, man, mankind, woman, child, children, boys, and girls. The language of application should be direct but tactful, straightforward but courteous, and all-inclusive yet personal.

When the sermon material permits, the preacher should keep the focus of application on the individual in the audience. By focusing on the individual rather than on a hundred or a thousand people, the minister may speak face to face in intimate dialogue with each one. A young student, upon trying to focus on the individual rather than the crowd for the first time, discovered with startling surprise that he did not have "to shout and scream" when he conversed with one. He applied his message with telling effect as he spoke to one person at a time.

Methods of Application

The method of approach to application is as important as the focus of application. In contrast to the procedure of making general remarks which seem suitable for the occasion, the thoughtful preacher will select specific methods of applying. Many choices are available. First, application may be made by affirming that the sermon data does relate to the hearer. Second, application may be made by showing how the message is related. This may be done by showing how the individual may receive the message and act on it. The preacher may present a chronology of possible action, may show steps in a process, may show the logical sequence for conduct, may indicate practical procedures for securing victory over temptations and problems, may present a factual course of action for that hour or for the following hours and days, may indicate how problems may be solved, or may detail the specific action to take place in the public invitation which will shortly follow.

A third method of application sets out the justification, the why, for the hearer's acting on the challenge of the message. The minister's task requires that he present the total sermon data so compellingly that the hearer must believe and respond. The minister will show the individual the imperativeness of the issue for himself. By using the thesis and specific objective, the preacher can achieve this result.

Again, application may be presented by showing the appropriate time—the when—for response. The preacher will seek for immediate commitment from his people. Immediate commitment may involve walking down the aisle when the public invitation is given; it may involve a decision to confer later with the preacher; it may involve a private decision or resolve in the heart which will be known but to God; and it may involve a commitment to go into the world and live for Christ. However the preacher desires the individuals to respond and in whatever manner they respond, the minister needs a note of urgency and immediacy in his feelings, words, and action. The preacher speaks about life or death, salvation or condemnation, victory or defeat, joy or sorrow, faith or failure, and he must speak with concern and feeling. He need feel no hesitancy in pressing individuals to believe and to act.

A fifth method of application allows the minister to describe the results which he believes flow from following the decision for which he speaks. By giving in concrete terms the specific and concrete advantages to be gained by the correct decision, the preacher will be effectively applying his message. The problem with this method is that ministers as a whole so earnestly desire that people make correct spiritual decisions they may exaggerate the possible results. In almost all cases, the exaggeration is not deliberate deceit, but it is eagerness pressed too far. Caution will cause the preacher to temper eagerness with honesty.

An additional method of application allows the minister to present the areas, the locations where a correct decision will permit the audience to serve or respond. It is literally true for Protestant congregations, as for so many other areas of life, that people prove the old proverb to be true: "One cannot see the forest for the trees!" Needs of all types abound in every community in the land, and it becomes the preacher's challenge to focus attention on them.

A seventh method, an ancient but still honorable one, is to exhort. The minister may use with effective results the procedure of giving exhortations to action. Exhortation must not be confused with the use of pressure tactics. They are not the same. Exhortation involves a sincere and earnest pleading by the preacher for the audience to act and to respond. Exhortation is the calling of the child back from the edge of a traffic-filled street, the calling of a sleeping man out of a burning house, and the calling back of a young man skating toward thin ice.

Moreover, an eighth method of application allows the preacher to extend a public invitation during which people are invited and urged to make decisions. The public invitation is application in action. By focusing on the specific objective, the minister will be able to give an invitation which matches his sermon and which should match the mood created in the persons in the audience.

In considering the methodology of application, the minister will not wish to overlook the fact that he may use the tools of explanation, argumentation, and illustration to assist him in any or all of the methods of application. Remember, the functional elements do overlap, blend into, and assist each other as needed.

Factors Influencing Application

Five factors influence the correct use of application in a sermon. First, the preacher has personal factors influencing and assisting him in application. The character of the minister, his knowledge of individuals in the audience, his concern and care for these persons, and his willingness to express warm feelings influence the nature and effectiveness of application in a sermon. Second, the minister has literary factors influencing and assisting him in application. This involves the correct use of the functional elements of preaching (explanation, application, and argument) and the attention given to style (clarity, appeal, and force). If it is true that the choice of the right word for a sentence is as profound as is the difference between lightning and the lightning bug, the minister will pay heed to the functional elements and to style.

Third, the minister has emotional factors influencing and assisting him in application. No speech or sermon can be effective unless it touches emotion and unless it motivates the hearer. In application, the minister may appeal to those desires and aspirations which assist men to be better men: the desire for approval, happiness, recognition and success, continuity of life, and service to others. Moreover, the minister may appeal to the individual to avoid trouble, problems, punitive judgment, disapproval, and failure. The preacher may also appeal to reason, fear, obligation, curiosity, and pride. In the use of any or all of these motivational factors, the preacher will point the individual to an obedience to the Lord Jesus Christ. All emotional factors should be used in good taste for the glory of God.

Fourth, the minister who preaches Biblical truth has Biblical author ity assisting him in application. The minister will be careful to avoid basing his sermonic application on a ministerial foundation or on church authority. The minister does not speak for self. people, or church. Rather, he speaks for God. This is his authority.

Finally, the minister has divine power assisting him in application. The Holy Spirit takes up the witness to God in self-disclosure and makes the witness understandable and acceptable to the hearer. Without this divine aid, effective application becomes impossible.

THE ELEMENT OF ARGUMENT

The third major functional element of preaching is argument. Argument means to persuade, to prove, to convince. or to refute. Argument means reason and discussion as well as controversy and dispute. In the homiletical sense, argument should be restricted basic ally to reason and discussion. Nevertheless, refutation. when used in good taste, is a legitimate part of homiletical argument.

Technically, controversy means a formal discussion between per sons who disagree and who attempt to settle the issue by means of writing and speaking. Dispute suggests contradicting one another rather than reasoning with one another. In homiletical argument the preacher knows or assumes that some type of difference in opinion between himself and various persons in the audience exists. Argument becomes the literary functional device to speak to the mind of the one or minds of the many who hold opinions in need of change or in need of strengthening. There are five methods of argument.

Argument from Testimony

One basic form of argument is argument from testimony. Argument from testimony is an ancient and still valuable form of persuasion. Certain standards must be affixed to this means of persuasion. Concerning the witness cited, the preacher must assure himself that this person is reliable and trustworthy, that he has had full and complete ability to know the truth about which he is quoted, and that he is an acceptable witness to the audience. Concerning the testimony, the preacher should be careful to distinguish whether the data he uses be fact, opinion, hypothesis, supposition, or illustration. As a test of the data cited, the preacher may wish to ask himself the same questions to be asked about the nature of illustrations.[1] In both instances credibility is the issue. An audience will accept various types of data by testimony provided they know the nature of the material cited. An audience does appreciate factual testimony, but it will accept testimony which is opinion, or even supposition, provided the distinction is clear.

Argument by Inference

Inference is the correct use of induction, deduction, and analogy in order to arrive at a decision. In argument by inference, the preacher uses inference in one of its three subforms in order to persuade or convince his audience concerning a view presented. In using induction the preacher will move from particular cases or incidents to a general answer or conclusion. In using deduction, the minister will begin with a general principle—the major premise; set out a true subfacet of that general principle—the minor premise; and then draw a conclusion. In using analogy, the preacher will reason by comparing and contrasting the relationship of two or more items. Induction, deduction, and analogy all lead to valid conclusions when properly managed.

Argument by Special Forms

There are eight special techniques or forms of argument: (1) argument *a priori*, which reasons forward from cause to effect; (2) argument *a posteriori*, which reasons from effect or result back to cause (as in a post-mortem or autopsy); (3) argument *a fortiori*, which reasons from weaker examples to strong ones, e.g., if a thing be true of an earthly judge, how much more will it be true of God?; (4) argu-

---

[1]See pages 67-68.

ment by the use of the dilemma which sets out two assumptions and calls for one choice, either one of which will be unpleasant, unfavorable, evil, or harmful; (5) argument *ex concesso,* which argues from that which has been granted or conceded; (6) argument by the concept of progress, which reasons that, as civilization and humanity advance, progress is made in various areas; (7) argument *reductio ad absurdum,* which reasons by reducing the issue under consideration to the absurd so that it must fail; and (8) argument *ad hominem,* which reasons by appealing to the personal feelings and interests of the hearer.

Even though these special forms of argument may appear to be formidable and difficult to use, they are often used by men who have had absolutely no formal training in argumentation and debate. Usually, those who make use of these forms do so without conscious effort. Not many ministers have had training or experience which qualifies them to reason technically. In a general sense, these eight forms of argument are the common property of free men who argue, debate, and dispute.

Argument by Refutation

Refutation consists of the correct use of *reductio ad absurdum, of ad hominem,* and of straightforward denial, negation, and rejection. Refutation is a difficult task to perform well because of the danger of aroused feelings and negative attitudes. Let the minister who uses refutation look to his own feelings and attitudes.

Argument by the Natural Development of an Assertion

In arguing from an assertion or a thesis, one should develop both the subject and predicate of the thesis. The affirmation that "Jesus is Lord" necessitates that the preacher show one of three things: (1) that Jesus is Lord because of His nature—because of who He is; (2) that Jesus is Lord because of His work—because of what He has done and is doing; or (3) that Jesus is Lord because of who He is and what He has done and is doing. In effect, to develop a thesis one may show the nature of the subject of the thesis (the noun which serves as the subject of the sentence), supply proof of the thesis, or show both of these things in the same message.

These three functional elements may be found in printed sermons used in five ways. First, they may be found in a group of two or more to build one paragraph. While one encounters this blending technique in numerous messages, it cannot be a recommended procedure. Confusion develops when explanation, argument, and application are not clearly marked out. Unless the minister knows with absolute certainty when he is presenting God's "then" or God's "now," and unless he presents them effectively, the audience will receive a blurred picture of Scripture and of its relationship to themselves. Occasionally, one finds a preacher who can blend the functional elements and make them clear, but this unique preacher is an exception to the rule.

Second, the functional elements may be found individually in effective paragraphs which develop the subpoints, or arabic points, of a message. This procedure is a most effective one. If the preacher would put "pure meat" on his structure, he must develop his subpoints with explanation, application, and argument. Third, the functional elements may be found individually in effective paragraphs which develop the major or roman points of a message. Again, good content can be developed for these major points by the use of the three functional elements of preaching. Fourth, the functional elements may be found individually in effective paragraphs which develop the sermon title as a whole. Remember that the title embraces the essence of the text, the central idea of the text, the thesis, and the purpose. In this form, the sermon has no specific points or divisions but is developed by paragraphs of explanation, application, and argument. This sermon is equal to the jewel sermon. Fifth, the functional elements may be found used in combination with the first four. Illustrations will make these clear.

Illustration one: Groups of functional elements *blended*. This form is not as desirable as the four which follow.

Introduction
    Text, central idea of the text, thesis, purpose, and title. (These five may be in any order.)
Sermon body
  I. Major point
    1. Subpoint or minor point
      One paragraph or more with explanation, application, and argument *blended* in each paragraph used. This is not a division of I. and 1., but a paragraph or more about it.*
    2. Subpoint or minor point
      Developed as I. 1.
 II. Major point
    1. Subpoint
      Developed as I. 1.
    2. Subpoint
      Developed as I. 1.
Conclusion
Invitation

---

*These functional elements may be used in any order; they may also be used more than one time; and one or more of them may be deleted.

Illustration two: Functional elements to develop subpoints.
    Introduction
            Text, central idea of the text, thesis, purpose, and title. (These five
            may be in any order.)
    Sermon body

        I. Major point
            1. Subpoint
                One or more paragraphs using singly as many of the func-
                tional elements as needed.*
            2. Subpoint
                Developed as I. 1.
        II. Major point
            1. Subpoint
                Developed as I. 1.
            2. Subpoint
                Developed as I. 1.
    Conclusion
    Invitation

Illustration three: Functional elements to develop major points.
    Introduction
            Text, central idea of the text, thesis, purpose, and title. (These five
            may be in any order.)

    Sermon body
        I. Major point
            One or more paragraphs using singly as many of the functional
            elements as needed.*
        II. Major point
            Developed as I. 1.
    Conclusion
    Invitation

Illustration four: Functional elements to develop the body without major
                    body points. This is the jewel sermon.
    Introduction
            Text, central idea of the text, thesis, purpose, and title. (These five
            may be in any order.)
    Sermon body
            The functional elements used to build the entire sermon.* In this
            sermon there are no points as such. Explanation, application, and
            argument are used as needed.
    Conclusion
    Invitation

Illustration five: Functional elements and outlining used in combination.
    Introduction

---

*These functional elements may be used in any order; they may also be used more than
one time; and one or more of them may be deleted.
    *These functional elements may be used in any order; they may also be used more than
one time; and one or more of them may be deleted.

Text, central idea of the text, thesis, purpose, and title. (These five may be in any order.)

Sermon body
    I. Major point
       1. Subpoint
       2. Subpoint
    II. Major point
       Developed by some combination of the functional elements. Explanation, application, and argument are used as needed.*

Conclusion

Invitation

Illustration five demands a special word. Many books of homiletics recommend that the same rhetorical procedures in regard to dividing or not dividing the title or major points be followed throughout the sermon. This rhetorical consistency is demonstrated in illustrations two through four above. Rhetorical consistency is a good and valid principle to practice. However, a cursory examination of printed sermons reveals that creative preachers allow at least one consideration to take precedence over rhetorical consistency. That one consideration is the nature of the text of the sermon.

What principles are available to guide one in the correct use of the functional elements of preaching? Seven guidelines are offered for the effective use of the functional elements of preaching. First, the minister should follow the best procedures he knows in completing the early steps in sermon preparation. These early steps, prior to the use of the functional elements, involve the personal spiritual preparation of the preacher, the selection of an idea to preach, the correlation of the idea with an adequate text of Scripture, the interpretation of the Scripture so as to discover the central idea of the text, the translation of the central idea of the text into a present-tense thesis or proposition, and the statement of purpose, both major and specific. Moreover, these early steps involve the securing by reading and research of all additional data needed for the sermon and the taking of adequate time to allow the sermon idea and materials to mature. Furthermore, the preacher will begin organizational work prior to the use of the functional elements. The title for the message will be constructed out of the essence of all the preceding data—the text, the central idea of the text, the thesis, and the purpose. In addition to the title, the preacher will frame the outline to be used. It also should grow out of and be composed of the essence of all preceding data, including the title.

---

*These functional elements may be used in any order; they may also be used more than one time; and one or more of them may be deleted.

Second, after these early steps have been made, the preacher should select the correct functional elements to fill out the sermon. How can he know whether to use explanation, application, or argument? He must decide which functional elements to use by considering the purpose of the message, by analyzing the nature of his congregation, by thinking about his personal preferences, and by considering his personal study habits. In a broad sense, the preacher will desire to use explanation and application in each sermon in some degree of balance. These two allow him to speak of God's "then" and God's "now." Illustrations will be freely used as the servant of both explanation and application. Argument may be used if the purpose of the sermon demands it.

Third, the minister should next select the proper methods to develop the particular functional elements chosen. Rather than to ramble through the entire field of exegetical and theological scholarship, the preacher will do his best sermonic work if he will select precise methods. A sharpness and distinctness may be brought to sermons by the careful choice of functional methods.

Fourth, the minister must prepare a topic sentence for each paragraph of functional data to be used. No one has ever invented or discovered a better device for preparing paragraphs than the development of the topic sentence. Many preachers could double their effectiveness in preparing sermons if they would but learn to write topic sentences and to develop them. The topic sentences are then developed by the supplying of data to fill out the functional methods selected.

Fifth, when the minister can do so, he should develop only one functional element in a paragraph. He may use more than one method of explanation to develop a paragraph of explanation provided he maintains the unity of his paragraph and provided the length of the paragraph does not become excessive.

Sixth, after the preacher has written his sermon manuscript with all points and parts developed to his satisfaction, he should test and polish the message. The preacher should read each paragraph carefully and objectively and ask himself, "Have I actually used the functional element and method recorded?" Again, he should ask himself, "In what ways may I polish and sharpen each paragraph so that the desired functional element and method may perform their work?" The minister must always remember that the mechanics of preparation exist solely to enable him to preach authentic and authoritative content.

Seventh, the minister will preach his message. All his labor points toward the hour of proclamation when he desires that God will speak through him to the waiting congregation.

Chapter 5

DIRECT BIBLICAL SERMONS

The reformation of preaching depends upon the proclamation of sermons saturated with true Biblical authority. One may find varying degrees of Biblical authority in sermons. Since Biblical authority is the key concept in understanding authentic sermons, the various degrees of Biblical authority must be clearly differentiated. There are five degrees of Biblical authority which may be seen in published sermons. These five degrees, of course, are not of equal worth. In fact, the last one represents a corruption of true Biblical authority.

The first of the five is the direct Biblical sermon. It uses Scripture in the message with the same meaning as it has in the text. The direct Biblical sermon employs the natural, grammatical, and historical meaning of the text in a direct, straightforward fashion. Only by moving correctly from the grammatical-historical "then" to the relevant "now" can a sermon be a direct Biblical sermon. The text and the direct Biblical sermon are parallel, harmonious, and correlate. The direct Biblical sermon says the same thing as its text.

Four subclasses of the direct Biblical sermon are identifiable.

USING COMMANDS AND IMPERATIVES OF SCRIPTURE

The direct Biblical sermon makes use of the commands and imperatives of the Bible. Although those things commanded or ordered by God through prophets, apostles, and Christ may be ordered and commanded by the preacher, he will remember that all imperatives and commands do not stand on the same plane of authority. Some commands in Scripture were given by evil men, fools, and the devil. Other commands and imperatives have been superseded by later orders. All commands and imperatives must be tested by the New Testament. Specifically, all commands and imperatives must be tested by the leadership of the Holy Spirit and by the relationship of the command to Jesus Christ, who came not to destroy but to fulfill the Old Testament and who is the central character of the New Testament.

Moreover, the preacher will remember to check carefully on the grammatical structure of each command. All apparent commands, as they appear in the King James Version, are not imperatives. The Great Commission, in Matthew 28:16-20, contains an imperative but not in the form as expressed in the King James Version. In verse nineteen we read: "Go ye therefore, and teach all nations, baptizing them in the name of the Father, and of the Son, and of the Holy Spirit. . . ." Much preaching stresses the imperative "Go." "Go," however, is not an imperative as Matthew wrote it. It is an aorist participle and should be translated "as ye go," or "going," or, even more to the point, as "having gone," indicating not a command by Jesus to go, but a confident expectation that His disciples would go. The command or imperative appears in the word "teach," or rather, "disciple," as it should be translated. Jesus said, in effect: "As you go about your normal travels and way of life, *disciple* all nations." However, participles in these verses convey the sense or force of imperatives and may be translated as such. Nevertheless, the stress does fall on the only imperative in the verses, "disciple." Careful exegesis will prevent confusion as to what is a command and what is not.

USING AFFIRMATIONS AND PROPOSITIONS OF SCRIPTURE

The direct Biblical sermon utilizes affirmations and propositions of the Bible. Those things affirmed, proposed, or declared by God through prophets, apostles, and Christ may be affirmed, proposed, and declared by the minister. Great care must be exercised to identify the spokesman who affirms something, for fools, evil men, and Satan also speak in Scripture. The fool did say, did he not, that "there is no God" (Psalm 14:1a).

Again, as with imperatives, the minister must interpret all affirmations, declarations, and propositions in the light of the New Testament, of Jesus, and of the Holy Spirit. Grammatical matters will also be checked to determine whether or not an apparent affirmation is such.

Can there be a propositional revelation? Did God give well-formulated propositional statements to the Biblical writers, or did He perform His great deeds and inspire His writers to see and to record their impressions of the events? Many modern theologians are convinced that the latter is the true explanation for the presence of propositional statements in Scripture. Modern scholars feel that the writers of Scripture are accountable and responsible for the various propositional statements in the Bible.

Whether God phrased the exact proposition or affirmation in each instance or whether God revealed Himself in deed and event and charged Paul and John with the responsibility for forming a valid and authentic account is largely, if not totally, beyond recovery. The evidence at hand is that we do have propositional truth in Scripture. This propositional truth has been placed in Scripture by God through the Holy Spirit speaking and writing through the Biblical writers.

These affirmations, declarations, and propositions, therefore, are valid content for authentic and authoritative Biblical sermons. Subject to the careful rules and principles of hermeneutics and to the leadership of the Holy Spirit, the preacher may and should preach the great affirmations of the Bible.

USING NEGATIONS OF SCRIPTURE

The direct Biblical sermon uses negatives and prohibitions, the "thou shalt nots" of Scripture. Those things denied, prohibited, or negated in Scripture may be also denied, prohibited, and negated by the preacher. As in the use of commands and affirmations, great care must be exercised to discern the spokesman and occasion surrounding the prohibition. Again, the grammatical and historical matters concerning negatives must be investigated in the light of the New Testament, of Jesus Christ, and the leadership of the Holy Spirit. Negatives should be checked to be sure that they are actually negatives.

USING ETERNAL TRUTHS OF SCRIPTURE

The direct Biblical sermon makes use of timeless and eternal truth of Scripture. These timeless and eternal truths may, of course, be cast as commands or imperatives, as affirmations and propositions, and as negatives and prohibitions. In addition to these three more obvious groups discussed above, there are numerous narrative, biographical, and historical events which contain timeless and eternal truth. Such historical sections of Scripture contain data on people, events, conflicts, deeds, and personal testimony. From these great passages of Scripture the minister may extract the timeless truth God has revealed.

In essence, the issue involves translating the past into the present, finding the eternal and timeless truth, and sharing that truth with the Smiths and Johnsons in the congregation. The preacher may preach about the strength of character and depth of faith of Peter, Paul, and

Moses and not speak one word of application. The preacher may preach without application because he believes that all texts are eternally relevant or because he has never thought about or discussed the need for contemporary application of Scripture.

Some passages are so direct in language and feeling that one may preach them in past tense (in the historical) and trust that they will carry an automatic application. When David transgressed and sinned so tragically, his cry for forgiveness, as found in Psalm 51, strikes the heart and mind so sharply and painfully that one can find himself involved by the mere reading or by hearing the reading of the total event in the historical setting.

Not all Scripture is easily read in the historical setting. Joshua 6:21 (ASV) records: "And they utterly destroyed all that was in the city, both man and woman, both young and old, and ox, and sheep, and ass, with the edge of the sword." This verse occurs at the end of the description of the events of the seventh day of Joshua's siege of Jericho. For the preacher to use Joshua 6:15-21, or a similar passage of Scripture, by merely reciting the historical data is to present an incomplete account. Joshua 6:21 stands in such complete contrast to the life, deeds, and teaching of Jesus Christ that the minister must show how and why this deed of Joshua belongs in the Bible. This, of course, can be done, and the preacher must do it.

How is timeless and eternal truth found in a narrative, historical, or biographical section of Scripture? First, eternal and timeless truth may be discovered by a careful use of the grammatical-historical method of interpretation. Because the details of how to use the critical method of interpretation will be set out in chapter nine, they will not be discussed at this point. The absolute necessity for a correct use of the critical method in investigating a text, however, cannot be overlooked. Second, following the careful exegesis of the text, the minister must state his historical thesis or the central idea of the text. The historical thesis and the central idea of the text are correlate. Third, the preacher must translate the historical thesis, central idea of the text, into a present-tense affirmation (a proposition or contemporary thesis). Fourth, the preacher must test this contemporary proposition as to its timeless and eternal quality.

In testing the proposition for its timeless quality one should ask five basic questions: (1) Has the text used an adequate portion of Scripture so that it is a fair example of the truth presented? If not, the preacher should start over with the selection of an additional text. If it is, he may continue. (2) Does the central idea of the text exactly state the historical meaning of the text? If so, the preacher may continue. (3) Does the present-tense proposition naturally and logically interpret the

text? One should determine whether or not the present-tense proposition covers the same type of principles, categories, situations, personalities, conflicts, struggles, or issues as occur in the text. This third test
also involves making certain that the proposition harmonizes with the
New Testament, with the life and teachings of Jesus Christ, and with
the leadership of the Holy Spirit. If the answer is negative, he should
subject the passage to further exegesis. If positive, he may continue.
(4) Is the present-tense proposition timeless in meaning? If it is not,
he should rewrite the proposition. If it is, he may continue. (5) Is the
present-tense proposition universal in meaning? He should discover
exceptions to the affirmation if possible. If there are exceptions, they
must be dealt with in the sermon or another proposition must be
written. If the answer is negative, he should rewrite the proposition.
If positive, he may continue.

How, then, may a narrative, historical, or biographical section of
Scripture be used as eternal truth? When Paul wrote to the Roman
Christians, he said:

> I am debtor both to Greeks and to Barbarians, both to the wise and to the
> foolish. So, as much as in me is, I am ready to preach the gospel to you also
> that are in Rome.[1]

How can Paul's determination to preach to the Christians in Rome
be used by a twentieth-century preacher? One answer is that you
cannot get from Paul, in this particular statement, to a modern preacher because Paul is merely expressing a personal desire which has no
direct influence on others. Another view states that you can use Paul
as an example or illustration, but that to use this Scripture as proof
that something must or even should be done involves poor exegesis and
application. Again, the claim is made that by process of analogy Paul
may be made to speak to twentieth-century preachers concerning
readiness to preach. As Paul was ready so should we be ready, runs
the argument. There yet remains one possibility, stronger and more
promising than any of the above views. By a process of generalization
this passage in Romans may be used as eternal truth in a direct Biblical sermon. Generalization is similar to induction. Technically, in the
process of using induction, all known facts and data should be collected
and analyzed before a valid conclusion is drawn. However, there are
instances when one case may be used as suitable data for the process of
arriving at a valid answer. This is the process of generalization: taking
one case and establishing a universal timeless principle.

It is said that diamonds are uniform in their essential nature and

---

[1]Romans 1:14-15; context 1:8-15, ASV.

that what you know about one, you know about all. Uniformity does not mean absolute identity, but it means that such variations as are present in diamonds do not change the diamonds into other minerals. Diamonds of various classes are still diamonds. The same process of generalization applies to a judicious and critical use of Scripture. Paul was ready to preach at Rome. Because of who Paul was, because of the nature of his commission and calling, because of the nature of the gospel, and because of the needs of men, Paul's statement can be generalized, translated, extended, and applied directly to ministers of the twentieth century. Indeed, we, too, should have the same readiness to preach that Paul had.

In attempting to discover the eternal truth in Scripture, one must remember that some texts of Scripture are by nature historical and local in meaning. They contain material which seems to be temporary, immediate, and nonrecurring. These passages may be used for teaching Bible history and background. Such a passage is Exodus 17:8-16, which describes Israel's war with Amalek. Moses, supported by Aaron and Hur, sent Joshua into the battle. While Joshua fought, Moses raised his hand and interceded with God. As long as Moses held up his hand, Israel prevailed, but as soon as Moses lowered his hand, Amalek prevailed. Therefore, Aaron and Hur placed a stone under Moses and supported him on each side. Israel won the battle.

In seeking the eternal truth of this passage, and others similar in nature, the preacher must present to his congregation from the passage truth which is eternal and which goes beyond that immediate and temporary situation of the text. Basically, this passage is historical and local. It is bound in the "womb of time." Yet, even in this text there is eternal truth. The eternal principle in this text is to be found in the obedience of Israel's leaders to God. To apply the text and say that we must support missionaries on the field of battle (i.e., Joshua), by holding up the hands of the pastor (i.e., Moses) is to do violence to the text. If this passage be missionary in import, it is strange missions indeed!

Other texts are by nature historical but eternal. They contain material which is cast in a historical setting, but which projects through time to eternity. Such a passage is Exodus 20:1-17, which contains the Ten Commandments. These commandments go beyond the local setting in which Moses received them from God and are eternal in value. As is true of this text, it is generally true that texts which are historical but eternal are given in positive or negative commands, as prepositional truth, as condemnations or commendations, or as timeless truth. Passages which are historical but eternal may be applied directly to the congregation.

Moreover, there are passages which have elements of the historical and local blended with the historical but eternal. Acts 2:1-47 demonstrates this double characteristic. In the setting at Jerusalem, with Jews from all the earth present, God wrought a miracle in making each Jew hear Peter's sermon in his own language. This act was not repeated in Acts, nor in the New Testament, nor since. The miracle of each Jew's hearing Peter in his own tongue was apparently local, immediate, and temporary. However, the content of Simon Peter's sermon, though cast out in time, was and is eternal. Peter declared, as Luke recorded it: "And it shall be, that whosoever shall call on the name of the Lord shall be saved" (Acts 2:21). This verse is historical but eternal in application.

The essence of discovering the eternal truth lies in the ability of the preacher to distinguish the abiding elements in a passage from the temporary. The preacher may think about the temporary elements as a vehicle which brings to us the cargo which is eternal. In no sense does the vehicle become unimportant. It is not fable, myth, fiction, or irrelevant form. It is vehicle, and it is important because it has aided in getting to man the cargo, the message, which is eternal. The preacher discovers by careful and prayerful study those positions of Scripture which are vehicle and which are cargo. He will use both in his sermons—the vehicle, largely used as background data, and the cargo, largely used as the heart of the message.

Must we teach only history? Must we never be prophets to say "the Lord speaks now in this Scripture"? Is the Bible shut and locked to a present-tense application? The answer is a resounding *no* to all three questions. By using imperatives and commands, affirmations and propositions, negatives and prohibitions, and eternal truths we may speak relevantly in our day. To preach with valid relevant application is to preach as did the prophets, apostles, and the Lord Jesus Christ. This is our challenge. This is our task.

The following sermon by Karl Barth, translated from German by M. Wieser, illustrates direct Biblical authority.[2] Furthermore, the message by Barth is evangelistic in purpose and a homily in form.

---

[2] Karl Barth, *Deliverance to the Captives*, trans. Marguerite Wieser (New York: Harper & Borthers, 1961), pp. 20-27.

UNTO YOU IS BORN THIS DAY A SAVIOR

LUKE 2:1-14

INTRODUCTION:

1. Barth addresses his hearers affectionately and summarizes the text for them. This is a simple form of *explanation* (exposition). Direct Biblical authority is present.

2. *Application* using illustration which confronts the hearers with the question of their involvement: (1) direct introduction, (2) supposition, (3) personal creation.

3. *Application* using illustration for confrontation: (1) direct introduction, (2) supposition, (3) personal creation.

4. *Application* using illustration for confrontation: (1) direct introduction, (2) supposition, (3) personal creation.

My dear brothers and sisters, now we have heard the Christmas story. We heard about Caesar Augustus and the governor of Syria, about Joseph and Mary and the birth of the baby in Bethlehem, about the shepherds in the fields and the appearance of the angel of the Lord in their midst, about the multitude of the heavenly host, praising God and saying *Glory to God in the highest, and on earth peace among men with whom he is pleased!*

I surely would like to know what went on in your minds when you heard this story! Perhaps two or three among you did not listen very carefully—this happens quite often —and the story passed over their heads like a cloud or a puff of smoke. Should I read the story again for the benefit of these people of wandering thoughts? It is worth repeating twice, even a hundred times!

Or perhaps there are those, men or women, who thought I was telling a nice fairy tale, far removed from the realities of life? Too beautiful to be true? What shall I tell them? Shall I debate with them? I shall gladly do so at any other time. But presently ours is a more important task.

Perhaps also some among you, when they heard the story, were reminded of the days of their youth long since gone by. They thought of Sunday school where they were told this story for the first time, of the Christmas tree, of the presents and the candies, of how beautiful things were, but are no longer and never will be again. What shall I answer? Shall I put on a serious face and say: Forget about Christmas trees and Christmas sentiments and concentrate on the Christmas story itself? This will not be my reply either.

5. *Application* showing how the sermon relates to the hearers.

6. *Application* by affirmation of relationship and by showing what to do.

7. *Application* showing relationship using explanation (exposition).
Application by illustration: (1) direct introduction, (2) art, (3) observation.
Explanation by exposition (assertion).
Application by illustration: (1) direct introduction, (2) poetry, (3) Christmas hymn.

I only intended to show you, my dear friends, that *these* are our human reactions to the Christ-story, which truly is the story of us all. It is much more important, more true and more real than all the stories in history books and novels and all the broadcast and printed news put together! A little absent-mindedness, a little unbelief and a little Christmas sentiment, these are our reactions, not only yours, but mine as well!

Until the *angel of the Lord* appears and shakes us up! The angel of the Lord most certainly passed this night through the streets and the homes and the squares of Basel. He was here for those who celebrated Christmas Eve in loneliness and distress, or on the contrary in fun and frivolity. He is here for all those who are still asleep and maybe have something to sleep off. He is passing through the churches of our town this morning. How does he tell the good news to all these people? How do they listen to him or do not listen at all? However, let us not refer to other people, but rather focus on ourselves. The angel of the Lord most certainly is here in our midst to speak and to be heard. It only remains for me to make you aware of his presence and attentive to his words, so that together we may listen, and ponder what he has to say.

An angel! That is—a *messenger*, who has some news for us. You might quite simply think—of the mailman bringing you some news. The angel of the Lord is God's messenger carrying the news of the Christmas story. You see, if *he* announces the news, absent-mindedness, unbelief and lofty sentiments are swept away, for the angel of the Lord descends directly from God to us. I recently saw a picture where he precipitates straight from heaven to earth, almost like lightning. Granted, this is an image, and yet it is real. If the angel of the Lord is the carrier of the news, the lightning strikes and illumines the

8. *Explanation* by transitional preview of text phrases to be used. This forecasts the homily form and direct Biblical authority. This is applied explanation.

BODY OF THE SERMON:
9. *Explanation* by division and exposition.

10. *Explanation* by illustration: (1) direct introduction, (2) factual, (3) observation of current news. A contrasting illustration. Also by *application* showing relationship.

11. *Explanation* by contrasting illustration: (1) direct introduction, (2) hypothetical, (3) personal creation. *Application* showing relationship.

truth: the glory of the Lord shone around them and the night was as light as the day. As a Christmas hymn has it: "Eternal light from heaven descends, the earth all new and bright extends, and vanquished is the darkest night, we all may be children of light."

And now let us try to hear and understand part of what the angel of the Lord told the shepherds and tells us now. *For to you is born this day in the city of David a Savior!* These words *you—this day—a Savior* contain the whole Christmas story. We shall meditate on each one of them.

"*To you* is born this day a Savior," says the angel of the Lord. This is already tremendously important.

First, the news of the birth of the child in Bethlehem is quite different from the news, let's say, of the arrival of the Emperor of Ethiopia in our country. You may have heard about this event. We were flattered that the emperor liked our country and that his hosts were equally impressed with their guest. But we hear this news—don't we?—thinking: "Why should I be concerned? This is entirely a matter between him and them." In contrast, the angel of the Lord points to Bethlehem, saying, "for *to you* is born this day a Savior." For your sake God was not content to be God but willed to become man; for you He emptied Himself that you may be exalted; for you He gave Himself that you may be lifted up and drawn unto Him. The wondrous deed brought Him no gain, fulfilled no need of His. It was accomplished only for you, for us. The Christmas story then is a story that is enacted with us and for us.

The news of the birth of the child in Bethlehem is not to be likened to a statement made in a textbook. The angel of the Lord was no professor as I am. A professor would perhaps have said: "To mankind is born a

Savior." So what? We are apt to deduce that mankind in general does not include me, is only meant for others. It is like in a movie or a play where we are confronted with people who are not ourselves. In contrast, the angel of the Lord points to the shepherds and points to *us*. His news is directly addressed to us: *"To you* is born this day a Savior!" You, regardless of who you are, whether or not you understand the message, whether or not you are good and pious people. The news is meant for you. For your benefit the Christmas story happened. Again, it does not take place without us; we are involved in it.

The news of the birth of the child in Bethlehem affects us differently than the morning mail. When the mailman arrives, we eagerly ask: "Anything for me?" And seizing the letter, we withdraw to read it. We resent intruders peeping over our shoulder and want to read the letter alone, since this is a private matter. In contrast, the event of Bethlehem is no private matter. *"To you* is born this day a Savior."* True, the angel of the Lord points to you and to me, individually, yet he addresses us corporately. His news ties us together like brothers and sisters who share a wonderful present from their father. No one is first, no one is last, no one gets preference, no one gets shortchanged, and most important, not a single one goes wanting. He who was born in Bethlehem is the eldest brother of us all. Therefore we pray in His name *"Our* Father." Therefore we do not pray, "Give me this day my daily bread," but rather, "Give us this day *our* daily bread." And forgive *us our* trespasses! And lead *us* not into temptation, but deliver *us* from evil! Therefore also we go to the Lord's Supper as to the table of the Lord, and eat from *one* bread and drink from *one* cup. "Take and eat! Drink ye all!" Therefore the Christian life is one great communion, a fellowship with the

12. *Explanation* by illustration of contrast: (1) direct introduction, (2) hypothetical, (3) personal creation. *Application* by showing relationship by using four illustrations (one family illustration and three Biblical illustrations — eldest brother, prayer, Lord's Supper): (1) all four direct introductions, (2) the family illustration created; the other three factual, (3) the first a personal creation and the other three Biblical.

This long involved paragraph uses direct Biblical authority.

Savior and hence a fellowship among brothers. Where there is no communion with the Savior, there is no communion among brothers, and where there is no communion among brothers, there is no communion with the Savior. The one is not possible without the other. This is the content of the angel's call "*to you*," and we should keep it in mind.

"To you *this day!*" says the angel of the Lord. When Christ was born it was *this day!* A new day dawned in the middle of the night. Christ Himself was and is the sun of this day and of everyday. The new day is not only Christmas Day, it is the day of our life.

This day refers not only to the *past*, to "once upon a time." Far from it. The angel of the Lord today announces the same news he then announced to the shepherds. We live in the new day which God has made. We hear of a possible new beginning in our human relations and conditions, in the history of our lives and even in the history of the world. We are told that yesterday's misery, guilt and fear, though still existing, have been mercifully covered and no longer harm us, because to us is born a Savior. We may take courage, pull ourselves together and venture a new start. Human experience does not warrant such confidence, yet this is the assurance of the angel of the Lord. Because the Savior is born, therefore a new day has dawned!

This day implies *not only tomorrow*. Certainly *also tomorrow!* He who was born on that first Christmas Day will not die ever again but lives and reigns eternally. Yet we ought not to dwell on the morrow. You know well enough the kind of people that love to repeat: *Morgen morgen, nur nicht heute!* (German proverb, in translation: Tomorrow, tomorrow, but never today!) "Let's wait and see" is a dangerous saying. Who knows if we shall be around tomorrow? Surely the Savior will be there, but what about us? Who knows

---

13. *Explanation* by division and exposition. *Application* affirming relationship.

14. Developed by *explanation* and *application*. Barth explains and applies the eternal relevance of the birth of the Saviour. Direct Biblical authority. This is existential explanation. It may also be called applied explanation.

15. *Explanation* by exposition (using an assertion), and by *application* using three illustrations—a proverb, a literary quotation, and a Biblical illustration: (1) direct introduction (all three), (2) proverb, literary opinion, factual, (3) literature, Bible. Direct Biblical authority.

whether we shall hear the good news once again tomorrow and shall be free to respond? The decision is not in our hands. Only yesterday I came across a word of our Swiss writer Jeremias Gotthelf: "Life is not a light; a light can be kindled again: life is a fire given by God to burn on earth just once and never more." My dear friends, let us pay heed lest we miss the hour of this fire right here and now. We are told elsewhere: "O that today you would hearken to his voice! Harden not your hearts!"

16. *Explanation* by division and exposition (assertion). Direct Biblical authority.

This is what the angel of the Lord has to tell us when he announces *"This day."* And now we hear: "To you this day is born *a Savior!"* This is the very heart of the Christmas story. To you this day is born *a Savior.* Of the many thoughts that come to mind here, I shall choose just one.

17. *Explanation* by exposition and by *application.* Direct Biblical authority.

What does the word *Savior* convey? The Savior is He who brings us *salvation,* granting us all things needed and salutary. He is the helper, the liberator, the redeemer as no man, but God alone, can be and really is; He stands by us, He rescues us, He delivers us from the deadly plague. Now we live because He, the *Savior,* is with us.

18. *Application* by showing relationship. Direct Biblical authority.

The Savior is also He who has wrought salvation *free of charge,* without our deserving and without our assistance, and without our paying the bill. All we are asked to do is to stretch out our hands, to receive the gift, and to be thankful.

19. *Application* by showing relationship. Direct Biblical authority.

The Savior is He who brings salvation to *all,* without reservation or exception, simply because we all need Him and because He is the Son of God who is the Father of us all. When He was made man, He became the brother of us all. *To you this day is born a Savior,* says the angel of the Lord.

CONCLUSION:
20. *Application* by showing relationship.

This, then, is the Christmas story. You see, we cannot possibly hear this story and not look away from ourselves, from our own life with its cares and burdens. There He is, our great God and Savior, and here we are, human beings, and now it is true that He is for me, is for us. Impossible to hear His story without hearing our own. It is the great *transformation* that has been worked in us once and for all, the great *joy* it has released in us, and the great *calling* we have received to set out on the way he shows us.

21. *Application* by a challenge.

What shall we do now? Shall we continue in our old ways, in absentmindedness, in disbelief, perhaps in some lofty Christian sentiments? Or shall we awake and rise, set out on our journey and turn about? The angel of the Lord does not compel anybody. Even less can I compel! A forced listening to the Christmas story, a forced participation in the story, is of no avail. We must willingly listen, and willingly participate.

22. Developed by *explanation* and by *application.* Direct Biblical authority.

And suddenly there was with the angel a multitude of heavenly host praising God and saying, "Glory to God in the highest, and on earth peace among men with whom he is well pleased." Our place is not among the angels; we live here on earth, in this city, in this house. Yet when we hear about this song of praise and when we realize that God did not send one angel alone, but that the multitude of the heavenly host was present with their song of praise, might we not be carried away just as we fall in step when a good band plays or unconsciously hum or whistle a well-known tune that falls on our ears? That would be it! Then we would freely listen to and freely participate in the Christmas story. Amen.

The strength of "Unto You Is Born This Day a Savior" is impressive: (1) the message correctly uses direct Biblical authority; (2) evangelistic or gospel purpose is revealed; (3) the homily form is simple and appealing in the hands of one of the great theological minds of the centuries; (4) the introduction is well developed; (5) the sermon body utilizes three phrases from the text for presentation rather than formal points. This is correct form for the advanced homily, which is discussed later in the book. Barth presents three paragraphs with explanation, ten paragraphs with application, and nine with a mixture of explanation and application. In the mixed paragraphs, Barth uses applied explanation or existential explanation. In style, the message reflects ample clarity, appeal, and vigor.

Concerning places for improvement, three suggestions are offered: (1) the conclusion is comparatively short in relation to the introduction: eight paragraphs for the introduction and only three for the conclusion; (2) for some readers the message would have been strengthened by utilizing formally stated points rather than by presenting Scripture phrases in sequence; and (3) again, for some readers, the message would have been strengthened by separating rather than blending the functional elements of preaching. Barth tends to confuse explanation when he mixes application with it.

Chapter 6

OTHER TYPES OF BIBLICAL AUTHORITY

In addition to direct Biblical authority, four other types of Biblical authority may be identified in sermonic literature. The four additional types, three of which are valid, offer less Biblical strength than does direct Biblical authority. The fourth, corrupted Biblical authority, represents a perversion of Biblical truth. How, then, may the additional types of Biblical authority be identified?

THE INDIRECT BIBLICAL SERMON

The indirect Biblical sermon uses Scripture in the message in an indirect way or with a variation from the meaning of the text. This sermon should begin with the natural, grammatical, historical "then" of the text. Unfortunately, it does not always do so before it departs with a variation from the central idea of the passage. In one sense the indirect Biblical sermon moves at a tangent from the central idea of the text. It does so by adding selected ideas to the central idea of the text. The preacher adds to, supplements, expands, or reduces the central idea of the text as well as compares and contrasts it in the indirect Biblical sermon.

There is an obvious danger in the use of indirect Biblical sermons in that any departure from Biblical truth introduces the possibility of theological error. In using this type of sermon, the minister should exercise care to be sure that his message is grounded in a critical study of Scripture and to be certain that when he departs from the central idea of the text, he does no violence to the text. The indirect Biblical sermon does not possess the total strength nor full authority of Scripture as does the direct Biblical sermon. Therefore, the indirect

Biblical sermon, though valid, is weaker and less desirable than the direct Biblical sermon. With some texts and for some occasions, however, the indirect Biblical sermon may be the preacher's best available choice.

The basic question to be asked about a sermon is: "Who said it?" That is, does the preacher speak from the Bible or merely from his own experience? If the Scripture presents the ideas of the sermon and the preacher speaks those ideas, the sermon is a direct Biblical sermon. When the preacher adds to or supplements the ideas of the text, the sermon is an indirect Biblical sermon. Therefore, one must always ask about a sermon, "Who said it? The preacher or the Bible?"

Three subclasses of the indirect Biblical sermon are identifiable. All three are, for all practical purposes, equally valid.

Completing an Implication in Scripture

The indirect Biblical sermon utilizes the process of completing implications in Scripture. Implication and inference, though commonly confused, are not synonymous. A valid implication must be present in the text in order for the preacher to complete the implication. Technically, a speaker, writer, or actor implies something; and, on the basis of the implication, a listener, reader, or observer completes that implication. The process of completing the implication is called *inference* and may be used to describe this process if desired. The important detail to keep in mind is that when the Scripture implies something, the preacher may complete the implication in his sermon.

When in Matthew 5:13-16, the disciples are called the salt of the earth and the light of the world, Christ obviously intended an implication. He did not state directly and positively that the earth should be arrested from decay and that the world is in darkness. However, one can hardly miss the intended implication that the earth must be preserved and that the world must receive light. Christ implied truths which the preacher may complete in his sermon. Some expositors insist that completed implications, as in Matthew 5:13-16, are as strong as if a direct teaching had been given. There are Scriptures of which this may be true. The preacher must beware, however, of equating his completed implication with direct Scriptural teachings.

The preacher may complete the implications involved in many passages used for direct Biblical sermons. By completing the implications of commands and imperatives (showing the *why* or *how* for commands), by completing the implications for negatives and prohibitions (again, showing why or how), by completing the implications for affirmations and propositions (showing the nature and/or proof of these affirmations), and by completing the implications of other truths in Scripture, the preacher may make a correct use of implications. For example, the negative commandment, "Thou shalt not kill" (actually it reads "Thou shall do no murder") implies a reverence for life. There is more than a negative here: there is a valid implication that human life is to be respected.

The minister should use the critical method of interpretation and be certain that he has found a valid implication. Moreover, after a valid implication has been found, the preacher must decide whether or not to use it or to use the central idea of the text. Unless there is a strong reason for turning to the implication, the preacher should develop the central idea of the text. In the excellent sermon by H. Gordon Clinard, which is used later in this chapter to illustrate the combination Biblical sermon, a portion of the first half of his message completes a valid implication while the second portion of the message is direct Biblical data. Since space will not permit the use of an entire message which completes a true implication, the sermon by Clinard will serve as an example of how valid implication may be used. Clinard, for example, could have used only the three arabic points under *I* for his entire sermon, and it would have been an indirect sermon which completed an implication. As he prepared his sermon, however, it is a valid combination Biblical sermon.

Particularizing a General Truth

The indirect Biblical sermon utilizes specific and particular truth drawn out of a broad general idea or truth. This broad or general truth is a truth which all Christians will approve. This broad truth serves as the source from which a restricted or limited idea is drawn. The syllogism (with major premise, minor premise, and conclusion) supplies the procedure for a correct use of particularizing a general truth.

In Romans 12:9 (AV), Paul declares: "Let love be without hypocrisy. Abhor that which is evil; cleave to that which is good." This verse, especially the second admonition, reveals an excellent Scripture for use in particularizing a general truth. A preacher may use Romans 12:9b and preach about "A Good Citizen Looks at Gambling," or "A Christian's Attitude Toward Pornography." Since gambling and pornography are not delineated by Paul, how can this verse be used for these titles? By a process of deduction or particularization, they may be used. The preacher can establish quite easily that gambling and pornography are evils and that they, by a process of particularization, come under the apostle's admonition of things to avoid.

The minister will take care to insure that he has a true broad principle from which to work, that he is legitimately drawing out a specific case, and that the entire sermon utilizes Scripture properly. All rules for critical Biblical study apply in particularization, and all safeguards of testing the passage in the light of the New Testament, of Jesus Christ, and of the leadership of the Holy Spirit obtain.

Comparing and Contrasting the Biblical Truth

The indirect Biblical sermon utilizes the process of comparison and/or contrast as a method for constructing a message. The preacher uses physical terms to explain spiritual truth and spiritual terms to explain physical data. In using comparison and/or contrast the preacher creates his own positive or negative analogy. He creates and uses analogy based on spiritual and physical data. This process of creating a sermonic analogy is *not* the same as the process of interpreting and preaching a Biblical analogy, i.e., one that has been written into the text. When the preacher uses an *analogy* from Scripture as it is written, he is preaching a direct Biblical sermon. However, when the preacher adds to or supplements a text by adding spiritual data to physical terms or physical data to spiritual terms, he is using comparison and/or contrast as a sermonic tool.

Analogy may be used by the preacher as a method of reasoning for proving a point at issue. Analogy is more commonly used, however, to explain or to illustrate something. When the preacher creates his analogical sermon structure through comparison and/or contrast, he is essentially using positive or negative analogy to explain or illustrate truth.

Since space in this book will not permit the use of three full sermons to illustrate the indirect Biblical sermon, the sermon "Spiritual Leprosy" by G. Campbell Morgan[1] has been selected for analysis.

---

[1]*The Westminster Pulpit* (Westwood; N. J.: Fleming H. Revell Company, n.d.), VIII, 48-60.

SPIRITUAL LEPROSY

INTRODUCTION:

1. *Explanation* by giving key verses of the text.

2. *Explanation* by medical illustration: (1) direct introduction, (2) factual, (3) current news and biography.

3. *Explanation* by medical illustration: (1) direct introduction, (2) factual, (3) current news and biography.

4. *Explanation* by medical illustration: (1) direct introduction, (2) factual, (3) current news.

5. *Explanation* by presentation of the actual text (Lev. 13-14), by e x p o s i t i o n (word study). Notice Morgan's use of leprosy as a symbol of sin. The

And the Lord spake unto Moses, saying, This shall be the law of the leper in the day of his cleansing.

LEVITICUS 14:1-2

Leprosy remains until this hour more or less a mystery to medical science.* In the New Year's Honors List a name included was that of Dr. George Turner, now Sir George Turner, whose story is one of splendid heroism and of pathetic interest. In Pretoria he did arduous work among the lepers, and on reaching the age limit gave himself to bacteriological research in the laboratories of this country, inspired by the ambition to find some remedy for the disease. Suddenly he discovered that he had contracted the disease himself, and now for over two years has been working in seclusion toward the same end.

Dr. Gerhard H. A. Hansen, of Bergen, Norway, who died last year, discovered the bacillus of leprosy, which was previously unknown. The exact value of the discovery cannot yet be known, but it is recognized as an important contribution.

These preliminary references are made in order to emphasize the mystery of the disease. It is, to say the least, an interesting fact, to which attention was drawn in *The Times* in an article on Sir George Turner, that the problem of the remedy for leprosy is an exceedingly difficult one because of the fact that none of the lower animals has yet been found to be capable of contracting the disease.

The Hebrew word for leprosy is derived from a root which means to strike down. It was looked upon as a stroke of God. There

---

*Medical science has made great strides toward the conquest of leprosy since this was written. It is now widely known as Hansen's disease from the name of the discoverer of its bacillus.

use of symbolism domi-
nates this sermon.

6. *Explanation* by illustration: (1) direct in-
troduction, (2) opin-
ion, (3) Lange.

7. *Explanation* by illustration: (1) direct in-
troduction, (2) opin-
ion, (3) Jewish expos-
itors.

8. *Explanation* by expo-
sition.
Application by an ap-
peal to action in health
matters.

was, however, nothing in the law itself to
give any ground for the view that it was
always such. In the thirteenth and fourteenth
chapters of Leviticus, which contain the law
of the leper, leprosy is dealt with on the
ground of health, simply as a disease; yet
it is quite evident that its mysterious character—its unknown origin and its insidious
and resistless progress—made it the fit type
or symbol of sin.

Lange graphically describes it as "a speaking picture of sin, and of evil the punishment
of sin—the plastic manifestation, the medical
phantom, or representation of all the misery
of sin."

Jewish expositors of these Scriptures were
quite explicit as to their spiritual suggestiveness. In dealing with these particular laws,
one of them said, "If a man considers this,
he will be humbled and ashamed on account
of his sin, since every sin is a leprosy; a spot
upon his soul."

The study of the law of the leper has for
us a twofold value. Its first teaching has to
do with the actual fact of the Divine interest
in the physical well-being of men. The general
good of humanity was sought by the segregation of the leper. The individual interest was
safeguarded in the extreme caution observed
in order that no person should thus be cut
off from communion with the people unless
he were actually leprous. I am not now
dealing with that aspect of the teaching of
these two chapters. I should, however, like
to say so much as this in passing, that in
each of these matters we have very much yet
to learn. We are a long way behind the
Hebrew economy in the recognition of God's
interest in the affairs of man's physical well-
being, and in the application of the principles
to which I have referred—the necessity for
the separation of all those in the grip of a

disease which constitutes a danger to the community. We are slowly moving toward it, but very slowly. There are some who describe legislation along these lines as grandmotherly. If it be grandmotherly, then may God increase it! We need to learn a good deal also before we arrive at the full realization of the importance of the second of these principles, that there must be strict justice: no person must be cut off from fellowship unless he actually is a peril to society.

However, when we turn from these general principles to the actual disease of leprosy, the only application possible to us is the symbolic, and that is supreme. There can be no reading of these chapters, especially of the fourteenth, without realizing that while in these laws there was provision for the physical well-being of the community, there was also a remarkable recognition of the spiritual.

It is important, therefore, that we consider quite briefly, and yet most carefully, the relation between the two parts of this law of the leper as we find it in Leviticus, chapters thirteen and fourteen. The thirteenth chapter is diagnostic. There is nothing more in it than instructions by which the priest was to discover whether what appeared to be leprosy was actually leprosy. In the thirteenth chapter there is no gleam of hope for the leper. The symbolic value of the chapter, therefore, is that sin demands the separation of the sinner, and is incurable by human agency.

Chapter fourteen opens with the words of my text. "And the Lord spake unto Moses, saying, This shall be the law of the leper in the day of his cleansing." The careful reader will immediately be arrested by the assumption that the leper can be cleansed. The thirteenth chapter contains no gleam of hope for the leper, but the fourteenth opens in the full flood of the light of hope. In the thirteenth the priest is to distinguish and differentiate

9. *Explanation* by exposition. Morgan defines his homiletical procedure for this sermon: symbolism. The first sentence of this paragraph is open to question. All Scripture does not need to be applied but may be simply understood and explained.

10. *Explanation* by exposition. Morgan interprets Leviticus 13 symbolically. Indirect Biblical authority.

11. *Explanation* by exposition. Morgan also interprets Leviticus 14 symbolically. Again indirect Biblical authority is used.

and separate, and make possible the return to the camp of the man who is not suffering from leprosy. The fourteenth says, "This shall be the law of the leper in the day of his cleansing." This is an admission of the possibility of what is not in the power of man to provide or produce. The chapter then contains instructions for that ceremonial procedure by which the cleansed man is to be restored to the privileges of the camp and of the tabernacle, the privileges of the economy of the theocracy, and fellowship with God in personal and direct worship. So far as the two chapters constitute a part of the Levitical code, we see that this code distinctly taught that leprosy is entirely incurable by human action; but it also recognized the fact that it may be cured by Divine action. As these chapters are viewed as symbolic, their suggestion concerning sin is the same: sin is incurable by any human process, but it is curable within the Divine economy.

12. *Explanation* by exposition. Symbolism again used. Indirect Biblical authority.

We at once recognize a gap between the two chapters, and the gap is great. Between the thirteenth and fourteenth chapters of this shadow of the old economy stands our great Christ, our great High Priest. In the thirteenth we have the unveiling of sin under the figure of leprosy, and in the fourteenth we have an unveiling of the way of salvation in the picturesque, and suggestive if vanishing, ritual of the old economy.

13. *Explanation* by preview of major points. Symbolism used. Indirect Biblical authority.

Let us consider what these chapters suggest pictorially. Our line of consideration will be twofold: first, leprosy as the symbol of sin; and, second, the way of cleansing from sin as revealed in the symbolic ceremonial.

BODY OF THE SERMON:

14. *Explanation* by preview of the division of I into four subdivisions.

Leprosy stands as a symbol of sin in four distinct particulars: first, in the mystery of its origin; second, in the method of its manifestation; third, in the nature of its effects; and, finally, in its treatment in this Hebrew economy.

15. *Explanation* by sub-division 1 of I. Also *explanation* by comparison and contrast. Symbolism again used which reveals indirect Biblical authority.
Also *explanation* by illustration: (1) direct introduction, (2) poetical, (3) common saying.

First, in the mystery of its origin. So far as leprosy is concerned, that may be dismissed by the simplest of statements already made, that even until this hour of scientific advancement, man has not been able to discover the origin of leprosy. There is nothing more appalling, shall I say, nothing more perplexing, nothing more certain, than the mystery of sin. I know we have our doctrine of original sin—in passing I should like to say that original sin is not a Scriptural phrase and therefore I hold no brief for it. But, granted the doctrine, believing in the doctrine in certain senses as I most certainly do, let it be remembered that it does not explain the nature of the persistent presence of sin in every human being; it states only the fact that sin is there, that in some form, sin is discovered in every human being. Moreover, it admits the fundamental truth that in human life sin is superinduced. The poetic declaration, "To err is human," is not true, though it is perfectly true if by human we mean humanity as we find it to-day. But if we think of humanity as in the purpose and economy of God, it is not human to err, not human to sin. Sin is a poison, sin is something within the soul that atrophies its powers and prevents the realization of all the deep and profound meaning of life. It is not part of essential humanity. Whatever terms we may employ in dealing with sin, we must remember that sin is superinduced.

16. *Explanation* by exposition and *application* showing how one can act.

Sin is a spiritual malady, the physical is but the expression of it; behind every physical act of sin is the spiritual attitude. There is no sin of the flesh which is not inspired by sin of the spirit. I cannot sin with my hand until I have sinned with my heart. I cannot sin physically, save as I have sinned spiritually.

17. *Explanation* by questions, answers, and

Then is it inherited? If so, how? The Bible teaches that every man is offspring of God illustrations: (1) direct introduction for both, (2) personal fact and Biblical, (3) observation and Bible.

18. *Explanation* of I. 1 by exposition and by two Biblical illustrations: (1) direct introductions, (2) both factual, (3) both Biblical.

19. *Explanation* by subdivision 2 of I, and by two illustrations: (1) both direct introductions, (2) the first, biographical; the second,

in his first creation, in his spirit life. Or is the spiritual malady of sin contracted in man? If so, when? I would have you clearly to understand that I am asking questions I do not propose to answer, for the simple reason that I cannot answer them. I ask them in order to affirm that there is no answer. Neither the theologian nor the philosopher has ever answered either of these questions. If sin is inherited, how is sin transmitted in the spirit realm? I am not spiritually the son of the man whose name I bear. "We had the *fathers of our flesh* to chasten us, and we gave them reverence, shall we not much rather be in subjection unto *the Father of spirits* and live?" Mark the clear distinction. If sin is of the spirit, and in the spirit, then some evil bacillus has been introduced poisoning the spirit.

The nature of that poison is discovered in Biblical definitions. Paul speaks of "the mystery of lawlessness"; John declares "sin is lawlessness." In the first we have the admission of the mystery. In the second we have a statement as to the true nature of sin. The sins which we denounce are but symptoms; sin lies deeper. Sin is "lawlessness," which does not mean being without law, but being in revolt against law. This evil germ within the spirit of man that affects all his mind and heart and soul is lawlessness; it has a thousand manifestations, but it is always the same in essence. It is indeed the *mystery* of lawlessness. How is it, why is it, that all men find this principle at work within the soul? I recognize the mystery; but I face the fact. As leprosy is a mystery as to its origin, so also is sin; but it is an appalling fact.

Leprosy is a symbol of sin in the method of its manifestation. The first appearance is at times discoverable only by the trained eye. Dr. Turner was a specialist, having a trained eye, yet the disease was on him and mania hypothetical case true to life, (3) biographical or current news; the second personal. Indirect Biblical authority.

20. *Explanation* by exposition (assertion).

21. *Explanation* by exposition (assertion).

22. *Explanation* by subdivision 3 of I, by *application*, by *explanation* (comparison and contrast), and by Biblical illustrations as word studies. Indirect Biblical authority.

23. *Explanation* by subdivision 4 of I and by comparison and contrast. Indirect Biblical authority.

festing itself before he knew it. One morning, while shaving, he caught sight of marks on his hands that arrested him; he was a leper! The first symptoms are discoverable only to the trained eye. In the little child there may be a thousand things that you count sin that are not proofs of sin at all; a child romancing up to a certain age is not sinning. It is exercising a faculty of mind which belongs to it.

The time comes when the first sign of sin is manifested in the child; it is lawlessness.

This leprosy of lawlessness is invariably progressive, never halting; it steals insidiously forward with varying degrees of speed, until, at last, the whole man is corrupt, mastered— strange paradox—by lawlessness; the whole life is in revolt against authority, against government.

Leprosy is the symbol of sin in the nature of its effects. It excludes from fellowship with our fellow-men. It renders the victim loathsome even to his fellow-men. Not always in the more vulgar forms of sensuality, but with cold, hard, cynical, devilish self-centeredness, infinitely more loathsome than vulgar forms of sensuality. Sin, like leprosy, ultimately renders its victim insensible to the pain of his own disease. We have in the Scriptures of Truth such arresting phrases as "hardened," "a conscience seared," "past feeling!" Leprosy ultimately completely destroys the physical frame; so also sin ultimately completely destroys the spirit life, and all its powers.

Once again, leprosy is the symbol of sin in its treatment in the Hebrew economy. Why was the leper separated not only from man but from God also as to outward worship? Surely because that in itself it was a symbol of sin, and there must be recognition of the fact that sin cuts a man off from fellowship with God, dims the vision, makes him in-

24. *Explanation* by summary.

25. *Explanation* by transition using questions and answers and by exposition. Symbolism used.

sensible to the fact of God. That necessarily means separation from the camp, exclusion from the fellowship of those who see the City of God and strive for its building; and that without respect of persons.

Sin is an appalling mystery as to its origin in the individual soul and life; in itself it is lawlessness, revolt against the law of God; and it expresses itself in a thousand ways as revolt against the law of man. Our age is particularly characterized by the restless spirit of lawlessness. Everywhere there are signs of mental, moral, social, theological, lawlessness; the refusal to recognize authority, or to be bound even by contracts which men make between themselves. Lawlessness is of the very essence of sin, a poison at the heart of man, a virus at the center of human life, that which prevents the realization of high ideals in individuals and in humanity. It is that which ultimately destroys man and destroys nations. I have never yet heard of a person being asked to sign a pledge against it. This is a very significant fact, revealing, first of all, that men do not as a rule deal with sin, but with sins; not with the malady but with the symptoms; we are always in danger of dealing with the surface of things, instead of getting down to the central trouble. On the other hand, perhaps, no pledge has ever been asked against it because of the subconscious conviction of humanity that it is something with which humanity cannot deal.

Is there a way of cleansing for the leper? Is there a way of cleansing for the sinner? Here we turn to the New Testament. I referred to a gap between the thirteenth and fourteenth chapters of Leviticus, and I declared that Christ stands in that gap, in the spiritual realm. In the fourteenth chapter we have the poetic symbols of His work, quite simple figures intended for that kindergarten period

26. *Explanation* by transition using numerous Biblical illustrations: (1) all direct introductions, (2) all true and factual, (3) all Biblical.

in the history of the people of God, yet all eloquent.

Passing into the New Testament, I find lepers, but I also find Christ; and the first general remark I desire to make is that never under any circumstances do we read in the New Testament of Christ *healing* a leper, never under any circumstances do we read of any writer describing a leper as being *healed*. The one word uniformly used is *cleansed*. That there is a distinction is evident from the fact when John asked, "Art Thou He that cometh, or look we for another?" Jesus said, Tell John the things you have seen, that "the blind receive their sight, and the lame walk, the lepers are *cleansed*, and the deaf hear, and the dead are raised up, and the poor have good tidings preached to them." At the foot of the mountain of beatitudes, when the Lord uttered the ethic that remains to this day startling and awful in its white holiness, He was immediately met by a leper, who said to Him, "Lord if Thou wilt, Thou canst make me clean." The hand of Christ was immediately stretched out, and the leper who could not be touched, was touched, the word was spoken, "I will; be thou made clean," and the leper was cleansed of his leprosy. Exactly the same scene was repeated later in one of the cities to which Jesus went. Again a band of ten lepers came, and He cleansed them all. These stories of the cleansing of the lepers must be interpreted as all the stories of healing are interpreted. According to New Testament teaching, Jesus never wrought a physical miracle wholly within the realm of the physical; such wonders were always associated with a spiritual activity far more wonderful. "Son, thy sins are forgiven," said He to the man sick of the palsy; and the people complained, "Why doth this man thus speak? he blasphemeth; who can forgive sins but One, even God."

Jesus replied to them, "Whether is easier, to say to the sick of the palsy, Thy sins are forgiven, or to say, Arise, and take up thy bed, and walk? But that ye may know that the Son of man hath power on earth to forgive sins . . . I say unto thee, Arise, take up thy bed, and go unto thy house." In the ministry of Jesus there was perpetual relationship between the physical and the spiritual; every physical miracle of healing or of cleansing was an outward sign of the spiritual marvel that He was able to work in the souls of men.

I glance back to Leviticus, to the fourteenth chapter, with which I am not proposing to deal in detail. Therein two great movements are revealed in the law of the leper on the day of his cleansing; they may thus be summarized. First, the priest meets the leper without the camp and leads him back into the camp. Second, the priest within the camp offers on behalf of the leper certain offerings, and anoints him with oil, and sets him at the door of the tent of meeting, the place of fellowship with God. The symbolism is perfect.

In the old economy the priest went without the camp where the leper had been driven on account of his leprosy, to certify the leper's cleansing, not to cleanse him; he could do no more than that. He then observed the ceremony which symbolized the way of his spiritual cleansing, and in doing so employed two birds, one to be sacrificed, the other to be set free, and cedarwood, scarlet, and hyssop. Do not be afraid of these pictures, they are very suggestive. The birds were for sacrifice; the cedarwood was the symbol of strength, for it was incorruptible wood; the scarlet, forevermore the color of earthly glory, spoke of life and health and beauty; the hyssop was the plant of fragrance and of healing. All these things in the old economy were brought by the leper; but none of them

27. Explanation by division II and by preview of the two subdivisions. Note another reference to the symbolic. Indirect Biblical authority.

28. Explanation by subdivision 1 of II, exposition, comparison and contrast, Biblical illustrations, and by appli- cation. Indirect Biblical authority.

cleansed him, neither did the priest cleanse him; but the man, having been cleansed by some act of God, was now to celebrate the physical cleansing, and that by such ceremony as suggested the method of spiritual cleansing. The disparity between all this and the method of Christ is more eloquent than the comparison. Our High Priest does not come without the camp to certify the leper cleansed; He comes without the camp to cleanse the leper. He comes to the place where the leper is cast out, the place where the leper is alone, excommunicated from the holy place, ostracized by all his familiar friends, shut out in his own loathsomeness for the sake of the health of those left behind. Coming to the leper there, in some infinite and amazing mystery, Christ takes into His own heart and nature the virus and poison of the leprosy, cancels it and by passion, by blood, the outward symbol of the profounder spiritual passion makes it not to be; and, lo, the leper is cleansed. His flesh come again as the flesh of a little child, and the spirit that was lawless utters its first word, and it is a word of submission: "Lord, what wilt Thou have me to do?" That is the death of lawlessness and the beginning of the law-abiding life. Our High Priest comes not to certify the leper cleansed, but to cleanse the leper, and to bring that leper back into the camp, into the theocratic economy, into right relationship with God, into the Kingdom of God.

29. *Explanation* by subdivision 2 of II, comparison and contrast and by Biblical illustrations. Indirect Biblical authority.

The priest not only brings the cleansed man back into the camp, he sets him at the door of the tent of meeting. Again we have the pictorial suggestions. In the old economy the priest offered the guilt offering, speaking of the reparation the man was making to God; he anointed the man with oil on ear and hand and foot, indicating his new consecration, then presented the Sin Offering and the Burnt Offering and the Meal Offering for him. Mark again the disparity: in the old economy the leper himself had to provide the offerings and bring the oil. In the new economy the one and only Priest provides against every aspect of human sin, all which aspects were suggested in these offerings of the old pictorial method. Sin is fraud; the man who is lawless is robbing God, defrauding God of his rights, rights that are always beneficent in purpose toward man himself, so that man robbing God of His rights is destroying himself in the infinite mystery of his being. For that the Guilt Offering or the Trespass Offering was provided. Sin is not only fraud, it is defilement finding its way into the life with its pollution and vileness. The Sin Offering provided for the removal of defilement. Sin is also failure in life, failure in the realization of the real meaning of life. The Burnt Offering suggests sacrifice that puts away the defilement, and issues in new dedication of the life. Sin is also failure in service. The Meal Offering covers it.

CONCLUSION:

30. *Explanation* by exposition and by *application*. Indirect Biblical authority.

Let the shadows pass and summarize the whole suggestiveness by declaring that our High Priest in His one offering for sin meets every aspect of human sin and deals with it. In this strange and wonderful economy of grace the offerings and the oil are provided by the Priest, forfeited life for life forfeit, spiritual power for spiritual death. A man is not a Christian merely because Christ has stood between him and some ultimate punishment. A man is a Christian when he has received from Christ the gift of life whereby lawlessness is checked, halted, mastered, dealt with, and life is related anew to God.

31. *Explanation* by exposition and by *application* using Biblical illusions and descriptive language.

There is another mystery, the mystery of godliness. The New Testament speaks of both. The mystery of lawlessness has many manifestations. It manifests itself in one man in reckless sensuality, in the plunge into the vulgar and bestial. It manifests itself in another man in cynical selfishness, selfishness which is so absolutely selfish that it dare not sin vulgarly, has not the courage to do it. Lawlessness expressed itself in one man in actual murder, and in another man in a cynical contempt for suffering and indifference to the agonies of men. As God is my witness I do not know which is the more terrible manifestation of lawlessness, but the latter I think. I can understand the rush of blood, the red passion that strikes a blow; that is lawlessness, and it is terrible; but, oh, the terror of the form of lawlessness which has so little recognition of the throne of God, and so little recognition of the claims of humanity, that it is content to live for self and minister to self, shutting its doors that it may never see the objectionable things outside. There may be all the perfumes of Arabia, and all the upholstery of Damascus; but in the sight of heaven whose God is love, and Who is prepared to die for humanity, it is the very ultimate of hell, and the most terrible form of lawlessness. The self-centered cynical man will say hard things about the sensualist and the murderer. We still measure ourselves among ourselves, and compare ourselves as with ourselves, and we find satisfaction while thus we put the little measurements of dust on our lives; but all the while God sees the leprosy of lawlessness and the rottenness of our godless culture.

32. *Explanation* by exposition and Biblical illustration: (1) direct introduction, (2) truefactual, (3) Biblical.

But there is another mystery. "Great is the mystery of godliness; He Who was manifested in the flesh, justified in the spirit, seen of angels [messengers], preached among the nations, believed on in the world, received up in glory." This mystery of godliness is also spiritual. There has been one manifestation of it in human history. Jesus Christ lived and wrought and served, not independently, but dependently on God. He manifested in the midst of human history the glory and beauty of true life, law-abiding and submissive. But He did infinitely more, He went outside the camp to meet the leper, and in some wonderful mystery of infinite compassion to place His pure life at the disposal of the impure man, so that being communicated to him his leprosy may be cleansed, and the man made to live.

33. *Application* by showing relationship. Indirect Biblical authority.

That mystery of godliness has been given to us as the norm of life, the type of what God would have other men to be; but more, blessed be God, or I am left a leper: not the norm alone but the germ also, and that communicated to my soul, so that the lawlessness is subdued, made not to be; and my feet are turned into the way of the Divine commandment, and my life at last conformed to the good and perfect and acceptable will of God. There is no other name given under heaven among men whereby we can be saved.

This sermon by Morgan is an *indirect Biblical sermon* (through comparing and contrasting the Biblical truth), *evangelistic* in purpose, and *rhetorical* in form. In strength these values are evident: (1) the title is interesting and appealing, (2) the title is properly divided and developed, (3) the introduction presents the text and stresses the symbolic use to be made of the text, (4) the body structure is set out under two major points with four subpoints under I and two subpoints under II. This is a simple and satisfactory use of form. (5) The conclusion stresses the purpose Morgan had in mind, and (6) the illustrations are sufficient and mostly Biblical.

In regard to possible improvement, it must be stated that this sermon by Morgan is not typical for him. Normally, G. Campbell Morgan is much more Biblical and appealing than this message represents him to be. This sermon was chosen because it illustrates effectively the comparison and contrast sermon. Morgan could have strengthened his sermon by the following changes: (1) The style is heavy and tedious; (2) in the movement from I to II Morgan's procedure is clumsy and awkward; (3) the sermon, though repeatedly stressing the fact that a symbolic use will be made of the text data on leprosy, does not move briskly and easily through the materials presented; (4) the comparison and contrast method, though valid, does not come off to a good advantage in this sermon. At times one is not sure just what

Morgan is attempting to do. *Biblical authority is weak* and confused because of the strain placed upon the comparison and contrast method. (5) The purpose of the text obviously is not evangelistic and therefore Morgan has stepped beyond his text in authority and purpose.

THE CASUAL BIBLICAL SERMON

The casual Biblical sermon makes a rather free use of the meaning of the text. This type of sermon should, but usually does not, begin with the historical meaning of the text before it proceeds to develop the message in a free and casual way. Most likely, more sermons of this type have been preached during the twentieth century than all other types combined. What a tragic commentary on the modern state of preaching! What a shallow regard this demonstrates for the Bible!

A valid question may be asked here. If this sermon represents such a weak and inferior use of Scripture, why discuss it in a book which seeks to have reformation in preaching? The casual sermon must be discussed for two basic reasons: (1) that men who use it may see this procedure, with its weaknesses, defined and illustrated, and (2) that those who use it may see this form in comparison to better forms and thereby be helped in changing to better methods and procedures. Those who preach casual sermons regularly should strive to move up to direct Biblical sermons.

Occasionally, a casual sermon will be so sparkling and fresh that it should be used. The tragedy of preaching casual sermons lies not in their occasional use, but in the constant, continuous, and routine use of such a casually-related Biblical form. Unless a preacher is as homiletically creative as Fosdick, he will surely starve his people on a diet of casual preaching. In regard to freshness of style, there are too few Fosdicks!

There is a rather large number of subclasses of casual sermons, but for practical purposes they will be grouped and discussed under two broad headings: (1) the rhetorical suggestion sermon and (2) the essay sermon with a text.

Using Rhetorical Suggestions

The rhetorical suggestion sermon makes use of any idea suggested by the text or some other source. The text, in its grammatical-historical relationships, may or may not furnish the spark for the sermon, but it most certainly does not share in the structure or development (i.e., outline and content) of the sermon. Horace Bushnell prepared his famous sermon "Unconscious Influence" by this method. He used

John 20:8a ("Then went in also that other disciple") as a text and
described the scene at the tomb on Resurrection morning. Bushnell said:

> In this slight touch or turn of history, is open to us, if we scan it closely,
> one of the most serious and fruitful chapters of Christian doctrine. Thus it
> is that men are ever touching unconsciously the springs of emotion in each
> other; thus it is that one man, without thought or intention, or even a con-
> sciousness of the fact, is ever leading some other after him. Little does Peter
> think, as he comes up where his doubting brother is looking into the
> sepulchre, and goes straight in, after his peculiar manner, that he is draw-
> ing in his brother apostle after him. As little does John think, when he loses
> his misgivings, and goes into the sepulchre after Peter, that he is following
> his brother. And just so, unawares to himself, is every man, the whole race
> through, laying hold of his fellow-man, to lead him where otherwise he
> would not go.[2]

Only the slightest touch of suggestion set Bushnell on his homiletical
way.

The evidence in available printed sermons indicates that almost
anything will spark a suggestion which will lead to a casual sermon.
A favorite passage of the casual-minded minister is Matthew 17:8, AV,
which reads: "And lifting up their eyes, they saw no one, save Jesus
only." Immediately the preacher fastens attention on the words "Jesus
only." He quickly produces an outline similar to this:

Text: Matthew 17:8
Title: "Jesus Only"
Introduction: Jesus is a unique person.
Body: I. Jesus only is Lord.
II. Jesus only is Saviour.
Conclusion: Trust Jesus for salvation.

In no way does *this text* reveal such thoughts. Why should the
preacher use a magnificent Scripture on our Lord's transfiguration
for the purpose of preaching the above outline? Since there are
Scriptures which teach directly and effectively the things which the
preacher says in this outline, why does he not go to the correct
Scriptures? But he protests, "This text is the one I must use!" He has
this choice, but he also has a serious responsibility, namely, to preach
Scripture as God gave it and not as he wishes to use it. This loose
and casual treatment of Scripture represents one of the serious weaknesses of the modern American pulpit. By this procedure, people are
led to believe that "any doctrine" may be preached from any text.

Another favorite Scripture of the casual-minded preacher is Matthew

---

[2]Horace Bushnell, "Unconscious Influence," *Sunday Half Hours with Great Preachers*,
ed. Jesse Lyman Hurlbut (n.p.: 1907), p. 357.

26:39a: "And he went a little farther. . . ." In the garden of Gethsemane Jesus left Peter, James, and John and "went a little farther" (away from the three apostles so that He could talk alone with God). The preacher, however, does not show us the Son of God in agony "sweating drops of blood." Instead, we hear an exhortation to "go a little farther in prayer, stewardship, witnessing, and church attendance." There is apparently no limit or end to the fancy of some men at this point. This Scripture does not teach the four items indicated. The preacher could have, and with just as much authority, pleaded for the people to go a little farther in the working with the babies, children, young people, and adults of the church. About all that can be said is that the text suggested something to the preacher. This type of sermon is weak and is virtually without Biblical authority when it appears.

Using an Essay with a Text

The complications of modern life occasion the use of data from ethics, philosophy, sociology, psychology, counseling, science, and other fields of knowledge. Because of the strong appeal of facts and information from these fields and because such data is readily relevant, ministers are tempted to overuse it. These fields of knowledge have much to teach the minister, and he should use all truth in preaching. At the same time, he should not become a public teacher of ethics, sociology, or psychology. There are ample ways to utilize all truth without ceasing to preach.

When the material is handled properly, the minister may speak to his people about ethical issues, sociological problems, and psychological disturbances. Since Scripture does not treat all these issues directly, some preachers choose to prepare an essay and use a text with their messages. This, of course, is a casual use of the text, but in certain selected cases appears to be justifiable. Some men make a rather full use of psychology and counseling in their pulpit work. Often, these sermons are essays with texts. The basic problem with this approach is not that a minister preaches sermons casually related to texts, but that he may preach such sermons almost exclusively.

An additional problem with this essay sermon is the use of a text with it. The listing and reading of a text with this sermon actually adds nothing to the sermon. Perhaps the preacher may cause some listeners to believe that he has Biblical authority, but Biblical authority is not present. A more straightforward approach calls for the preacher to tell his people that for this sermon he will not use revealed truth but ethical truth. In this event, the preacher simply presents a moral essay or a moral speech to his people. Biblical authority, therefore, is absent. For the minister who excels in and enjoys essay preaching, a periodic homiletical check upon himself is advisable to prevent majoring on this type preaching.

A lack of space prohibits the use of both a rhetorical suggestion sermon and an essay sermon. Therefore, the excellent rhetorical suggestion sermon of Harry Emerson Fosdick, "The Power to See It Through," will be analyzed.[3] In this sermon, Fosdick creatively uses the casual sermon with multiple passages for its text.

---

[3]Harry Emerson Fosdick, *Riverside Sermons* (New York: Harper & Brothers, 1958), pp. 28-37.

THE POWER TO SEE IT THROUGH

INTRODUCTION:

1. *Explanation* by exposition (giving the text) and by *application* relating Demas to us.

There is one character in the New Testament, mentioned only three times, concerning whom one suspects that many Christians have not even heard. His name was Demas and, alas, some of us are much more like him than like the great New Testament figures we know so well. First, in Paul's letter to Philemon, we read, "Demas, Luke, my fellow-workers." So Demas, along with Luke, and named first at that, was standing by Paul in his Roman imprisonment, a devoted and promising disciple. Second, in Paul's letter to the Colossians, we read, "Luke, the beloved physician, and Demas." Reading that, one wonders why Demas and Luke, who were praised together at the first, were separated in this passage as though Luke indeed retained Paul's confidence as "the beloved physician" but Demas had become merely "Demas." Third, in the Second letter to Timothy, incorporating, we suppose, one of the last messages Paul ever wrote, we read, "Demas forsook me, having loved this present age." Three points on a curve, that enable us to plot its graph! For here is the story of a man who made a fine beginning and a poor ending: Demas, my fellow-worker; Demas; Demas forsook me.

2. *Explanation* by exposition and by illustration: (1) direct introduction, (2) factual, (3) Biblical.

One's imagination plays about this condensed biography, especially the relationships between Demas and Luke. Intimate companions of Paul in the Roman circle, they must have known each other very well. Now, Luke is the only narrator of Jesus' life whose gospel records the parable about the man who started to build a tower and was not able to finish. Matthew did not remember that, nor Mark, nor John; only Luke recalled it. One wonders if he remembered it because of Demas. Demas was slipping, let us say.

Through Paul's little group in the Roman prison anxious apprehension ran that Demas was not holding out, and one imagines Luke pleading with his friend. The Master Himself, he might have said, warned His first disciples about the peril which is besetting you. For once He said, "Which of you, desiring to build a tower, doth not first sit down and count the cost, whether he hath wherewith to complete it? Lest haply, when he hath laid a foundation, and is not able to finish, all that behold begin to mock him, saying, This man began to build, and was not able to finish." So one thinks of Luke pleading with his friend, and at least Luke, alone among the evangelists, put the parable into his gospel. He had seen its truth too vividly illustrated in the life of a friend ever to forget it. Demas, my fellow-worker; Demas; Demas forsook me.

3. *Explanation* by exposition (presentation of facts) and by illustration: (1) direct introduction, (2) figure of speech, (3) personal creation.

As one considers this familiar experience of a fine beginning and a poor ending, it is obvious, for one thing, that the qualities which make a good start possible are not identical with the qualities that see life through to the end. Starting power and staying power are not the same thing in any realm. A ship can make a grand get-away at the launching only to make a poor stand later against the fury of the waves and winds when the northeasters are unleashed. So one sees in Demas a character—how familiar—capable of fine impulses, generous responses, idealistic loyalties, and eager loves; only he lacked staying power.

4. *Application* by illustration: (1) direct introduction, (2) hypothetical case of a child, (3) personal observation; and by showing relationship.

One thinks of this not simply because of the New Year season, which is naturally a festival of fresh beginnings, but because our generation, above every other generation in history, has stressed the gospel of a good start. How we have emphasized the importance of childhood and of the influences that play on childhood! To give a child a good start, we have said, is the most essential benediction that can be bestowed upon a human life. So we have thought and accordingly have labored. Now, that gospel of a good start is profoundly important and it tells the truth; only, not the whole truth. For many of us here had a good start. We have no complaints about that. In family and church, in school and early Christian training, we had a fine beginning. But for all that, some of us are Demas and all of us know we could have been. Over what thin ice have we skated! How easily we could have broken through! How many of us here have already fallen far from a faith that once was strong and a character that once was clean. We know Demas. The mirror shows him to us. Introspection reveals the process of his downfall. Nearly two thousand years ago he lived and died, his very name barely preserved, as though by accident, and yet how vivid he is in our imaginations! Demas, my fellow-worker; Demas; Demas forsook me, having loved this present age.

5. *Explanation* by exposition and by illustration: (1) direct introduction, (2) factual, (3) Biblical.

Another general truth concerns our thought: namely, that however beautiful one's start, nothing matters much in human life without a good ending. Of course one does not mean that we may demand an outwardly successful and fortunate conclusion, as in old sentimental novels where everything had to come out all right. But without a *good* end, without morale and staying power and steady character to see a man through to a worthy conclusion what else in human life can be much worth while? Jesus could have spoiled everything in the Garden of Gethsemane and, had He done that, all for nothing would have gone His unremembered Sermon on the Mount and His unselfish months of ministry. The career of Jesus was like splitting a log. Every previous blow of the ax is indispensable but it is the last blow that splits it. So we know there was a Christ, and the rich meanings of His ministry have come to us because He had staying power to go through to the end, where He could say, "It is finished."

What would you consider the most lamentable tragedy in human life? To face suffering, to be cruelly handicapped? Surely not! For we have seen some terribly handicapped people who had moral staying power so that they came through to a great conclusion, all their flags flying when they came into port. But there is a tragedy so appalling that when one has seen it in the circle of one's friends the very reminiscence of it makes one's blood run cold—to be so fortunately born, to have so glorious a boyhood, to rise to such responsible position, to be so loved, so trusted, and then to crack as though all the time the shining metal had had a flaw in it, to betray one's trust, deceive one's friends, blow out one's brains! Whether it be in dramatic fashion like that or in homelier wise, where a fine beginning lapses by slow degrees into a disheveled ending, Demas is the tragedy.

In this regard life is like marriage. How beautiful love begins! With what romantic launchings can it get its start! But we elders, who watch the young folks at their lovemaking and their weddings, habitually ask a deeper question. They have qualities that can start a home; have they the qualities that can keep one—the deep fidelity, the long-term loyalty, the steady and abiding love that can keep a home? For in marriage, as in all life, a good beginning only makes more tragic an unhappy end.

On this first Sunday of the New Year, therefore, let us talk together not about starting power—there is no soul here that has not more than once made a fine beginning—but about staying power. I celebrate the qualities of faith and character that enable a man to see life through.

BODY OF THE SERMON:

9. *Explanation* by division, exposition, and illustration: (1) direct introduction, (2) factual, (3) biographical (Chopin).

For one thing, staying power is always associated with a certain central integrity of conscience. Whatever else life may give or may deny, one thing is absolutely indispensable to a man—that he should not break faith with himself, that he should not inwardly be a failure. Such quality of conscience, making it indispensable that a man live on high terms with himself, whatever happens, is of the essence of staying power, and it is the glory of great artists that so commonly in their art they have exhibited it. Elsner was a teacher of music in Warsaw to whom came, one day, a young man for music lessons, and at the end of the first term one finds this in Elsner's record: "Lessons in musical composition: Chopin, Fryderyk, third year student — amazing capabilities, musical genius." That was a fine start. But to finish that career was costly. It cost hard work—one would take that for granted. It cost discouraged hours— one would expect that. Once Chopin was so disheartened he talked of turning to interior decorating instead of music. But, deeper yet, Chopin's career cost conscience. He would not, for popularity's sake, write music that violated his own interior standards. One thing was absolutely indispensable, no matter what happened: he must not break faith musically with himself. So Chopin became "Chopin." As another put it, "the artist's conscience is a fearful thing."

10. *Explanation* by comparison and contrast, and by exposition.

Now, as we see Paul and Demas in Rome, it is obvious Paul had *that*. He would have liked outward good fortune and success could he have had them on honorable terms—of course he would! But whether fortune or misfortune befell, one thing was absolutely indispensable—he must not break faith with himself and the Christ within him. Not simply as a matter of duty but as a matter of happiness, that was indispensable. Demas, however, was of another sort. He soon found something else that was indispensable. "Demas forsook me," wrote Paul, "having loved this present age." So that was it! Roman civilization was brilliant like our own. It had ugly aspects, but for agile minds and grasping hands there were prizes to be gained. All around Paul's poor prison house was Rome. So Demas, no Chopin in his character, wrote his music down. He did not have an artist's conscience; Christ had never dug so deep as that into Demas. To be loyal to the royal in himself was not absolutely indispensable. He loved this present age.

11. *Application* by affirmation of relationship, by challenge, and by multiple illustrations.

You see, I am not really talking about Demas now, but about us. One would not minimize the sacrifices that such a conscience as we are speaking of often costs in a world like this, but the great souls who have most possessed such conscience have commonly thought of it not as a burden of duty but as a gospel of liberty. Listen! No man ever needs to be a failure. Trouble, outward breakdown of hopes, may come, but a man who cares most that he should not be a failure can capitalize trouble. "All sunshine," say the Arabs, "makes Sahara." Men may give the hemlock to Socrates, nail Jesus to the cross, behead Paul outside the gates of Rome. Livingstone may die in the heat of Africa, his work unfinished, and Lincoln may be shot by a crazy man. All such souls have known an inner liberty. Whatever happened, they did not need to *be* failures. That was within their control. Still they could be loyal to the royal in themselves and come to their last port with flags a flying.

12. *Explanation* by exposition using comparison.

That is the final difference between people. Paul faced many kinds of failure but he himself was no failure. If, however, the old legend is correct, Demas went back to Thessalonica and became a priest of idols in a pagen temple. He himself was a failure.

13. *Explanation* by division, by illustrations:

In the second place, staying power is always

(1) formal introductions for all, (2) arts, philosophy, missions, and history, (3) biographical reading for all four; and by exposition.

associated with the experience of being captured by a cause, laid hold on by something greater than oneself to which one gives one's loyalty—an art, a science, a vocation, a social reform, an object of devotion which one conceives to be more important than oneself. This was the common property of those to whom we have turned as illustrations of persistent character—Chopin in music, Socrates in philosophy, Livingstone as a missionary, Lincoln as a statesman with a cause. They all cared for something so much superior to themselves, to which they gave their long-term loyalty, that they stood the gaff, as we say, so far as their individual fortunes were concerned, and followed through to a strong conclusion for their cause's sake. All staying power in character is associated with that.

14. *Explanation* by description of process.

Christ had never gotten so deep as that into Demas. Demas had laid hold on some of the more comfortable aspects of the Christian gospel, but the Christian gospel had never laid hold on Demas. Demas had possessed himself of this or that detail of Christ's message, but Christ had not possessed Himself of Demas. So the man's Christianity was a superstructure easily put up, easily taken down—jerry-building on slim foundations. For the foundation of enduring character is laid in something greater than oneself which one will serve through life and death.

15. *Explanation* by contrasting one text idea with another Scripture.

There is a fascinating contrast between two phrases in the New Testament: the first, Paul's description of Demas—"having loved this present age"; the second, the description of a true Christian in the Epistle to the Hebrews as one who has "tasted the . . . powers of the age to come." So, *that* is the difference, as the New Testament sees it. An apostate is a man who loves the *status quo*, this present age, a Christian is a man who has tasted the powers, been laid hold on by the hopes, of the age to come.

16. *Application* by affirmation and *explanation* by exposition.

When some one tries to tell you that the Christian social gospel is a modern innovation not in the New Testament, face him with that. The Christian social gospel is in the very heart of the New Testament—set, to be sure, in mental frameworks appropriate to the first century and different from ours but indubitably there. The primary emphasis on the Kingdom of God in Jesus' teaching and in the first church was so dominant that they tested Christian discipleship by it. A man who loved this present age was an apostate, a man who had tasted the powers of the age to come was a Christian. Whenever we see a New Testament Christian carrying through to the finish, one fact is always apparent: he had set his devotion on a coming Kingdom of God on earth for which he was willing to live or die.

17. *Explanation* by illustration: (1) direct introduction, (2) hypothetical, (3) personal observation.

The upshot is that one often sees today outside the church men who seem closer of kin to New Testament Christianity than many inside the churches. Sometimes a downright unbelieving scientist who gives himself to his science and for the sake of humanity stands by it, serving it through thick and thin to the end, seems closer to a New Testament Christian than many of us in the churches. At any rate, he has tasted the powers of the age to come.

18. *Explanation* by illustration: (1) Direct introduction, (2) hypothetical, (3) personal observation.

Or here is a man who puts his conscience above narrow nationalism, who not simply on Sunday, as in the Navy, but every day runs the white flag of the gospel to the top of the mast with the Stars and Stripes under it. He will no longer subjugate his conscience before God to the mad paganism of nationalistic policies that even now, by old familiar steps, are leading mankind to another holocaust. Such a man may be very disturbing, but he is closer akin to a New Testament Christian than many in our churches. At least he has tasted the powers of the age to come.

19. *Explanation* by illustration: (1) Direct introduction, (2) hypothetical, (3) personal observation.

Or here is a man who will not surrender to the abominable and often savage pressures of racial prejudice. He knows that in God's eyes the sons and daughters of mankind are not seen in terms of their skin's color or their ethnic origin. He cannot deny what both his conscience and his intelligence affirm, that despite our outdated discrimination and segregation the future belongs to mankind conceived as one family under the fatherhood of God. This difficult and disturbing conviction he holds to and, what is more, he puts into practice. He may be an irritating neighbor in our bitterly prejudiced world, but he is much nearer New Testament Christianity than many of us are. He has tasted the powers of the age to come.

20. *Application* by showing relationship.

I suspect that this is the outstanding challenge to us in the churches—our attitude not on theological questions but on practical, ethical, social questions. We find it easy to love this present age. We make fine beginnings, especially at New Year's time, but then some comfortable corner of this present age invites us and we nestle down. So our Christian profession lapses, our faith grows formal, and we do not amount to much in the end as Christians. If I should accuse some of you of being Judas Iscariot you would be indignant. You would never deliberately sell anybody out. But Demas—ah, my soul, how many of us have been that!

21. *Explanation* by division and illustration: (1) Direct introduction, (2) true event, (3) personal knowledge of the preacher; and by *application* showing relationship. Also, *explanation* by exposition.

Finally, staying power is commonly associated with profound resources of interior strength replenished by great faiths. There is a phrase in the Bible on which a colleague of mine once preached a sermon entitled "An Appalling Alternative"—"I had fainted, unless I had believed." That is true of life. We do faint, peter out, go flat, lose our morale unless our interior resources are replenished by faith in something. We may be sure that Demas, before he left Paul, had lost some of his first convictions about Christ and the God whom Christ revealed.

Suppose that some one should ask you what your faith in the Christian God really does for you. What would you say? For one thing, I should say that when a man believes in God he does not need to worry about the universe any more. That is off our minds if God has it on His. If I imagined the universe as without any God, aimless, purposeless, an accidental dance of atoms, spiritually meaningless, then I would worry about it. As Carlyle said, a cosmos like that is "one huge, dead, immeasurable steam-engine, rolling on, in its dead indifference to grind me from limb from limb." But if a man believes in God, that is off his mind. He can concentrate upon the task in hand, get on with his moral business here on earth with some high hopes about its outcome, and not be haunted by a huge, cosmic apprehension.

Deeper yet, a vital faith in God means a faith in an eternal moral purpose in the light of which a thousand years are as yesterday when it is past and as a watch in the night. That gives a man wide horizons, long outlooks, steady hopes, so that when people lose heart over the disappointment of some immediate expectation, such faith still has standing ground and carries on. Of all mad things in history can you think of anything madder, with Nero upon his throne and Paul in his prison, than to have believed that the gospel for which Paul stood would outlast and wear down the empire? That is, of course, what "got" Demas: the tremendous power of Rome on its eternal hills, with its inveterate and triumphant evils, against the seeming weakness of Christ's gospel. Who in a sober and realistic hour could have supposed that Paul would outwear Nero? But that, you see, is exactly what happened. A man who has faith in God always expects that to happen, though

22. *Explanation* by question and answer, division 1 of III, exposition, and illustration: (1) direct introduction, (2) opinion, (3) Carlyle; and by exposition.

23. *Explanation* by division 2 of III, by *application* showing benefits, and by *explanation* again by exposition. Also, *application* again showing conduct.

24. *Explanation* by division 3 of III, description, and exposition.

it take a thousand years. So, of course, he carries on.

Deeper yet, a vital faith in God gives a man available resources of interior power. We never produce power. We always appropriate it. That is true from the harnessing of Niagara to eating a dinner or taking a walk in the fresh air. We never create power; we assimilate it. So, a man with a real faith in God senses around his spiritual life a spiritual presence as truly as the physical world is around his body, and as truly from that divine companionship he draws replenished strength. He knows the deep wells of staying power.

CONCLUSION:

25. *Explanation* by restatement of thesis.

26. *Explanation* by question and answer and by exposition (thesis).

I celebrate the resources of a Christian faith to see a man through.

If faith in God means such things, how do men live life through without it? How do they meet the shocks of fate, the ugliness of evil, the shame of man's inhumanity to man, the disheartenment of moral failure, the impact of personal sorrow, and still keep their morale? I celebrate the resources of Christian faith.

27. *Explanation* by illustration: (1) direct, (2) hypothetical cases, (3) personal observation; and by *application* showing desired results.

Technically I know little or nothing about music. I venture this comment, however, about the difference between the best of the old music and the ordinary run of the new. The trouble with so much of the new music, as an older man at least sees it, is not its noisy cacophony but something deeper; it never seems to believe in anything enough so that it thinks it worth while to say it over and over again. It picks up a trivial theme and drops it. It never goes through with anything. It lacks sustained convictions. It is fulfilled with unimportant discontinuities. But when one hears a great symphony by Tschaikowsky, let us say, or Beethoven, *there* are convictions so profoundly believed that the music goes through with them to the very end. One says to himself, Surely that theme has been said as beautifully as ever it can be said. Yet that theme returns again and again, elevated and resplendent beyond our dreams. A man says to himself, now, surely, all the possibilities have been exhausted and, lo, at last the theme marches back once more into the music glorious like an army with banners. Whatever may be your judgement about music, great living is like that. Is there anything a man could wish for his friends at New Year's time better than a life like that —great convictions which life develops, expands, elevates, and glorifies, fine at the beginning, loveliest of all at the last? And is there anything that a man could better pray against for himself or his friends than the opposite?—Demas, my fellow-worker; Demas; Demas forsook me.

The virtues of "The Power to See It Through" are as follows: (1) a fresh and creative use of the casual Biblical sermon, (2) a correct use of the supportive objective, and (3) satisfactory rhetorical form with three major divisions and three subdivisions under III (it is pleasing to note that Fosdick felt free to use subdivisions under III though he had not used them under I and II), (4) a correct and sparkling use of multiple passages of Scripture as the text, and (5) as is usual with sermons by Fosdick, a style which is fresh, creative, and appealing.

In regard to places for improvement, three are evident: (1) most of the fabric of the sermon is not text-centered. This is normally a weakness with a casual sermon. (2) The three subpoints under III need attention in wording and language. Surprisingly, Fosdick occasionally uses run-on sentences for points. (3) There is a slight imbalance in length between the introduction and conclusion.

THE COMBINATION BIBLICAL SERMON

The combination Biblical sermon possesses the possibility of making the second strongest use of Biblical authority. This is especially true when the combination sermon uses a generous portion of direct Biblical material. Since no one knows how many ways the combination sermon may be put together, only a few ways will be indicated.

The combination Biblical sermon combines and uses direct Biblical data, indirect Biblical data, and casual Biblical data. Regrettably, some men include corrupted data also. The combination Biblical sermon appears as follows:

Introduction
Body of the sermon
 I. Indirectly from the text
  1. Develops I
  2. Develops I
 II. Directly from the text
  1. Develops II
  2. Develops II
Conclusion

Or, the combination sermon appears thus:

Introduction
Body of the sermon
 I. Casually from the text
 II. Indirectly from the text
Conclusion

Perhaps an all-too-frequent picture of the combination sermon appears like this:

Introduction
Body of the sermon
 I. A corruption of the text
 II. A casual use of the text
 III. A casual use of the text
Conclusion

The last outline of the combination sermon presents a weak and inferior type of sermon which is all too common. If those who desire to use the combination sermon will major on the direct and indirect areas, with only an occasional point from the casual, they will use the combination sermon to its best advantage.

The sermon "Be Angry and Sin Not" by H. Gordon Clinard illustrates the combination Biblical sermon.[4]

---

[4] H. C. Brown, Jr. (ed.), *More Southern Baptist Preaching* (Nashville: Broadman Press, 1964), pp. 4-11.

BE ANGRY AND SIN NOT

INTRODUCTION:

1. *Explanation* by exposition—the text.

2. *Explanation* by exposition, by two illustrations: (1) both direct introductions, (2) both are opinions, (3) James Robinson and George Buttrick; and by exposition again.

Be ye angry, and sin not: let not the sun go down upon your wrath: Neither give place to the devil.

EPHESIANS 4:26-27

Is it true that we are largely ignored? What of the image of the minister? In some places, at least, it has never been more frustrating. James Robinson has said of us, "The nation rushes by, and we draw solace from the fact that as they pass they tip their hats in a hurried, vestigial gesture of respect."[1] More often than we like to admit George Buttrick has described our frenzied ineffectiveness:

> To many he [the preacher] is a pathetic figure, an anachronism, a stage joke—an inoffensive little man jostled by the crowd, and wearing the expression of a startled rabbit. With one hand he holds a circular hat on a bewildered head and with the other desperately clutches an umbrella. The crowd pushes him from the sidewalk; the traffic shoots him back into the crowd. Some curse him; a few laugh; most are unaware of his existence.[2]

It is time for us to be disturbed by the comparative ineffectiveness of our Christian witness. We are more silent than vocal, ignored than heard, tolerated than respected. The day of the rebirth of a prophetic ministry and a prophetic church is long overdue.

3. *Explanation* by exposition and by illustration: (1) direct introduction, (2) theological literature, (3) Kierkegaard; and by exposition again.

Our big problem is not that we are rejected. A prophetic voice never has a promise of being welcomed. Our problem is that we are not even recognized. We have walked with the world so long that they do not see anything offensive in us. Our position is that of Kierkegaard's Pierrot: We have enter-

[1] *Adventurous Preaching* (Great Neck, New York: Channel Press, 1956), p. 22.
[2] *Jesus Came Preaching* (New York: Charles Scribner's Sons, 1932), p. 4.

tained the audience so well that when we desperately shout that the theater is on fire they only applaud. In short, we are not sufficiently different to offend our culture. How can we expect to prophesy against it?

The problem of conformity is not new. In Ephesians 4:26-27 Paul is in the midst of a reminder that Christians are to be different. The old man is to be put off and the new man in Christ put on. The old walk with the spiritually darkened is to be forsaken, and a walk which is worthy of the Christian calling begun. The fruits of conversion are set forth in terms of distinctive conduct. Vices of the old life are to be refused. The virtues which belong to the community of believers are to be assumed.

Nestled in the list of practical distinctives is a strange command, "Be angry, and sin not." In this text are two imperatives which are boldly pertinent to our decreasing ability to speak to our world. No other words of the passage have a greater significance for the minister who would be a prophet of God.

Here Is a Command—"Be Angry"

There is a need for holy anger. Or is there? We immediately recognize a difficulty in the text. Paul quotes Psalm 4:4, translated in the King James Version, "Stand in awe and sin not." But in the Septuagint it reads. "Be angry and sin not." Some would interpret Paul's words as a prohibition of all anger, or they would insist that the first imperative is a permissive, "If you are angry, don't sin." The command is thus said to be only against sinning as the peril in anger. There is sound scholarship, however, to favor the view that the imperative, "be angry," is also a jussive which commands a habitual displeasure with evil.

A further difficulty is that the word for "angry" is that used in Ephesians 4:31, as we

---

4. *Explanation* by exposition—the text. This is applicatory explanation or existential explanation.

5. *Explanation* by exposition, preview, and *application* showing relationship.

BODY OF THE SERMON:

6. *Explanation* by division I.
7. *Explanation* by exposition of text.

8. *Explanation* by exposition of text, con-

text, and related Scriptures.

are told to "put away" anger. Also, it is the same word of the warning of Matthew 5:22, "Everyone who is angry with his brother shall be liable to judgment" (RSV). It is the same word of Colossians 3:8 where we are enjoined to "put off" anger. But the sense of an imperative is not destroyed, for anger is also attributed to God, and in Mark 3:5 to Christ. The fact is, the same term is used in the New Testament to refer to a Godlike anger which is virtuous and an anger mingled with malice which is sinful. The command of the text, is "have a habitual holy anger."

9. *Application* by urging anger.

Such an imperative is mandatory if we are to stand against the stream of our culture. One of our paralyzing weaknesses is an inability to be angry about the right things. Such anger is no vice. The ethics which forbid all anger was more Stoic than Christian. The man who cannot be angry has no strength for good.

10. *Explanation* by three illustrations: (1) all direct introductions, (2) all factual, (3) all Biblical.

The Old Testament prophet knew how to be angry. You feel the holy heat of indignation as Elijah challenged Ahab's idolatry. You feel holy wrath in Isaiah's judgment, "Woe to those who join house to house, who add field to field, until there is no more room" (Isaiah 5:8, RSV). Anger is in the nostrils of Amos as he thunders, "Hear this, you who trample upon the needy, and bring the poor of the land to an end . . . [who] buy the poor for silver and the needy for a pair of sandals" (Amos 8:4-6, RSV).

11. *Explanation* by illustration: (1) direct introduction, (2) factual, (3) Biblical.

Jesus was angry. Mark records that He looked with anger on them who in their hypocritical self-righteousness thought more of legalism than mercy. He drove the moneychangers from the Temple. He was indignant against those who offended the weak, the poor, the "little ones." His great soul revolted against sham, and pretense and pride and sin. His was an anger that was the very wrath of God.

12. *Explanation* by illustrations: (1) all direct introductions, (2) factual, (3) Biblical.

13. *Application* by showing relationship and with a challenge.

14. *Application* by use of a caution. Also, transition is made pointing to subdivisions. The preacher moves from direct to indirect Biblical authority in paragraph 16.

15. *Explanation* by exposition and *application* presenting a challenge.

16. *Explanation* by division 1 of I and by illustrations: (1) both d i r e c t introductions, (2) both factual, (3) both Biblical.

For our God is a God of anger. A study of the Bible reveals that He is angry at idolatry, unbelief, affliction of the helpless, the abuse of his people, pride, sin, "for the wrath of God is revealed from heaven against all ungodliness and unrighteousness of men, who hinder the truth in unrighteousness" (Rom. 1:18, ASV).

The lesson is clear. If we are to witness for God we must recover the manliness of holy anger. Our weakness is in our silence. Our powerlessness is in our neutrality. Paul leans across the centuries to shake us from complacency—"Be angry!"

But let us be sure it is the anger of God. Our problem is that we are angry about the wrong things. We are like the world; the real foes raise no holy anger in us. If we would be certain that our anger is the holy wrath of the text, we best be angry at the things about which God is himself indignant. I venture to mention some contemporary objects of holy anger.

It is not beyond possibility that Paul has in mind an anger against the wickedness of the Gentile walk which is prominent in the passage. God's anger is raised against those who turn away from Him to walk in the darkness and ignorance of alienation. Therefore, a prophetic voice must always be raised against vanity, uncleanness, greed, lying, filthy communication, bitterness, malice, clamor, slander. Perhaps we take pride that against these our pulpits ring. But we need to be more specific about the modern means by which these sins are expressed.

Let us be angry at materialism, the idolatry of our generation. God's first commandment is that we shall have no other gods before Him. It is no wonder that God's anger is raised against idolatry. How many times are the sentiments of Deuteronomy 11:16-17 repeated in Scriptures, "Take heed to your

17. *Explanation* by exposition, descriptive language, and illustrations: (1) both direct introductions, (2) the first opinion and the second a news story, (3) the first by Luccock and the second from *Time*. Again existential explanation used.

selves, lest your heart be deceived, and ye turn aside, and serve other gods, and worship them; and the anger of Jehovah be kindled against you" (ASV).

About modern idolatry we must be angry The idol of our day is not a golden calf, but it is gold nonetheless. Halford Luccock has suggested that the big lie that life consists in the abundance of things which we possess is the mark of our age. Our idol is not Baal but it is fertility nonetheless. Ours is a culture immersed in a sensual materialism which has made success, sex, and goods its gods. *Time* recently carried a story on the success of the editor of a lurid magazine. In describing the $400,000 Victorian home into which this publisher had recently moved, the writer said:

> The American boy lies, on his left side dreaming.
> Someday, when I have enough money, I am going to have a house with a massage room a steam room, a bar, and a bedroom big enough for two 707s. The floor will be covered with a white rug four inches thick, with polar-bear skin near the hi-fi. And the bed, oh maneroonian, the bed will be adequate for a exhibition match between the Green Bay Packers and the Los Angeles Rams.
> Downstairsville, there is a two-story chandeliered, oak-paneled living room with teakwood floors and a trap door through which you can drop twelve feet into a kidney-shaped indoor pool. "That," I'll tell my visitors, "is where we throw the old, discarded girls."[3]

Against this culture, no prophetic voice can fail to cry in holy anger.

18. *Application* showing relationship, developed by questions and answers, by descriptive language, and by illustration: (1) direct in-

But how shall we speak when the same materialism marks our ministry and our ecclesiology? Shall we fail to be angry at the minister's own involvement in materialism? We have become so affected by the materia

---

[3]"The Boss of Taste City," March 24, 1961, p. 55.

troduction, (2) opinion, (3) Floyd Shafer.

security cult that, enjoying pleasant living, we cannot without awkwardness articulate the gospel. Instead of being doctors who detect and treat the maladies of our age, we have contracted the disease.[4] Shall we be able to be angry at the materialism about us so long as we have no anger at the idol of success and institutionalism within our own household? There may be new money-changers in the temple who turn God's house from a house of prayer into an "organization church" which may be as efficient as an IBM but just as powerless spiritually. The fact is that we cannot judge materialism so long as we are materialists—so long as we are more prone to judge ministers by Chamber of Commerce standards than by spiritual perspectives, so long as we are more interested in success in suburbia than in speaking for God. I take it Floyd Shafer is angry about it all. He suggests that to save the minister we must

> rip out his telephone, burn up his ecclesiastical success sheets, refuse his glad hand, and put water in the gas tank of his community buggy. Give him a Bible and tie him in his pulpit and make him preach the Word of the living God. . . . humiliate him for his ignorance of things divine, and shame him for his glib comprehension of finances, batting averages, and political-infighting.[5]

About materialism, our new idolatry, be angry!

19. *Explanation* by division 2 of I and by multiple illustrations: (1) all direct, (2) all factual, (3) all Biblical.

Let us be angry at false discipleship, the hypocrisy of our generation. God's anger has continually risen against religion without spiritual life. Isaiah spoke of God's anger against external religion without internal reality: "To what purpose is the multitude of your sacrifices unto me? saith the Lord: I am

[4]Lee C. Moorehead, *Freedom of the Pulpit* (New York: Abingdon Press, 1961), p. 13.
[5]"And Preach as You Go!" *Christianity Today,* Vol. V, No. 13 (1961), p. 9.

full of the burnt offerings of rams, and the fat of fed beasts . . ." (1:11). It was the empty legalism of the Pharisees that continually aroused the anger of Jesus. They watched to see if He would heal the man with the withered hand on the sabbath and He "looked round about on them with anger" (Mark 3:5). The hypocrisy of men who, like sepulchers, appeared to be beautiful on the outside but were black within brought Jesus to his greatest outrage: "Ye serpents, ye generation of vipers, how can ye escape the damnation of hell?" (Matt. 23:33). It is the persistent evil of false religion which brings God to anger. So it should be with us.

20. *Application* using illustrations: (1) both d i r e c t introductions, (2) one opinion and the other factual, (3) one from Bonhoeffer and the other from the Bible; showing relationship and with a challenge.

It is time for us to be angry about a discipleship which costs nothing. To use Bonhoeffer's unforgettable term, we have a preference for "cheap grace." "Too often ours is a discipleship that leaves a Christian content with his worldliness—a grace that offers forgiveness without repentance, baptism without church discipline—grace without a cross."[6] We are often powerless to speak to our world because many of us see no vital connection between Christian discipleship and the affairs of life. When will we be bold enough to let Jesus say, "Whosoever doth not bear his cross, and come after me, cannot be my disciple" (Luke 14:27). When will we really practice the discipline of regenerate church membership? Only when we do will holy anger qualify us to judge the world.

21. *Application* showing relationship and with an exhortation.

It is time for us to be angry about the idea that Christianity is to be identified with our culture. The gospel will never be able to prophesy against our way of life so long as we identify the gospel with our way of life. It is a false discipleship which snuggles into the comforts of the status quo, believes that

---

[6]Dietrich Bonhoeffer, *The Cost of Discipleship* (New York: The Macmillan Company, 1948), p. 36.

God is irrevocably on our side without bothering to find if we are on God's side, and which bends God to conform to our ways. We shall pervert Christian discipleship and be without witness in the world so long as we identify the kingdom of God with culture. About false discipleship, our new hypocrisy, we must be angry!

Let us be angry at silence in the presence of injustice, the cowardice of our generation. There are many who insist that the pulpit has no right to speak on the burning injustices, social and political, of our day. These people would insist that there are many things which the pulpit cannot do: preach in words which hit like hammers and burn like fire, interpret the life situation in which we find ourselves, assert the lordship of Christ in every area of life.[7] But such ideas are foreign to the Word of God. The prophet's voice can still be heard crying out against the social injustices of his day. The concern of Jesus for the needs of men puts a sob in your throat yet. The courage of the saints of Christian history who have caused kings to tremble and nations, like America, to be free rises up to shame our silence.

There is a big difference between the social gospel, which we despise, and the social implications of the gospel. The Christian who feels no anger when men are exploited by political demagogues who think more of votes than of virtue, when men are robbed of basic freedoms by greed and prejudice, has no power to witness to our revolting world. The minister who lets his voice be stilled by fear needs to hear the words of Phillips Brooks:

> If you are afraid of men and a slave to their opinion, go and do something else. Go and make shoes to fit them. Go even and paint pic-

22. *Explanation* by division 3 of I and *application* by descriptive language showing relationship and with an exhortation.

23. *Application* showing relationship using three illustrations: (1) all direct introductions, (2) the first an opinion of Brooks, the second an e x p e r i e n c e of Thompson, and the third a Scripture, (3) B r o o k s , Moorehead, and Ezekiel.

[7] Franklin H. Littell, *The German Phoenix* (Garden City, New York: Doubleday and Company, 1960), p. 157.

tures which you know are bad but which suit their bad taste. But do not keep on all your life preaching sermons which shall say not what God sent you to declare, but what they hire you to say.[8]

Joseph Thompson was the heroic preacher of the Broadway Tabernacle in New York. One day he was shot at from the balcony by a fanatic who was enraged at his preaching on a moral evil of the day. Thompson did not even duck. But standing straight in his pulpit, he said, "The man who stands in this pulpit must be the first to see, the first to feel, the first to move against all forms of moral evil in the world."[9] It sounds strangely like God's shout to Ezekiel—"I have set thee to be a watchman over the house of Israel" (33:7, author's translation).

24. *Explanation* by summary and transition.

If we would witness to our day we need to learn the ability to be angry.

25. *Explanation* by division II.

Here Is a Corrective—"And Sin Not"

26. *Explanation* by exposition. This is applicatory explanation.

Anger has a way of becoming sinful. We must be angry, but we must never permit anger to be other than God's kind of anger. The second imperative of the text is actually the stronger—"be angry and stop sinning."

27. *Explanation* by exposition and by *application* showing relationship.

Anger is often selfish. If so, it is not of God. The text adds, "Let not the sun go down upon your wrath." The term "wrath" speaks of a sudden temper, a flash of wrath that comes bathed in uncontrolled selfishness. It is typical of the anger which takes offense quickly when the ego is involved. How much of our so-called prophetic utterances are filled with anger like that!

28. *Explanation* by illustration: (1) direct introduction, (2) factual, (3) Biblical; and

The anger of Jesus was never selfish. Never once, when men reviled Him, did he revile again. When they lashed out at Him, he never sought revenge. When they nailed Him to

[8]*Lectures on Preaching* (New York: E. P. Dutton and Company, 1880), p. 59.
[9]Moorehead, *op. cit.*, p. 51.

by *application* showing exhortation.

29. *Application* showing consequences.

30. *Application* showing what to do and using illustration: (1) direct introduction, (2) factual, (3) life of Christ.

CONCLUSION:

31. *Application* by showing what to do and using illustrations: (1) both direct introduction, (2) both factual, (3) both Biblical.

32. *Application* by presenting an exhortation, using descriptive language, and using an illustration: (1) direct introduction, (2) factual, (3) Biblical.

the cross, it was not hatred but love that spoke with every dying word. A prophetic anger which speaks out of a selfish interest to protect ourselves and our institutions will never witness to the world. We, like Jesus, must lose ourselves in others if anger is to have power.

Anger is often needlessly embraced. Even justifiable anger can degenerate into sin. The prophet easily becomes a complainer, the angry Christian easily becomes a pessimist, always searching for negatives.

In short, anger must be the servant of compassion if we are to sin not. Jesus somehow found the way to be angry with sin and to love the sinner, to despise sin and to give Himself for the sinner. The greatest compliment ever paid Him was, "He is the friend of sinners" (Matt. 11:19). He knew that man's greatest need was redemption, and He became involved even unto death with those whose sins repulsed His divine being. He only hated sin because of what it did to the sinner.

How deep is our need for His compassion! If we need His anger, we need His compassion even more. We must not be mere social reformers. We must be heralds of salvation. We must not be selfish, easily offended, unloving, unforgiving, coldly indignant, without involvement with men, angry about the wrong things. If we are, our witness falls on empty ears. We drive men from Christ rather than to Him. But if our compassion is bigger than our anger, than the world will hear. It may not heed, but it cannot ignore. Men cannot be ignored who only "seek to save that which is lost."

We do not have to be ignored. We can make a difference. We do not have to be inoffensive little men, stage-jokes, jostled and unnoticed by the crowd. We can be courageous, compassionate prophets for God. We can be once more a people with power. We

can be, when we learn to be angry against
evil, when we learn to care for men with the
compassion of him of whom it was said:
He "emptied himself . . . and became obedient, unto death" (Phil. 2:718, RSV). Be
angry and sin not.

The strength of "Be Angry and Sin Not" impresses one upon a
careful reading. Five virtues stand out: (1) The message is a strong
example of the combination Biblical sermon. As Clinard has prepared
it, this form ranks only slightly below the full and complete direct
Biblical sermon. Since the text did not supply needed details for
specific development of I, Clinard has correctly completed the implication of the text. (2) The purpose is actional or consecrative which
equals the thrust of the text. (3) In form, this message is a rhetorical
sermon with two major divisions and three subdivisions under I. Like
Fosdick, Clinard felt free to use subpoints under one heading without
using them under the other. This freedom from the tyranny of false
scholastic rules is refreshing. (4) The introduction presents the title,
text, and proposition in five attractive paragraphs which represents
a good balance with the conclusion which has two paragraphs. (5)
In style, Clinard is comparable to Fosdick in that his sermon possesses
clarity, appeal, and force in good measure.

Concerning improvement, two items are noted: (1) more explanation could have been used; (2) I uses eighteen paragraphs as over
against five for II, which represents an imbalance in content distribu-
tion between I and II. The second suggestion represents the more
important item for improvement.

THE CORRUPTED BIBLICAL SERMON

The corrupted Biblical sermon does not use but rather abuses the
Bible. An inexhaustible number of ways have been devised for
twisting, misusing, and corrupting texts. The more prominent methods
are: (1) to allegorize the text—to assign to Scripture double, triple,
or quadruple meanings, none of which, or one, at the most, can be
true; (2) to corrupt the text through sheer carelessness; (3) to abuse
the Bible by pressing the casual sermon too far; (4) to destroy the
worth of the text through wooden, mechanical, and dead patterns;
(5) to destroy Biblical authority by making the Bible a textbook on
science, atomic chemistry, astronomy, or other sciences; (6) to corrupt Biblical authority through rejection of and disbelief in the plain

teachings of the supernatural and miraculous in Scripture; (7) to twist Scripture through cultural accommodation, as in attempting to make the Bible support white supremacy claims; (8) to pervert doctrine through denominational accommodation, as in attempting to prove that Peter was the first bishop of Rome or that one's own and only one's own millennial view is correct; and (9) to destroy Biblical authority through proof-texting sermons without regard to true interpretation.

Chapter 7

PRIMARY BIBLICAL PURPOSE

Not only should the preacher secure Biblical authority in his sermon, he should also secure Biblical purpose. To secure Biblical purpose means to secure the true meaning and intent of Scripture. Meaning and intent, in relation to Scripture, mean that the natural grammatical-historical truth of Scripture has been determined (the meaning) as well as the purpose (the intent) for which the passage was originally given.

When Jesus told the Pharisees and publicans, as recorded in Luke 15, that "God loves sinners," He gave material whose meaning and intent demand that the passage be used in one basic way, namely, *evangelistically*. Of course, Luke 15 may be used doctrinally just as all Scripture may be so used. However, Luke 15 sets out a meaning and intent so distinctly evangelistic that one abuses this passage of Scripture to neglect this gospel aspect. For one to use Luke 15:11-24 (the lost boy who left home, or the prodigal son) as a sermon to depict backsliders is to damage the passage. To insist that the passage means apostasy or backsliding is to insist on a corruption of Scripture. The passage does not teach that a Christian left home (i.e., the Kingdom of God), sinned, awakened, returned, confessed, and was restored. The passage declares that one sins when he rebels against God, awakens when he sees his state in comparison to a better state with the loving Father, goes to the Father, confesses his sin, and receives forgiveness and salvation from the loving Father. Luke 15 presents over and over again the theme, "God loves sinners."

Therefore, the preacher must determine the meaning and intent of Scripture when he prepares sermons. Both the nature of homiletical purpose and biblical meaning and intent must be explored.

THE NATURE OF PURPOSE IN HOMILETICS

Over the centuries preachers and teachers have attempted to sharpen the thrust of sermons by defining as sharply as possible the purpose of sermons. This purpose must be stated so that it matches the interpretation of Scripture and the needs of the congregation.

The Basic Term

Purpose may be understood to mean the objective, the intent, or the goal for the sermon. Purpose is *that* which the preacher attempts to accomplish through the preaching of his sermon.

To attempt to accomplish something through a sermon lends concreteness to the thrust of the message, creates a vivid sense of expectancy in the mind and heart of the preacher, tends to stimulate the congregation, and casts light upon the entire sermon. Henry Ward Beecher said, in effect, that when he discovered purpose (taking aim, he called it) he learned to preach.

> When I had lived at Indianapolis the first year, I said: "There was a reason why when the apostles preached they succeeded, and I will find it out if it is to be found out." I took every single instance in the Record, where I could find one of their sermons, and analyzed it and asked myself "What were the circumstances? Who were the people? What did he do? And I studied the sermons until I got this idea: that the apostles were accustomed first to feel for a ground on which the people and they stood together; a common ground where they could meet. Then they heaped up a large number of the particulars of knowledge that belonged to everybody; and when they had got that knowledge, which everybody would admit, placed in a proper form before their mind, then they brought it to bear upon them with all their excited heart and feeling. *That was the first definite idea of taking aim that*[1] I had in my mind.
>
> "Now," said I, "I will make a sermon so." I remember it just as well as if it were yesterday. First, I sketched out the things we all know. "You all know you are living in a world perishing under your feet. You all know that time is extremely uncertain; that you cannot tell whether you will live another month or week. You all know that your destiny, in the life that is to come, depends upon the character you are forming in this life." And in that way I went on with my "you all knows," until I had about forty of them. When I had got through that, I turned around and brought it to bear upon them with all my might; and there were seventeen men awakened under that sermon. I never felt so triumphant in my life. I cried all the way home. I said to myself: "Now I know how to preach."[2]

[1]Italics added.
[2]Jesse Burton Weatherspoon, *Sent Forth to Preach* (New York: Harper & Brothers, 1954), pp. 125-26.

Aspects of the Word "Purpose"

Because the word "purpose" or "objective" contains many aspects, one must understand these in order to understand the word.[3]

The total objective. Total purpose or total objective represents that ultimate goal or end a man desires that his ministry accomplish. J. B Weatherspoon, for forty years professor at three seminaries (Southwestern Baptist Theological Seminary, Southern Baptist Theological Seminary, and Southeastern Baptist Theological Seminary), said on numerous occasions that nothing less than the purpose of Jesus Himself would suffice for the minister's ultimate purpose. And what was this purpose of Jesus? "I came that they may have life, and may have it abundantly" (John 10:10b). "Life for the people," said Jesus, brought Him into this world. This life included eternal life and abundant life. Thus, the minister seeks to serve people so that they may have life eternal and life abundant.

The major objectives. The major objectives are six in number: (1) evangelistic, to win unsaved men to Christ; (2) doctrinal, to lead men to a better knowledge of God; (3) ethical, to lead men to a better relationship with other people based on a correct relationship with God; (4) actional, to lead men to serve God through total dedication of time, talent, and resources; (5) supportive, to lead men to depend upon God for grace and strength; and (6) devotional, to lead men to love, honor, and worship God. These six major objectives are all subfacets of the total objective.

The specific objective. The specific objective is one aspect of one major objective for one sermon for one particular audience on one specific occasion. The specific objective is the last of three steps from general to particular in the use of purpose in preaching: total, major, and specific. The specific objective is always true to the total objective and represents a true and valid subdivision of one major purpose. Moreover, the specific objective is the "partner" of the proposition. When the minister begins his sermon through the selection of a text, subjects that text to exegesis, states the central idea of the text (the historical thesis), and translates that central idea into a present tense proposition, he has created the ground for the specific objective. The proposition no more stands alone than does man. As man finds unity and completion when he marries a wife, so does the proposition find completion with the creation of the specific objective.

Moreover, the specific objective should meet a current vital need

---

[3]This discussion has been strongly influenced by Jesse Burton Weatherspoon through his lectures and writings.

for the congregation and will do so if the best procedures of homiletics be followed. In each sermon there should be only one specific purpose, and this purpose should be the center and focus of the preacher's attention from the first word of the introduction through the last word of his conclusion.

THE NATURE OF BIBLICAL PURPOSE

The Meaning of Scripture

Before one may comprehend the teaching of a particular text, he should state his understanding of the meaning and intent of all Scripture. In the wording of the man on the street, "What is the meaning of the Bible from cover to cover? Does the Bible have a meaning?" It does.

God's story of how He came to men. The Bible states two wonderful truths, the first of which is that God came to men. Read the words of the writer of Hebrews as he described God's self-disclosure.

> When in former times God spoke to our forefathers, he spoke in fragmentary and varied fashion through the prophets. But in this the final age he has spoken to us in the Son whom he has made heir to the whole universe, and through whom he created all orders of existence: the Son who is the effulgence of God's spendour and the stamp of God's very being, and sustains the universe by his word of power. When he had brought about the purgation of sins, he took his seat at the right hand of Majesty on high, raised as far above the angels, as the title he has inherited is superior to theirs.[4]

The story Scripture first tells is that God in ways and times of His own choosing came to man. Man did not make the glad discovery that "God is." Such knowledge is beyond the ability and power of man to invent or to discover. God came to man and told man who He was and what He was doing.

God's story of how man can come to God. There is more to God's story than the fact of his sacrificial self-disclosure, as marvellous as this is. The additional fact of God's story is that God has provided salvation for man, told him how to receive this salvation, how to conduct himself along the path of life, and how to spend eternity with God.

Allow the apostle Paul to describe the procedure for us as he told the Ephesian Christians how salvation came to them, was continuing in them, and would be completed in them:

---

[4]Hebrews 1:1-4, NEB.

Time was when you were dead in your sins and wickedness, when you followed the evil ways of this present age, when you obeyed the commander of the spiritual powers of the air, the spirit now at work among God's rebel subjects. We too were of their number: we all lived our lives in sensuality, and obeyed the promptings of our own instincts and notices. In our natural condition we, like the rest, lay under the dreadful judgement of God. But God, rich in mercy, for the great love he bore us, brought us to life with Christ even when we were dead in our sins; it is by his grace you are saved. And in union with Christ Jesus he raised us up and enthroned us with him in the heavenly realms, so that he might display in the ages to come how immense are the resources of his grace, and how great his kindness to us in Christ Jesus. For it is by his grace you are saved, through trusting him; it is not your own doing. It is God's gift, not a reward for work done. There is nothing for anyone to boast of. For we are God's handiwork, created in Christ Jesus to devote ourselves to the good deeds for which God has designed us.[5]

The Homiletical Use of Scripture

The homiletical use of Scripture connotes not special privileges but practical procedures in the use of Scripture. The preacher's way of reading, studying, and using Scripture is the meaning of the homiletical use of Scripture. The minister has no rights in regard to interpretation that an exegete or theologian does not possess. The common belief prevails that the preacher has more liberty and freedom in using and preaching Scripture than does the Biblical interpreter and the careful theologian. But surely this cannot be true! The true and natural meaning of Scripture sets the bounds and limits on the use of the Bible. Simply because the minister preaches sermons does not grant to him special hermeneutical privileges. The minister should observe all critical procedures carefully and accurately in his exegesis and preaching. When the preacher points out God's way of salvation, he must be sure that he is right. The only way he can be right is to preach the Bible correctly.

The homiletical use of Scripture involves discovering meaning and intent of Scripture and matching homiletical purpose to the Biblical meaning and intent. Specifically, the homiletical use of Scripture involves discovering which of the six major objectives (evangelistic, doctrinal, ethical, actional, supportive, and devotional) matches the meaning and intent of each passage of Scripture under study. At times, this task is quite simple (as with Luke 15), and at times it is extremely difficult (especially with Old Testament passages). In spite of difficulties, however, the minister must attempt to secure as perfect a correlation as he can for Biblical meaning and intent and homiletical purpose.

---

[5]Ephesians 2:1-10, NEB.

What, then, are the characteristics of the major objectives? Two are examined in this chapter and four in chapter eight.

THE EVANGELISTIC OBJECTIVE

The evangelistic objective seeks the salvation of sinners. The evangelistic objective is also called the *kerygmatic* objective or the gospel objective. This objective, the basic one in preaching, secures its validity from the fact that "all have sinned, and fall short of the glory of God" (Romans 3:23, ASV). Paul, when speaking before King Agrippa, said that God appointed him to lead people out of darkness to light and to salvation. He related the words of Jesus to him at the time of his conversion and commission:

> I have appeared to you for a purpose: to appoint you my servant and witness, to testify both to what you have seen and to what you shall yet see of me. I will rescue you from this people and from the Gentiles to whom I am sending you. I send you to open their eyes and turn them from darkness to light, from the domination of Satan to God, so that, by trust in me, they may obtain forgiveness of sins, and a place with those whom God has made his own.[6]

The commission Jesus gave to Paul becomes the commission of each called minister. Evangelistic work was not the only work of Paul, nor is it the only work of a modern preacher even though evangelistic work remains the basic work of each minister. It is through preaching or witnessing to the gospel in public or private that a minister carries out the evangelistic work of his ministry. What is the meaning of gospel preaching, or more simply what is the meaning of the gospel?

Not any truth about God, nor any truth spoken emphatically, nor "hell fire and brimstone" preaching, nor just any truth agreed upon, will define gospel preaching. Paul said, "It was God's good pleasure through the foolishness of *the* preaching to save them that believe" (I Cor. 1:21b, ASV). Paul did not say that foolish preaching saved them that believed, but he said that *the thing preached* saved them that believed. In essence the verse declares: "It was God's good pleasure *through the foolishness of gospel preaching to save them that believe.*" Salvation comes to those who hear God's gospel declared and then believe it. Thus, the preacher who would use the evangelistic purpose properly must preach or witness to the gospel of Jesus Christ.

What is the gospel? The gospel is good news about a new age which came with Jesus Christ. The old age began in Eden and con-

---

[6]Acts 26:16-18, NEB.

tinued until Jesus came.[7] Throughout the ages, the prophets looked for the coming of a new age; they longed for a new dominion over nature and over all creatures; Ezekiel talked of the river of life (47:1-2); Isaiah saw all nature at peace (chapter 11); the prophets longed for a real fellowship with God and Jeremiah talked about a new covenant (31:31); Hosea (2:19) and Ezekiel (36:26) looked to a bright future; Daniel discussed eternal life (chapter 12); and Isaiah (chapter 65) and Zechariah (chapter 3) talked of conquering evil. Peter, at Pentecost, declared that Jesus Christ brought a new age: "But this is that which hath been spoken through the prophet Joel" (Acts 2:16, ASV).

The gospel is good news about the personal ministry of Jesus Christ: His birth was in fulfillment of prophecy in that He was born of the seed of David (Acts 2:29-31; Rom. 1:3; Psalms 132:11); His works demonstrated good news (Acts 3:22; 10:36-39; John 21:5; Acts 2:22); He died for our sins (Acts 2:23; 3:13-15; I Cor. 15:3); He was buried (Acts 13:29; I Cor. 15:4); and He was victorious over sin, Satan, and the grave through His resurrection (Acts 2:24, 31, 32; 4:10; 3:15; I Cor. 15:4).

Moreover, the gospel is good news about the exaltation of Jesus. He is at God's right hand (Acts 2:33; 5:31); He is both Lord and Christ (Acts 2:36); He is the Son of God with power (Rom. 1:4); He is the stone which is the head of the corner (Acts 4:10-11); and He is a Prince and a Savior (Acts 5:31).

The gospel, furthermore, is good news about the continued activity of Jesus in heaven: He makes intercession for us (Rom. 8:34b), and He pours out the Holy Spirit on us (Acts 2:17-21; 2:33; 5:32).

Again, the gospel is good news about the Second Coming of Christ. He is coming as judge (Acts 10:42; Rom. 2:16; I Cor. 4:5; II Cor. 5:10; Rom. 14:10); and He is coming as Savior (I Thess. 1:9-10).

Therefore, because these things are true, the gospel calls for repentance. The gospel is good news in that men may repent and be saved (Acts 2:37-39; 3:19; 4:12; 5:31; 10:43).

> Now when they heard *this* [Peter's sermon at Pentecost], they were pricked in their heart, and said unto Peter and the rest of the apostles, Brethren, what shall we do? And Peter *said* unto them, Repent ye, and be baptized every one of you in the name of Jesus Christ unto the remission of your sins; and ye shall receive the gift of the Holy Spirit.[8]

The evangelistic objective seeks the salvation of lost men. Men are

---

[7]See C. H. Dodd, *The Apostolic Preaching and Its Development* (New York: Willett, Clark & Co., 1937).
[8]Acts 2:37-38, ASV.

saved by hearing the gospel preached or explained and by committing themselves to Jesus Christ. If the preacher would be faithful in his evangelistic work, therefore, he will preach the gospel of Jesus Christ.

The following sermon by Wayne E. Ward, "The Gospel of Jesus Christ," is a direct Biblical sermon using a multiple text, with an evangelistic purpose.[9] It is rhetorical in form.

[9]H. C. Brown, Jr. (ed.), *More Southern Baptist Preaching* (Nashville: Broadman Press, 1964), pp. 134-140.

THE GOSPEL OF JESUS CHRIST

INTRODUCTION:

1. *Explanation* by exposition (the text).

> *The beginning of the gospel of Jesus Christ, the Son of God. As it is written in Isaiah the prophet, "Behold I send my messenger before thy face, who shall prepare thy way; the voice of one crying in the wilderness: Prepare the way of the Lord, make his paths straight."*
>
> *Now after John was arrested, Jesus came into Galilee, preaching the gospel of God, and saying, "The time is fulfilled, and the kingdom of God is at hand; repent, and believe in the gospel."*
>
> MARK 1:1-3, 14-15, RSV.

2. *Explanation* by illustration: (1) direct introduction, (2) observation of an event, (3) personal to the preacher.

"That's what I call really preaching the gospel!" Amid such comments and a chorus of "Amens," a renowned preacher had concluded a conference address and taken his seat. His eloquent and forceful message had been a scathing attack upon sin in high places and low. It was, doubtless, a much needed and very effective indictment of wrong doing and was, for the most part, quite true to the facts. Yet, although it was received as a glowing example of gospel preaching, it never touched one tiny note of the gospel! How can men who are "called to preach the gospel" be so careless about what the gospel is? Surely our time would be well spent if we took a few moments to go back to the "beginning of the gospel" and learn something about the gospel from the One who brought it to us.

3. *Explanation* by exposition. Direct Biblical authority and evangelistic purpose.

One of the most beautiful words in the English language is the word "gospel." It comes from an Anglo-Saxon root which means "God's story" and serves as a very effective translation of the New Testament word for good news—the good news of the saving work of God which culminated in the cross and resurrection of Christ. From the Greek word for gospel we get the words "evangel" and "evangelist," terms which denote the thrilling story of God's redemptive love, in which He took upon himself our humanity and bore our sins on Calvary's cross. Many Christians refer to themselves as "evangelicals," because they consider it their highest calling to proclaim to a lost world the good news of salvation in Jesus Christ.

4. *Explanation* by exposition and by Biblical illustration: (1) direct introduction, (2) factual, (3) Biblical.

Yet, as often happens, a word that is so well known is almost never really understood. Its very familiarity breeds careless ignorance of its meaning. Could anything be more unfortunate than the loss or impairment of the true meaning of the greatest news in all human history, simply because it was buried under a commonplace term? Would this, indeed, violate the commandment: "Thou shalt not take the name of the Lord thy God in vain"? (Ex. 20:7). If God's act in Jesus Christ is the greatest event in all history, if we rightly divide our calendar in such a way as to make this the central point in time, it should be worth our while to spend the time necessary to strip away the crust of the commonplace and seek to penetrate the inner meaning of the Christ event. What is the gospel by which men may know Jesus Christ and thereby obtain eternal life?

BODY OF THE SERMON:

5. *Explanation* by division I.

Incarnation

6. *Explanation* by exposition and by *application* using an illustration: (1) direct introduction, (2) supposition, (3) personal creation by the preacher; and by *explanation* again using descriptive language and two illustrations: (1) both direct introductions, (2) poetry and factual, (3) James Weldon Johnson and the Bible;

The heart of the gospel is found in a straw-filled manger. The gospel is the good news that a baby was born in Bethlehem long ago. Perhaps someone is saying, "News, indeed! We have heard this all our lives; we sing about that old story every Christmas." Yet, this is the most earthshaking, incredible news which has ever come to the ears of men; and it is always news. Earth has certainly had one "visitor from outer space." But we have heard it until we no longer listen to its meaning. We are so sure we know this story and by *application* again showing relationship. Also, *application* by illustration: (1) direct introduction, (2) factual, (3) Biblical.

7. *Application* by illustration: (1) direct introduction, (2) an anecdote, (3) the preacher's personal experience.

that we do not ask what God is trying to say to us. If once this good news could break in upon us as it did upon the shepherds, if once the angel song could come down out of the Christmas sky and strike the lost chord in our hearts, its message would overwhelm us. What does the coming of this baby mean? It means no less than this: that the living God who made this universe, who put the stars in their places, who "pushed the mountains up and hollowed the valleys out," who made your life and holds it in His hand— this living God came down to earth, taking upon Himself human flesh, cradled by the lowly virgin of Galilee, becoming bone of our bone and flesh of our flesh. Forevermore, lost humanity can hear the most glorious news which ever reached earth's ears: Our God has come to us, to live with us, to share our human plight, to fight our tempter, to bear with us our burdens. He is not far away, a God transcendent, untouchable! He has drawn near in Jesus Christ for "God was in Christ, reconciling the world unto himself" (2 Cor. 5:19). This is the most overwhelming good news lost sinners ever heard. We do not walk this rocky road alone; there are the footprints of Jesus, going on before.

Men of every religion, and men of no religion, are waiting in the depth of their being for this gospel word. One group of Christians will never forget the earnest young Moslem guide who displayed the glories of the Citadel of Saladin in Cairo, Egypt, and revealed a justifiable pride in the simple beauty of the ancient mosques. On every side were helpless supplicants, calling upon a God who was always far away, who could never be "touched with a feeling of their infirmities." Allah was the unmoved, distant deity—Mohammed, his somewhat unaccountable prophet. But the young Moslem beamed, "We all seek the same God. You Christians may call him God; we

8. The illustration continued.

call Him Allah. You follow His prophet Jesus; we follow His prophet Mohammed. Does it not all come to the same thing?"

But one Christian in that group could not let this pass unchallenged: "No, Abou, you have misunderstood us Christians; we do not follow Jesus simply as a prophet. We believe Allah Himself came down! We believe God came to this earth as a man among men! He lived, He died, He rose again—and Jesus of Nazareth is His name!" To this devout Moslem it was blasphemy. Allah çome down? What sacrilege! And yet this wonder-working message wrestled with his mind and heart. What a glorious, incredible thought! Because man could not climb the long road to a holy God in a faraway heaven, the God of love came down to man. In such a gracious deed there was hope—even for the guilty sinner.

9. The illustration continued.

Later that evening Abou came to say, "Yes, professor, I have checked on you. Other Christians do believe what you said. It is surely the most wonderful thought that ever came to me. If only it could be true!" With what soul-searching wonder this devout Moslem heard the thrilling news of the incarnation for the first time; with what carelessness some Christians leave the good news of this gospel story untold, unsung, unheard.

10. *Explanation* by division *II.*

Atonement

11. *Explanation* by exposition (applied explanation) using numerous Biblical phrases as descriptive language; and by *application:* using an illustration: (1) direct introduction, (2) poetry, (3) Watts.

Nor is this all: the gospel is the good news that on the hill called Calvery, God was in Christ pouring out His life for the sins of the world. He bore our sins, in His own body, on the old rugged cross. How can sinful men be unmoved by such news as this? Estranged from God, rebellious in sin, men would not come that they might have life. But God came to men, and He who knew no sin was "made to be sin" for us. We like sheep had strayed from the fold of God, but the Good

Shepherd came out into the wilderness of sin and gave his life for the sheep. At the crossroads of the world stands Calvary. It represents the highest point of man's proud rebellion, because when God came to man in righteous love, He was by man rejected, beaten, and pilloried there. That cross marks also the depth of the divine humiliation to this unthinkable shame he would come, in the love that would not let men go. Who can stand before this cross unmoved or feel self-righteous in this place?

> When I survey the wondrous cross,
>   On which the Prince of glory died,
> My richest gain I count but loss,
>   And your contempt on all my pride![1]
>   Isaac Watts

12. *Explanation* by illustration: (1) direct introduction, (2) stage drama, (3) the preacher's observations of "Green Pastures."

In one of the great southern cities an all-Negro cast of players once enacted its own free version of "Green Pastures." To some Christians sitting there, the careless language and the unorthodox portrayals, such as "de Lawd" with the long black "seegar" puffing smoke rings around his head, bordered on the sacrilegious. But near the last scene of the play, a bolt of heavenly light broke through. The Lord was sitting on His great white throne, high and lifted up. Before Him marched a blustering angel, up and down the golden balcony of heaven, in his hands a silver trumpet with a golden bell! Now and then, impatient Gabriel would lean far out over the golden balustrade pleading, "Lawd, let me blow this here trumpet! Look at them poor, missable sinners, a-fightin', and a-killin'—Lawd, they's in an awful shape. Let me blow one toot on this horn and wind up the whole shebang."

13. The illustration continued.

But the Lord protested, "Hold on, Gabriel, de Lawd am thinkin'. Do you reckon all that suffering down there might jus' mean de

---

[1]Hymn, "When I Survey the Wondrous Cross" by Isaac Watts.

14. The illustration continued.

15. The illustration continued.

16. The illustration continued.

17. *Applied explanation.*

18. *Explanation* by division III.

19. *Explanation* by exposition and by *application* using exhortation.

20. *Application* using descriptive phrases and showing relationship.

Lawd Himself gotta get down there an' suffer, too?"

In shocked disbelief Gabriel remonstrates, "Lawd, *you* suffer! Why, Lawd, you ain't no missable sinner, you is the King of the whole creation."

And then it happened! Blinding streaks of lightning flashed, and thunder rolled across the scene. Slowly darkness fell over the shuddering earth. Far in the distance "the shadow of a cross arose, upon a lonely hill." Above the muffled roaring of a crowd and the whistling of the wind came one woman's piercing cry: "Oh, Lawdy, look at 'em! Look at 'em nail Him to dat cross!"

Back to the center of the scene came one light to play upon the face of "de Lawd" upon the throne. Gone was the golden crown and in its place—a crown of thorns! Down the agonized face came the livid streams of His own blood. His lips moved: "Yes, Gabriel, that's jus' what it means. It means de Lawd Himself gonna suffer *most* of all!"

God is the greatest sufferer! God was in Christ, bearing your sins and mine, on that old rugged cross. Did ever burdened sinners hear such news as this?

Resurrection

But no presentation of the gospel would be complete without the greatest victory of all. The preaching of the early church does not leave the Savior on the cross. The supreme note of the gospel is the glorious news that on that third morning after Calvary there was in Joseph's garden an empty tomb! Let all heaven and earth join in this greatest song of triumph: "He is not here: He is risen!"

Every grave this world has ever seen was filled, or just about to be, with the body of a mortal—a loved one, a friend. Every pastor knows that this world is one big graveyard. As he winds his way, day by day and week by week, to the last resting place of a church member, a friend, he ponders the grim fact of suffering and death—the lot of every man, great or small. At long last, each must come to this—this grave which is so final. But the good news of Easter rings with the assurance that one grave is empty. One grave could not hold its prey! Death itself was dealt a fatal blow that Easter morning: because he lives, we shall live also. Did ever a weary and dying world hear such news as this?

21. *Explanation* by exposition and by *application* showing relationship using questions.

The resurrection is God's glorious vindication of the ministry, the life and death of His Son. We know that God is truly "well pleased" with His Son, because through the resurrection He is exalted and given the "name which is above every name.". This is the life upon which sin and death can make no claim— this is truly eternal life. Who is the man that would hesitate to give everything for such a life as this? And yet men stumble on through sin toward death, as if such news had never come. Have they never heard? Can it be that they do not understand what this news means? Are they afraid to believe it—this mind staggering news? Do they need more proof than His insistent knock at their heart's door, saying, "I am the way, the truth, and the life?"

22. *Application* by illustration: (1) direct introduction, (2) an anecdote, (3) an experience of the preacher.

When a young couple moved into an old tenant house on my church field, I went as pastor to invite them to church. In answer to my knock, as little feet came running toward the door, Mother called out from the kitchen, "Jimmy, come back from that door! Don't you touch that door!"

23. The illustration continued.

Not often do I pray for little boys to disobey their parents, but this morning I slipped. I found myself praying, "Lord, let this boy open this door, I need to talk to these people. They need Jesus, and they need the church."

24. The illustration continued.

25. The illustration continued.

26. The illustration continued.

27. The illustration continued.

28. The illustration continued.

29. The illustration continued.

30. The illustration continued.

I was counting on the prayer, and a little boy's curiosity, and, sure enough, in a flash he grabbed the door and swung it open.

"Hi, Mister," he said, with a smile to melt an iceberg.

"Hi, Jimmy," I responded to his expansive greeting. "I'm the Baptist preacher at the red-brick church up the road. We want you to come with the other boys and girls and hear stories and sing songs about Jesus."

"You're the *what?*"

"I'm the preacher." Imagine my shock when he turned around abruptly and called back to the kitchen, "Mommy, what's a *preacher?* They's one at the front door."

Mommy and Daddy never came. But five-year-old little Jimmy was there almost every Sunday that fall—and always smiling. The Sunday before Christmas he missed. Two days before Christmas, about five o'clock in the morning, the phone rang: "Hurry, Preacher, to the hospital!" There I found (in the oxygen tent) Jimmy, slipping away. Before it was discovered, pneumonia had done its deadly work. And the doctor was lamenting, "If only you had brought him a little sooner."

There was snow on the hillsides that Christmas Eve, as we laid that little body to rest. When we came back into that humble home through the kitchen door, I remember seeing the calendar behind the kitchen stove with the red letters "December 25," mocking the box of toys in the corner—toys which Santa had already brought for a little boy who would not be there to play with them. Have you ever gone home with such hopeless sorrow as this? I knew that Christmas could not come to that home that year. But would it ever come? I knelt in the kitchen floor and prayed about the babe of Bethlehem.

It was the month of April when, one Sunday, the father and mother came down the aisle to give their lives to the risen Lord!

CONCLUSION:

31. *Explanation* by summary and by *application* showing relationship.

By their request I baptized them in a river—in a beautiful setting of trees and sparkling cold water. Their baptism witnessed to their faith in the crucified, buried, and risen Savior. We came back to kneel by a little grave now turning green in the springtime and thanked God for the resurrection!

This is the gospel: a manger, a cross, and an empty tomb! God's good news! How can we rest until we have told this glorious news to every person on earth?

"The Gospel of Jesus Christ" is a direct Biblical sermon (a thematic Biblical message using several passages of Scripture), with evangelistic purpose. The form is rhetorical with three major points and no subpoints. Each major point is developed by the functional elements of preaching. The introduction, which is fully developed (with four paragraphs), presents the text (at least the key verses) and sets out the dominant idea of the message. The body is divided into three parts, each of which is effectively developed by the functional elements. In matters of style this sermon has clarity, appeal, and force in good measure. In regard to improvements, three needs are evident: (1) more Biblical explanation could be used, (2) more application is needed, especially in the conclusion, and (3) the text is not handled firmly and clearly. In all probability, Ward gives only his key verses but makes use of virtually all the four Gospels, if not all the New Testament, in setting out his message. By specifying exactly how Scripture was used, Ward could have strengthened his sermon.

THE DOCTRINAL OBJECTIVE

The doctrinal objective seeks for Christians to understand God better through a proper understanding of the facts and teachings of the Bible. Systematic theology, Biblical theology, and all areas of Biblical study contribute to a proper use of doctrinal purpose.

The need for the doctrinal objective is that since man does not discover or invent theological truth, he must be taught revealed truth. This process of teaching revealed truth began with the prophets and apostles, and it continues in our day through the preaching and teaching of the message of the same prophets and apostles.

The doctrinal objective is the one true dual objective among the six major objectives. It is a valid dual objective in that each passage of Scripture may be taught for the sake of the data in the passage.

Moreover, each passage of Scripture, in addition to its meaning, carries an "intent" which must be discovered. This intent is not something separated from or in addition to the basic meaning of a passage of Scripture, but is simply the logical purpose for which the passage was revealed and retained. The passage may be preached according to its *meaning* and *intent*, and there must never be a conflict in the two.

The sermon to follow, by Helmut Thielicke, "The Parable of the Seed Growing Secretly," contains direct Biblical authority and doctrinal purpose.[10] The preacher presents a dramatic explanation of one aspect of the Kingdom of God. In form this message is a simple homily without points. In terms of special forms, it is a jewel type sermon in that Thielicke simply presents the central idea of his text from many perspectives but without the use of even one division.

---

[10]Helmut Thielicke, *The Waiting Father,* trans. John W. Doberstein (New York: Harper & Brothers, 1959), pp. 83-92.

THE PARABLE OF THE SEED
GROWING SECRETLY

1. *Explanation* by exposition (the text).

And he said, "The kingdom of God is as if a man should scatter seed upon the ground, and should sleep and rise night and day, and the seed should sprout and grow, and he knows not how. The earth produces of itself, first the blade, then the ear, then the full grain in the ear. But when the grain is ripe, at once he puts in the sickle, because the harvest has come."

And he said, "With what can we compare the kingdom of God, or what parable shall we use for it? It is like a grain of mustard seed, which, when sown upon the ground, is the smallest of all the seeds on earth; yet when it is sown it grows up and becomes the greatest of all shrubs, and puts forth large branches, so that the birds of the air can make nests in its shade."

With many such parables he spoke the word to them, as they were able to hear it; he did not speak to them without a parable, but privately to his own disciples he explained everything.

MARK 4:26-34

2. *Explanation* by illustration: (1) direct introduction, (2) scientific opinion, (3) Robert Jungk; and by exposition.

In his widely read book, *The Future Has Already Begun,* Robert Jungk tells of a lecture given by an American specialist in aeronautical medicine. In this lecture the statement was made that measured by the tasks which he faces in aeronautics—that is, breaking through the sound barrier and later in space travel—man is from a biological point of view a misconstruction. What the blunt frankness of this statement really means is that the body given to us by the Creator, with its sensitive circulatory system and its even more sensitive nervous system, is no longer equal to the possibilities opened up by the technical ingenuity of man. We can express this even more pointedly: the contribution which God has made to our existence (by putting a body at our disposal) has now been outstripped by the contribution of man and his technical intelligence. Now, man has invested the larger share of capital in the firm of "creation." He has acquired the majority of shares. The divine partner has been pushed to the wall and the directorate of creation will undoubtedly work out in such a way that from now on the human voice will be given more weight.

3. *Explanation* by exposition.

Now, what will this human voice say? It will say: Man must be biologically re-bred. The obsolete apparatus of the created human organism must be modernized. "Biometrics" (as this new method is called) will take these long-since outworn designs of the Creator, this hoary and somewhat antiquated old dodderer, and breed the new man, the space man.

4. *Explanation* by exposition and by description. This is applied explanation.

Why do I mention this little story? Because it expresses a feeling about life which is shared more or less by all of us, even though it may not be stated as drastically as it is here. We can describe this feeling by reference to an idea which has already become almost a commonplace: we are convinced that we can make anything. Good heavens, what have we not made with our technology! We can see things that happen a thousand miles away, we can even produce rain artificially, we can make stockings out of coal, we can change the course of rivers, transform landscapes, produce test-tube babies— why shouldn't we be able also to change the biological construction of the *author* of all these things, man himself? After all, this is what the Marxists have always wanted to do. All you need to do—this is their formula— is to change the social conditions and man will change. Then you can turn him from a human person with an unpredictable will and an unmanageable conscience into a compliant marionette, indeed, into an insect which will conform without friction to the termite state. The possibilities are endless. No rules are laid down for us, nothing is prescribed as far as creation is concerned; we are not limited by any alleged Lord of the world.

5. *Explanation* by exposition.

"Everything is created," you say. Nonsense! *Everything can be made!* You haven't seen anything yet. And Adam and Eve, the human beings of the first morning of creation, will still marvel at what we shall make of this world supposedly made by God, at how we shall turn it upside down.

6. *Explanation* by pertinent question.

What place do these statements have in a sermon?

7. *Explanation* by exposition and description. This is applied explanation.

They have their very proper place in it because all this concerns our soul. For anybody who holds that everything can be made must also *want* to make everything. And anybody who has taken everything in hand must then keep on moving that hand. He can no longer be still. Our over activity, which constantly keeps us on the merry-go-round and yet, no matter how fast we go, gets us nowhere, but only makes us dizzy, is not caused by the fact that we were so nervous or that we had no time. It is just the opposite. We are nervous and we have no time because we think everything will stop without us and because we think we are so tremendously important—we parvenus in this old business of creation! And this is why we can never let anything get out of our hands and be entrusted to others. That's why we hold on to everything convulsively and thus wear ourselves out all over again. Undoubtedly, all this is connected with the ultimate decisions of our life and not so much at all with medicine or with the problem of our modern way of life. And because we have thus taken over the management of the bankrupt assets of creation, because now we do everything ourselves and therefore must always be producing somthing, we never get away from constant care and concern. For anybody who takes everything upon himself finds that everything depends upon him.

8. *Explanation* by exposition and descrip-

That's why we go about worrying over how we shall pass tomorrow's examination, what

tion. Again, this is applied explanation.

will happen to our children, and what will happen when the market turns. We are literally beset by threatening possibilities. We have forgotten how to rely on the fact that it is God who clothes the lilies and feeds the birds of the air, that He provides our daily ration of bread, and that His kingdom comes no matter what happens. God the partner on whom we used to depend has become insolvent, and now we stand alone, utterly alone, on the commander's bridge as the wild weather blows up, and nobody is there with authority to command the waves and bring us through winds and icebergs to safe harbor. The *Titanic,* our world, is unsinkable and our navigation is perfect. What can be made has been made and we can dispense with this "Christian navigation." Christian! Nonsense! We don't need the Man who walks the waves. "Nearer, my God to thee?" No, nearer to the statue of liberty! We and our children will win history's blue ribbon—what glorious things we have accomplished!

9. *Explanation* by exposition, description (applied *explanation),* and many short illustrations.

But why is it then that the captain keeps pacing the bridge so anxiously? After all, it must be a grand thing to have control of this smoothly vibrating, powerful ship and guide it over the ocean—that ocean which is no longer, as Gorch Fock once expressed it, a tiny pool in the hand of the Savior but an element that challenges the omnipotence of man and offers him chances of undreamed-of triumphs. "Hast thou not accomplished all things, O holy, glowing heart?" Why doesn't this Promethean assurance cheer the captain? Why does he worry? Because now there is nobody there upon whom he can cast his cares. Why is he active and overwatchful? Because he no longer sees the eyes that watch over him. Why can't he sleep? Because he can no longer let himself go. For the world has become a weird place. Whatever happens without him and when he is not there himself

10. *Application* by showing relationship.

11. *Application* by illustration: (1) direct introduction, (2) an anecdote, (3) biography—Moltke.

12. *Application* of the illustration by showing relationship.

he cannot trust. So he has to be everywhere. That's why he can no longer *let* things happen; he must always be on deck. Not for one moment can he live like a lark or a lily. He can never let down or let up. Perhaps when he is drinking he gets away from himself for a moment. To drink or to pray: that is the question. (And drinking need not always mean the consumption of alcohol.)

Yes, the *Titanic* is our world. We and the captain are no longer able to *let* things happen. For this you can do only if you know that somebody is in control and if you know who that somebody is. But we stand alone on the bridge. We have taken charge of the firm and the ship, and now we are dying of our privileges and prerogatives.

Count von Moltke when he was an old man was asked what he was going to do in the quiet closing phase of his life after years of great activity and responsibility. His reply was: "I want to see a tree grow."

Would Moltke, we may ask, have been able to say such a thing in his old age if during the years of greatest responsibility he had not already found time for quietness, time to see that Another and Higher Being was carrying out *his* plans and guiding events to *his* goals quite independent of what Moltke did or left undone? The man who doesn't know how to let go, who is a stranger to this quite, confident joy in *him* who carries out *his* purposes without us (or also through us and in spite of us), in him who makes the trees grow and the rainbows shine—that man will become nothing but a miserable creature in his old age. For, after all, what is he good for if he can no longer produce what can be produced and his two eyes, on which he staked everything, have grown dim? Can the reason why many aging people are melancholy and fearful of having the door shut upon them be that for decades they have never been able to "let go and let God" and now can no longer see a tree growing, and therefore are nothing but run-down merry-go-rounds?

13. *Explanation* by exposition.

All this may sound almost as if we were going to discuss today the question of the art of living or talk about mental hygiene. But the art of living and mental hygiene are only the by-products of something altogether different, a by-product of the very thing our parable means when it says that God lets His seeds sprout in this namelessly quiet way, that this miracle occurs without any aid whatsoever from man and apart from any agricultural intervention — in that natural, old-fashioned way in which God carries forward His work despite all human efforts.

14. *Explanation* by summary.

Everything we have said so far, which at times may have sounded like an analysis of our culture, has been seen and said in the light of this theme. We have been standing as it were behind the preacher, Jesus Christ, trying to follow his eyes and see the world as He saw it.

15. *Explanation* by exposition of the text and by *application* showing blessings.

Here is a man who has sowed his fields. When he has done this, he leaves them, feeds the cattle, makes some repairs on his house, drives to town on errands, goes to bed at night, and rises up early. And while he is doing all this, the seed grows, without his moving a hand; first the blade from the seed and from the blade the ear and then the kernels in the ear. What an unspeakable comfort it is to know that in the midst of man's mischief, in the midst of his scheming and bad speculations, his shaping and misshaping, his activism and his failures, there is still another stream of events flowing silently on, that God is letting His seeds grow and achieving His ends.

16. *Explanation* by illustration: (1) direct introduction, (2) true event, (3) Biblical; by

When the Flood subsided and the rainbow sign of reconciliation appeared against the skies still dark with clouds, God pronounced a very strange word of consolation upon this

exposition, and descrip-
tion. Again, applied
explanation used.

poor, guilt-laden earth whose wounds were
now to be closed: "While the earth remains,
seedtime and harvest, cold and heat, summer
and winter, day and night, shall not cease."
We should certainly miss the comfort in this
assurance if we saw in it nothing more than
an invitation to man to find respite from all
the busyness of his daily grind and also from all
the folly and confusion of human life by
contemplating the constancy of nature, observing the orderly rhythm of the seasons in their
coming and going, pondering the perfect
mathematical harmony of the stars in their
courses, by simply letting God's sun shine
upon him and enjoying the lyrical beauty of
moonlight shining upon the sea. Certainly this
can be a very good thing. But we dare not
expect too much from these exercises in spiritual nature-cure. If nature is our sole physician; it may be that we shall only become more
miserable. For then we may suddenly feel
that we are excluded from its peace and its
measured orderliness. Then we may shake
our heads and go back to our store, our office,
our classroom, and say: "Wherever man is
absent, in a quiet forest clearing, in the orbits
of the planets, all is well. But wherever this
'beast' appears there is confusion and restless-
ness. He spoils the loveliest landscapes with
his picnic invasions; he desecrates the sub-
limest of mountain scenes with his heel
marks; and where he is all by himself, with
his asphalt streets and his neon lights, it is
worst of all." So, if we are honest, nature
also has something altogether different from a
message of comfort to speak to us.

17. *Explanation* by ex-
position and descrip-
tion. Again, applied
explanation used.

But this is not at all the intention of God's
message of comfort after the Flood. Summer
and winter, day and night, seedtime and harvest—here these are not to be understood as
manifestations of natural law at all, but
rather as signs that point to the *Lord*, who is
at work here. What this passage says to us is

this: The one fixed pole in all the bewildering confusion is the faithfulness and dependability of God. Insane as we men are with our idea that everything can be made, however madly we try, we shall never destroy God's creation. And we shall not be able to smash it, not because it is indestructible (for one day it will be destroyed, and the sea will be no more; the sun and moon will cease to give their light, and the stars will fall from heaven), but simply because God's love, God's faithfulness can never falter. All the confusions of men in their personal lives and the politics of the world, all the many dodges and futilities which only take us farther from the goal, still do not divert God from *His* purposes. In the end, despite all the chaos, all the stupidity, all the sin, it will not turn out to be a hopelessly tangled skein; but rather straight through all the labyinths of history, even though the conflict between East and West, and also through all the confusions of our personal lives there runs the red thread of God's purpose. He knows what He wants, and He does what He knows.

18. *Application* by showing ideal action.

One day, perhaps, when we look back from God's throne on the last day we shall say with amazement and surprise, "If I had ever dreamed when I stood at the graves of my loved ones and everything seemed to be ended; if I had ever dreamed when I saw the specter of atomic war creeping upon us; if I had ever dreamed when I faced the meaningless fate of an endless imprisonment or a malignant disease; if I had ever dreamed that God was only carrying out His design and plan through all these woes, that in the midst of my cares and troubles and despair *His* harvest was ripening, and that everything was pressing on toward His last kingly day— if I had known this, I would have been more calm and confident; I would have been more cheerful and more tranquil and composed."

19. *Explanation* by illustrations: (1) formal introduction for the first and direct introduction for the second, (2) factual for the first and opinion for the second, (3) Biblical and Manfred Hausmann.

If we want an illustration of how this certainly works out in a human life, we have only to look at the Lord Himself. What tremendous pressures there must have been within Him to drive Him to hectic, nervous, explosive activity! He sees—Manfred Hausmann has given this magnificent literary expression in his essay "One Must Keep Watch"—as no one else ever sees, with an infinite and awful nearness, the agony of the dying man, the prisoner's torment, the anguish of the wounded conscience, injustice, terror, dread, and beastliness. He sees and hears and feels all this with the heart of a Savior. And this means that distress and misery are not merely noted and registered as with a tabulating machine but actually suffered in compassionate love, as if all this were happening in his own body and His own soul. Must not this fill every waking hour and rob Him of sleep at night? Must He not begin immediately to set the fire burning, to win people, to work out strategic plans to evangelize the world, to work, work, furiously work, unceasingly, unrestingly, before the night comes when no man can work? That's what we would imagine the earthly life of the Son of God would be like, if we were to think of Him in human terms.

20. *Explanation* by illustration: (1) direct introduction, (2) factual, (3) Biblical.

But how utterly different was the actual life of Jesus! Though the burden of the whole world lay heavy upon His shoulders, though Corinth and Ephesus and Athens, whole continents, with all their desperate need, were dreadfully near to His heart, though suffering and sinning were going on in chamber, street corner, castle, and slums, seen only by the Son of God—though this immeasurable misery and wretchedness cried aloud for a physician, He has time to stop and talk to the individual. He associates with publicans, lonely widows, and despised prostitutes; He moves among the outcasts of society, wrestling for the soul of individuals. He appears not to be bothered at all by the fact that these are not strategically important people, that they have no prominence, that they are not key figures, but *only* the unfortunate, lost children of the Father in heaven. He seems to ignore with a sovereign indifference the great so-called "world-historical perspectives" of His mission when it comes to one insignificant, blind, and smelly beggar, this Mr. Nobody, who is nevertheless so dear to the heart of God and must be saved.

Because Jesus knows that He must serve His neighbor (literally, those nearest here and now), He can confidently leave to His Father the things farthest away, the great perspectives. By being obedient in His little corner of the highly provincial precincts of Nazareth and Bethlehem He allows Himself to be fitted into a great mosaic whose master is God. And that's why He has time for persons; for all time is in the hands of His Father. And that too is why peace and not unrest goes out from Him. For God's faithfulness already spans the world like a rainbow: He does not need to build it; He needs only to walk beneath it.

So, because Jesus knows which way the switches are set, because He knows what the outcome of growth and harvest will be, the words He speaks are not prepared, tactical propaganda speeches. The propaganda of men, even when it masquerades as a kind of evangelism and becomes an enterprise of the church, is always based on the accursed notion that success and failure, fruit and harvest are dependent upon our human activity, upon our imagination, energy, and intelligence. Therefore the church too must guard against becoming merely a busy enterprise, and pastors must beware of becoming religious administrators devoid of power and dried up as far as spiritual substance is concerned.

Jesus is not a propagandist. And there is

21. *Explanation* by illustration: (1) direct introduction, (2) factual, (3) Biblical.

22. *Explanation* by illustration: (1) direct introduction, (2) factual, (3) Biblical; and by *application* showing relationship and presenting a challenge.

23. *Explanation* by il-

24. *Explanation* by illustration: (1) direct introduction, (2) factual, (3) Biblical.

25. *Explanation* by illustration: (1) direct introduction, (2) factual, (3) Biblical; and by *application* showing relationship.

26. *Explanation* by illustration: (1) direct introduction, (2) anecdote, (3) history — Luther; and by *application* showing what we can do.

lustration: (1) direct introduction, (2) factual, (3) Biblical.

one fact which shows that He is not, and that is that for Him speaking to His Father in prayer is more important than speaking to men, no matter how great the crowds that gather around Him. Just when you think that now He must seize the opportunity, now surely He must strike while the masses are hot and mold them to His purpose, He "passes through the midst of them" and withdraws into the silence of communion with the Father.

Why was it that He spoke with authority, as the scribes and Pharisees did not? Because He was rhetorically gifted, because He was dynamic? No; He spoke with such power because He had first spoken with the Father, because always He came out of silence. He rested in eternity and therefore broke into time with such power. That's why He is so disturbing to time. He lived in communion with God; that's why His speech to men becomes an event of judgment and grace which none can escape.

Jesus' powerful speech derives from the power of His prayer life, and the very reason why He can afford to pray so diligently and give the best hours of the day to this communion with the Father is that He knows that while He rests in eternity it is not that nothing is happening but that in doing this He is rather giving place to God's Spirit, that then God is working and the seed is growing. Woe to the nervous activity of those of little faith! Woe to the anxiousness and busyness of those who do not pray!

Luther once said, "While I drink my little glass of Wittenberg beer the gospel runs its course." That is truly the finest and most comforting thing I have ever heard said about beer. The conversion of a man is not something that can be "produced." The new life comes into being only by letting God work. Therefore, Luther can cheerfully and trustfully step down from the pulpit; he doesn't need to go on incessantly crying, shouting, and roaring around the country. He can quietly drink his little glass of Wittenberg beer and trust in God. The Lord "gives to his beloved in sleep." In most cases today we do not sin by being undutiful and doing too little work. On the contrary, we ought to ask ourselves whether we are still capable of being idle in God's name. Take my word for it, you can really serve and worship God simply by lying flat on your back for once and getting away from this everlasting pushing and producing.

27. *Application* using rhetorical questions about how to achieve desired conduct.

Now, some of you may say, "All this may be so, but how do I go about achieving this detachment in which I stop allowing myself to be carried away by busyness and simply let God work?" This is the problem, after all. How can we attain this stillness?

28. *Application* by illustration: (1) formal introduction, (2) hypothetical, (3) Thielicke relates his truth to himself.

There are some things which cannot be appreciated merely by understanding them, they must be practiced. For example, I may have listened to a piano concert of Mozart music and had a clear insight into its musical structure, I may even have plumbed its spiritual depths intuitively or intellectually; but I am still miles away from being able to play this piano concert, for I have not practiced it. In *exactly* the same way it is possible for me to have understood the mystery of the seed growing secretly and still not be able to let God's seed really grow in *my* life. I know very well that I should drink my little glass of Wittenberg beer now, that I should be trusting enough to disconnect the gears and let myself relax. But I cannot do it; I cannot find the switch by which I can turn off my own activity and my own compulsive desire to do everything myself.

29. *Application* by showing relationship and by *explanation* using exposition.

I should like to close therefore by suggesting a little prescription, even though prescriptions in a sermon always have something shady about them, since they may give the impression that there are certain tricks, certain forms of self-training by which one can learn the art of faith. As if faith were an "art" at all! Faith is nothing but being quiet and receptive when God speaks, being still when God acts. What I have to say, then, applies only to this quiet receptiveness. Or, to express it in a different way, it is suggested only in order to help us stop putting ourselves in the limelight and asserting ourselves when God wants to turn on His light and enlighten us.

30. *Application* by showing how to have quiet receptiveness and by illustration: (1) direct introduction, (2) poetry — music, (3) Gloria Patria.

When we are sitting in a train or bus or the back set of our car, when the telephone is silent for a moment and secretaries and appointment books are gone for a time, we should try for once not to reach for the newspaper or the next file folder or for some kind of button, be it a radio knob or a bell push. Then we should try taking a deep breath and saying, "Glory be to the Father, and to the Son, and to the Holy Ghost; as it was in the beginning, is now, and ever shall be, world without end." This will give a sense of distance and peace.

31. *Application* using explanatory methods and by showing how.

We may then go on and ponder these words meditatively. Glory be to "the Father." This means: Glory be to Him who has brought me to this moment in my day's work, who has entrusted to me my fellow workers, and in the last analysis makes the final decision with regard to every decision I am now obliged to make.

32. *Application* by explanatory methods and by showing relationship.

Glory be to "the Son." The Son is none other than Jesus Christ, who died for me. Dare I—for whom He suffered such pains, for whom He opened the gates of heaven—dare I go on frittering myself away on trifles and futilities? Must not the *one* thing needful be constantly present in my mind, and must it not show up the merely relative importance of these *many* things which I do? For whom, or for what, did Christ die; for my cash register, for the roving eye of the boss whom I must please, for my television set, or for any other such trivialities? Or did he not rather die for the fellow beside me who is struggling with some burden in his life or for my children whom I hardly ever see? And as far as the children are concerned, did He die for their food and clothing or for their souls, which I do not know at all, because the "many things" are always getting between me and their souls?

Glory be to "the Holy Ghost." Oh, I'm full of spirit, I am not unenlightened. I also have feeling, heart, sentiment, and imagination. But do I ever hold still in order that the wholly Other may fill me with His Spirit and give me a sense of the true priorities in life?

"As it was in the beginning, is now, and ever shall be, world without end." Here we are encompassed by the everlasting arms. overarched by the rainbow of a faithfulness we can trust, founded upon a foundation which the shifting sands of daily routine can never provide.

If we perform this little exercise repeatedly, we shall soon find that it is not merely a mystical rigmarole and much less an inward flight by which we escape from daily duties. Oh, no; we shall go back to our job renewed; we shall become realists in a new way, for then we shall know how to distinguish what is great from what is small, the real from the false. The fanatics who believe that man can "make" everything are really fools at bottom. They are not realistic at all, even though they have the cold, sober eyes of hardheaded men of fact. But the man who has grasped the mystery of the seed growing secretly and, like the farmer in the parable. goes out and does his part of the job and then commits the fields to God and lies down to sleep in His name—that man is doing not only the most godly thing but the wisest

33. *Application* by explanatory methods and by showing relationship.

34. *Application* by explanatory methods and by showing relationship.

35. *Application* by explanatory methods and by showing relationship.

thing. For godliness and wisdom are far more
closely related than our philosophy and the
wisdom of the "managers" ever dream.

Helmut Thielicke's sermon, "The Parable of the Seed Growing Secretly," presents numerous interesting perspectives and elements of
strength: (1) In some ways the sermon resembles a symphonic sermon
in that the theme, "The Seed Growing Secretly," occurs over and
over. (2) Language and literary qualities are exceptional. (3) The
range of illustrations is both enlightening and appealing. (4) Clarity,
appeal, and vigor—the basic marks of effective style—stand out. The
preacher resembles the conductor of a great orchestra in moving his
audience from mood to mood. One has the feeling that everything
which can be said about the silently growing seed has been said. Paragraph eighteen, in the sermon, is as beautiful a paragraph of sermonic
literature as one could wish to read. (5) A most effective and appealing
use of application is made throughout the message.

Concerning improvements, three seem to be needed: (1) More direct
explanation of the text would be beneficial. At times one feels that
Thielicke has forgotten his text. With a larger use of explanation this
deficiency would be corrected quickly. (2) The length of the sermon
is excessive. The listener would be required to display great powers
of concentration in order not to be lost in the dramatic mood changes
of the preacher. This observation may be tested by reading the sermon
a second and third time and noticing how much more one receives
upon each new reading. For one hearing the message for the first
time, much quality content would be lost in a sermon of this length.
(3) For some readers, the absence of a fairly well marked introduction,
body, and conclusion would be distracting.

Chapter 8

ADDITIONAL TYPES OF BIBLICAL PURPOSE

In addition to evangelistic and doctrinal purpose the minister will employ other major objectives in his preaching. These include the ethical, consecrative, supportive, and devotional objectives.

THE ETHICAL OBJECTIVE

The ethical objective seeks to strengthen the conduct of Christians. The essence of the ethical objective may be found in the word "relationship." Christian ethics is concerned with the proper relationship of husbands and wives, parents and children, boys and girls, and young men and young women. Moreover, Christian ethics is concerned with the relationship of Christians to other Christians, of Christians to non-Christians, of Christians to employers or employees, and of Christians to state and/or all lawful authority.

All relationships must be grounded in an adequate relationship with God. Apart from the divine foundation, relationships can be no stronger than the moral standards of the individuals. In modern society one may have strong reasons to doubt that personal moral standards will suffice as codes for personal guidance. Unless one's conduct be guided and controlled by Christian principles, he will have no sure standard.

Sermons on love, courtship, marriage, divorce, parenthood, church and state. military service, race relations, labor relations, federal support for education, alcohol, our system of laws, capital punishment, and narcotics—all depict aspects of ethics which concern minister and people. These crucial issues concern each citizen in this great nation.

Among the most challenging issues of the late twentieth century are the critical ethical issues. The burning concern of minorities to secure equality in a nation where all citizens are constitutionally equal in principle but are not environmentally equal in fact has aroused the Christian conscience. Unfortunately, while some Christian consciences are disturbed by the plight of Negroes, Indians, Jews, and other minorities, other Christians are aligned in councils, clubs, and clans for the suppression of minorities and the prevention of true and equal freedom for all men. It is a strange time which sees American citizens denied basic human rights because of race, color, and creed, while visiting communists and atheists have the red carpet of hospitality rolled out to them. Two hundred thousand ministers with the concern of Jeremiah, the vision of Isaiah, the courage of Amos, and the truth of Jesus Christ could smash racism completely. American Christianity could then march in the army of kingdom soldiers without shame and embarrassment about racial matters.

In the sermon which follows, "Christ's Teaching on Divorce," D. Martyn Lloyd-Jones confronts another vital ethical issue of the late twentieth century.[1] Divorce threatens the foundations of home, community, church, and nation. A nation, church, community, and home are no better than the people in each home in the land. This sermon is a direct Biblical sermon with an ethical objective.

---

[1]Martyn Lloyd-Jones, *Studies in the Sermon on the Mount* (Grand Rapids: Wm. B. Eerdmans Publishing Co., 1962), pp. 252-261.

CHRIST'S TEACHING ON DIVORCE

INTRODUCTION:

1. *Explanation* by exposition (the text).
Matthew 5:31-32 appears to be the text, but Lloyd-Jones broadens this to include two other Scriptures, or he uses these other passages as supportive Scriptures. Applied exposition used.

We now come to consider our Lord's statement in verses 31 and 32 on the subject of divorce. Let me begin by pointing out that, when we come to a subject and passage like this, we see the value of a systematic study of the teaching of Scripture. How often do we hear an address on a text such as this? Is it not true to say that this is the kind of subject that preachers tend to avoid? And thereby, of course, we are guilty of sin. It is not for us to study some parts of the Word of God and to ignore others; it is not for us to shy at difficulties. These verses that we are now considering are as much the Word of God as anything else which is to be found in the Scriptures. But because of our failure to expound the Bible systematically, because of our tendency to take texts out of their context and to choose what interests and pleases us, and to ignore and forget the rest, we become guilty of an unbalanced Christian life. That in turn leads, of course, to failure in actual practice. It is a very good thing, therefore, that we should work our way through the Sermon on the Mount in this manner, and so find ourselves face to face with this statement.

2. *Explanation* by exposition. This is applied exposition.

For some reason or another many commentators, even though they may have set out to write a commentary on the Sermon on the Mount, slide over this and do not deal with it. One can easily understand why people tend to avoid a subject like this; but that is no excuse for them. The gospel of Jesus Christ concerns every part and portion of our life, and we have no right to say that any part of our life is outside its scope. Everything that we need is here provided for us and we have clear teaching and instruction upon every aspect of our life and being. But at the same time, anyone who has ever troubled to read up on this subject and the various interpretations will realize that it is a matter that is surrounded by many difficulties. Most of these difficulties, however, are man-made, and can be traced ultimately to the particular teaching of the Roman Catholic Church about marriage as a sacrament. Having started by taking up that position she manipulates statements in Scripture to suit her theory. We should thank God, however, that we are not left to ourselves and our own ideas, but have this clear instruction and teaching. It is our business to face it honestly.

3. *Explanation* by exposition of the context of Matthew 5:31-32.

As we approach these verses, let us once more remind ourselves of their background or context. This statement is one of six statements made by our Lord in which He introduces the subject by the formula "Ye have heard . . . but I say unto you". It comes in the section of the Sermon on the Mount in which our Lord is showing the relationship of His kingdom and teaching to the law of God that was given through Moses to the children of Israel. He began by saying that He has not come to destroy but to fulfill; indeed He says, till heaven and earth pass, one jot or one tittle shall in no wise pass from the law till all be fulfilled. Then comes the following: "Whosoever therefore shall break one of these least commandments, and shall teach men so, he shall be called the least in the kingdom of heaven: but whosoever shall do and teach them, the same shall be called great in the kingdom of heaven. For I say unto you, That except your righteousness shall exceed the righteousness of the scribes and Pharisees, ye shall in no case enter into the kingdom of heaven." He then proceeds to display His teaching in the light of this background.

4. *Explanation* by exposition of context.

Bearing all that in mind, let us also remember that in these six contrasts which our Lord draws, He is comparing not the law of Moses, as such, with His own teaching, but rather the false interpretation of this law by the

Pharisees and scribes. Our Lord obviously does not say that He had come to correct the law of Moses, because it was God's law, given by God Himself to Moses. No, our Lord's purpose was to correct the perversion, the false interpretation of the law which was being taught to the people by the Pharisees and scribes. He is therefore honoring the law of Moses and displaying it in its great fullness and glory. That, of course, is precisely what He does with regard to the question of divorce. He is especially concerned to expose the false teaching of the Pharisees and scribes with regard to this important matter.

5. *Explanation* by preview of body.

The best way to approach the subject is to consider it under three headings. First of all we must be clear in our minds as to what the law of Moses really did teach about this matter. Then we must be clear as to what the Pharisees and scribes taught. Lastly we must consider what our Lord Himself teaches.

BODY OF THE SER-MON:

6. *Explanation* by division I, by broadening the text to include Deuteronomy 24 and Matthew 19, and by exposition.
These two additional Scriptures could be supportive Scriptures, but in spite of the text listing by Lloyd-Jones it appears that they are now part of the text. Also, *Explanation* by exposition.

First, then, what did the law of Moses really teach concerning this problem? The answer is to be found in Deuteronomy xxiv, especially verses 1-4. In Matthew xix our Lord again refers to that teaching and in a sense gives us a perfect summary of it, but it is important that we should look at the original statements. There is often a good deal of confusion about this. The first thing to notice is that in the old Mosaic dispensation the word adultery is not mentioned in the matter of divorce, for the good reason that under the law of Moses the punishment for adultery was death. Anybody under that old law who was found guilty of adultery was stoned to death, so there was no need to mention it. The marriage had come to an end; but it was not brought to an end by divorce but by punishment by death. That is a very important principle to have clearly in our minds.

7. *Explanation* by exposition using Deu-

What then was the object and purpose of the Mosaic legislation with regard to divorce?

teronomy 24 and Matthew 5:32-32.

You see the answer at once, not only as you read Deuteronomy xxiv, but especially when you read our Lord's pronouncement upon, and exposition of, that legislation. The whole object of the Mosaic legislation in this matter was simply to control divorce. The position had become entirely chaotic. This is what was happening. In those days, you remember, the men generally held a very low and poor view of women, and they had come to believe that they had a right to divorce their wives for almost any and every kind of frivolous and unworthy reason. If a man, for any reason whatsoever, was anxious to get rid of his wife, he did so. He brought forward some trumpery excuse and on the basis of that he divorced her. Of course, the ultimate cause of it all was nothing but lust and passion. It is interesting to observe how, in this Sermon on the Mount, our Lord introduces this subject in immediate connection with the subject that went before it, namely, the whole question of lust. In the Authorized Version of the Bible, these two things are put together in one paragraph. That may not be right, but it does remind us of the intimate connection between the two. The Mosaic legislation, therefore, was introduced in order to regularize and control a situation that had not only become chaotic, but was grossly unfair to the women, and which, in addition, led to untold and endless suffering on the part of both the women and the children.

8. *Explanation* by division 1 of I and by exposition.

In the main, it laid down three great principles. The first was that it limited divorce to certain causes. It was only to be permitted henceforth when there was some natural, moral or physical defect discovered in the wife. All the various excuses which men had been using and bringing forward were now prohibited. Before he could obtain a divorce a man had to establish that there was some very special cause, described under the title of uncleanness. He not only had to prove that, he had also to establish it in the sight of two witnesses. Therefore the Mosaic legislation, far from giving a number of excuses for divorce, greatly limited it. It dismissed all the frivolous, superficial and unjust reasons, restricting it to one particular matter.

9. *Explanation* by division 2 of I and by exposition.

The second thing it enforced was that any man who thus divorced his wife must give her a bill of divorcement. Before the Mosaic law, a man could say he no longer wanted his wife, and could turn her out of the house; and there she was, at the mercy of the whole world. She might be charged with unfaithfulness or adultery and so be liable to being stoned to death. Therefore, in order to protect the woman, this legislation provided that she should be given a bill of divorcement in which a statement was made that she had been dismissed, not because of unfaithfulness, but because of one of these reasons which had been discovered. It was to protect her, and the bill of divorcement was handed to her in the presence of two witnesses whom she could always call in any case of need and necessity. Divorce was made something formal, something serious, the idea being to impress upon the minds of those people that it was a solemn step and not something to be undertaken lightly in a moment of passion when a man suddenly felt he disliked his wife and wanted to get rid of her. In this way the seriousness of marriage was emphasized.

10. *Explanation* by division 3 of I and by exposition.

Then the third step in the Mosaic legislation was a very significant one, namely, that a man who divorces his wife and gives her a bill of divorcement is not allowed to marry her again. The case was put like this. Here is a man who has divorced his wife, and given her a bill of divorcement. With that in her hand she is entitled to marry somebody else. Now the second husband may also give her a bill of divorcement. Yes, says the law of

Moses, but if that does happen and she is free to get married once more, she must not marry the first husband. The whole force of that enactment is again exactly the same; it is to make these people see that marriage is not something you can walk in and out of at will. It tells the first husband that, if he gives his wife a bill of divorcement, it is a permanent enactment.

11. *Explanation* by summary, exposition, and illustration: (1) direct, introduction, (2) factual, (3) Biblical.

When we examine it like that, we can see at once that the old Mosaic legislation is very far indeed from being what we thought it was, and especially what the Pharisees and scribes thought it to be. Its object was to reduce to a certain amount of order a situation that had become utterly chaotic. You will find that this was the characteristic of all the details of the Mosaic legislation. Take for example the matter of "an eye for an eye, and a tooth for a tooth." The Mosaic legislation enacted that. Yes, but what was the object of it? It was not to tell the people that if a man knocked out another man's eye, the victim must retaliate in the same way. No; its purpose was to say this: You are not entitled to kill a man for that offence; it is only an eye for an eye, or if a man knocks out another's tooth, all you are entitled to is a tooth. It is restoring order in a state of chaos, limiting the consequences and legislating for a particular condition. Now the law concerning divorce was exactly the same as that.

12. *Explanation* by division II and by exposition of Matthew 19 and 5:31-32.

Next we must consider the teaching of the Pharisees and scribes because, as we have seen, it was to this especially that our Lord was referring. They said that the law of Moses commanded, indeed urged, a man to divorce his wife under certain conditions. Now, of course, it never said anything of the kind. The law of Moses never commanded anybody to divorce his wife; all it did was to say to a man: If you do want to divorce your wife you should do so only under these conditions. But the Pharisees and scribes, as our Lord makes particularly plain in Matthew xix when He was speaking on this same subject, were teaching that Moses commanded divorce. And, of course, the next step was that they were again demanding divorce and insisting upon their right to it, for all kinds of inadequate reasons. They took that old Mosaic legislation with regard to this question of uncleanness and had their own interpretation as to what was meant by it. They actually taught that, if a man ceased to like his wife, or for any reason found her to be unsatisfactory to him, that, in a sense, was "uncleanness." How typical this is of the teaching of the Pharisees and scribes, and their method of interpreting the law! But in reality they were avoiding the law in principle as well as in letter. The result was that at the time of our Lord terrible injustices were again being done to many women who were being divorced for most unworthy and frivolous reasons. There was only one factor that really mattered to these men, and that was the legal one of giving a bill of divorcement. They were very punctilious about that, as they were careful about other legal details. They did not, however, state why they were divorcing her. That was unimportant. But what did matter supremely was that she be given a writing of divorcement! Our Lord puts it like this: "It hath been said" —that is the sort of thing you have been hearing from the Pharisees and scribes. What is the important thing for "whosoever shall put away his wife?" "Let him give her a writing of divorcement." Well, of course, that is important, and the law of Moses had enacted it. But you see that is not the main thing, or the thing to be stressed and emphasized. But it was in the center of the picture as far as the Pharisees and scribes were concerned and, in emphasizing this, they had been failing to see the real meaning of marriage. They had failed

13. *Explanation* by division III and by exposition of Matthew 19:3-9 and 5:31-32.

Explanation by division 1 of III, by exposition, and by illustrations: (1) all direct introductions, (2) all factual, all Biblical.

to consider this whole question of divorce, and the reason for it, in a true, just and righteous manner. Such was the perversion by the Pharisees and scribes of the Mosaic teaching. They were avoiding it and circumventing it with their clever interpretations and traditions which they added to the law. The result was that the ultimate object of the Mosaic legislation had really been entirely concealed and nullified.

That brings us to our third and last main heading. What does our Lord say about this? "But I say unto you, That whosoever shall put away his wife, saving for the cause of fornication, causeth her to commit adultery: and whosoever shall marry her that is divorced committeth adultery." Now the statement in Matthew xix: 3-9 is most important and helpful in interpreting this teaching, because it is a fuller explication of what our Lord puts here in a summarized form. The Pharisees and scribes said to Him—they were trying to trap Him—"Is it lawful for a man to put away his wife for every cause?" They were really giving themselves away in asking such a question for they themselves were actually sanctioning this. And here is our Lord's answer. The first principle He emphasizes is that of the sanctity of marriage. "Whosoever shall put away his wife, saving for the cause of fornication." You notice that He goes back beyond the law of Moses to the law that was given by God at the very beginning. When God created woman to be a helpmeet for man He made that great pronouncement. He said, "They twain shall be one flesh." "What therefore God hath joined together, let no man put asunder." Marriage is not a civil contract, or a sacrament; marriage is something in which these two persons become one flesh. There is an indissolubility about it, and our Lord goes right back to that great principle. When God made woman for man that was

His intention, that was what He indicated, and that was what He ordained. The law which God laid down was that a man should leave father and mother and be joined to his wife and that they should become one flesh. Something new and distinct has taken place, certain other ties are broken and this new one is formed, This aspect of "one flesh" is all-important. You will find that it is a principle running right through Scripture whenever this subject is dealt with. It is seen in I Corinthians vi, where Paul says that the terrible thing about fornication is that a man becomes one flesh with a harlot—a most solemn and important teaching. Our Lord starts there. He goes back to the beginning, to God's own original view of marriage.

14. *Explanation* by exposition of Matthew 5: 31-32 and Matthew 19.

"If that is so," asks someone, "how do you explain the law of Moses? If that is God's own view of marriage why did He allow divorce to take place on the conditions which we have just considered?" Our Lord again answered that question by saying that, because of the hardness of their hearts, God made a concession, as it were. He did not abrogate His original law with regard to marriage. No, He introduced a temporary legislation because of the conditions then prevailing. God controlled it. It was exactly the same as we have seen with regard to "an eye for an eye, and a tooth for a tooth." It was a tremendous innovation at that time; but in reality it was God leading the people back in the direction of His original pronouncement. "Because of the hardness of your hearts," says our Lord, "Moses gave you this concession." It was not God advocating divorce, or commanding anybody to divorce his wife; it was God just reducing the chaos to a certain amount of order, regularizing what had become utterly irregular. We must keep in the forefront of our minds in these matters God's original object and intention with regard to this whole estate of marriage: the one flesh, the indissolubility, and the coming together in that way.

The first principle leads us to the second, which is that God has never anywhere commanded anybody to divorce. The Pharisees and scribes were suggesting that this was so with Moses' law. Yes, he certainly commanded them to write that bill of divorcement if there was to be a divorce. But that is not the same thing as commanding them to divorce. The idea taught by God's Word is not only that of the indissolubility of marriage, but that of the law of love and forgiveness. We must get rid of this legalistic approach which makes a man say, "She has spoiled my life, therefore I must divorce her." As unworthy and undeserving sinners we have all been forgiven by the grace of God, and that must enter into and control our view of everything that happens to us with respect to all other persons, and especially in the relationship of marriage.

The next principle is one which is of the utmost importance. There is only one legitimate cause and reason for divorce—that which is here called "fornication." Now I need not emphasize the urgent relevance of all this teaching. We are living in a country in which conditions have became chaotic in this matter of divorce, and there are still further bills proposed which are designed to make divorce easier and which would aggravate the position still further. Here is our Lord's teaching with regard to the subject. There is only one cause for divorce. There *is* one; but there is only one. And that is unfaithfulness by one party. This term "fornication" is inclusive, and it really means unfaithfulness on the part of one party to a marriage. "Whosoever shall put away his wife, saving for the cause of fornication, causeth her to commit adultery." We must realize

15. *Explanation* by division 2 of III, by exposition, and by *application* showing relationship.

16 *Explanation* by division 3 of III, by exposition, and by *application* showing relationship.
Also developed by exposition and by illustration: (1) direct introduction, (2) factual, (3) Biblical.

the importance of this principle. It was particularly important in the days of the early Church. If you read I Corinthians vii you will find there that this matter is referred to again. In those early days the problem presented itself to many Christians in this form. Imagine a husband and wife. The husband is suddenly converted, the wife is not. Here is a man who has become a new creature in Christ Jesus, but his wife still remains a pagan. These people had been taught the doctrine about separation from the world and sin. They, therefore, immediately jumped to the conclusion which forced them to say, "It is impossible for me to go on living with a woman like that who is a pagan. Surely, if I am to live the Christian life, I must divorce her because she is not a Christian." And many a wife who had been converted and whose husband was not, was saying the same thing. But the apostle Paul taught these people that the husband was not to leave his wife because he was converted and she was not. You see, even that is not a ground for divorce. Take all this modern talk of incompatibility of temperament. Can you imagine anything more incompatible than a Christian and a non-Christian? And according to modern ideas, if ever there was cause for divorce surely there it is. But the plain teaching of Scripture it that even that is not a ground for divorce. Do not leave the unconverted one, says Paul. The wife who has been converted having an unbelieving husband sanctifies that husband. You need not worry about your children; if one party is Christian they are covered and have the privilege of Christian nurture within the life of the Church.

17. *Application* by showing relationship. This is explanatory application.

Now that is a most important and vital argument. It is the way of impressing upon us this great principle which is laid down by our Lord Himself. Nothing is a cause for divorce save fornication. It does not matter how difficult it may be, it does not matter what the stress or the strain, or whatever can be said about the incompatibility of temperament. Nothing is to dissolve this indissoluble bond save this one thing. But I emphasize again that this one thing does. Our Lord Himself says that this is a cause and a legitimate one for divorce. He says Moses granted certain concessions "because of the hardness of your hearts." But this is now laid down as a principle, not as a concession to weakness. He Himself tells us that unfaithfulness is a cause for divorce and the reason for this is surely obvious. It is this question of the "one flesh" again; and the person who is guilty of adultery has broken the bond and has become united to another. The link has gone, the one flesh no longer obtains, and therefore divorce is legitimate. Let me emphasize again, it is not a commandment. But it is a ground for divorce, and a man who finds himself in that position is entitled to divorce his wife, and the wife is entitled to divorce the husband.

18. *Explanation* by applied exposition.

The next step makes this even clearer. Our Lord says that if you divorce your wife for any other reason you cause her to commit adultery. "Whosoever shall put away his wife, saving for the cause of fornication, causeth her to commit adultery." The argument is this: There is only one thing that can break this bond. Therefore, if you put away your wife for any other reason you are putting her away without breaking the bond. In this way you are making her break the bond if she should marry again; and she is therefore committing adultery. So that a man who divorces his wife for any reason but for this is thereby causing her to commit adultery. He is the cause, and the man who marries her is in like manner an adulterer. Thus our Lord enforces this great principle in this positive and clear manner. There is only one cause for divorce, and no other.

CONCLUSION:

19. *Explanation* by summary exposition This is applied exposition in part.

20. *Application* by showing relationship and results. Also, *application* by exhortation using an illustration: (1) direct introduction, (2) factual, (3) Biblical.

What, then, is the effect of this teaching? We can summarize it in this way. Our Lord here shows Himself to us as the great Lawgiver. All law comes from Him; everything appertaining to this life and world has come from Him. There was temporary legislation for the children of Israel because of their peculiar circumstances. The Mosaic penalty for adultery was death by stoning. Our Lord abrogated that temporary legislation. The next thing He has done is to make divorce for the cause of adultery legitimate; He has established the law on this matter. These are two main results of His teaching. From that time onwards men and women are not stoned and put to death for adultery. If you want to do anything you are entitled to a divorce. Out of that we may legitimately draw one very important and serious deduction. We can say not only that a person who thus has divorced his wife because of her adultery is entitled to do so. We can go further and say that the divorce has ended the marriage, and that this man is now free and as a free man he is entitled to re-marriage. Divorce puts an end to this connection, our Lord Himself says so. His relationship to that woman is the same as if she were dead; and this innocent man is therefore entitled to Christian re-marriage. But he alone is in that position and she is not, or vice versa.

"Have you nothing to say about the others?" asks someone. All I would say about them is this, and I say it carefully and advisedly, and almost in fear lest I give even a semblance of a suggestion that I am saying anything that may encourage anyone to sin. But on the basis of the gospel and in the interest of truth I am compelled to say this: Even adultery is not the unforgivable sin. It is a terrible sin, but God forbid that there should be anyone who feels that he or she has sinned himself or herself outside the love of God or outside His kingdom because of adultery. No, if you truly repent and realize the enormity of your sin and cast yourself upon the boundless love and mercy and grace of God, you can be forgiven and I assure you of pardon. But hear the words of our blessed Lord: "Go, and sin no more."

21. *Application* by showing relationship and by exhortation.

There, then, is our Lord's teaching on this important subject. You see the state of the world and of society round about us today. Is it surprising that our world is as it is while men and women play fast and loose with God's Word in this vital matter? What right have we to expect nations to stand to their bonds and keep their vows if men and women do not do it even in this most solemn and sacred union of marriage? We must start with ourselves; we must start at the beginning, we must observe the law of God in our own personal, individual lives. And then, and then only, will we be entitled to trust nations and peoples, and to expect a different type of conduct and behavior from the world at large.

"Christ's Teaching on Divorce" is a direct Biblical sermon with an ethical objective. In form, this message is rhetorical with three major points and three subpoints under I, no subpoints under II, and three subpoints under III. While the absence of subpoints under II may be disturbing, no real problem exists here. The introduction and conclusion are in good balance, with five paragraphs for the introduction and three for the conclusion. In matters of style, "Christ's Teaching on Divorce" is, at times, rather tedious and heavy. However, clarity, appeal, and force are apparent even though they could be improved.

As to general improvements, Lloyd-Jones could brighten his style, reduce the length of his paragraphs or divide them in some fashion, and add additional paragraphs of illustration and application. The weakest portions of the sermon are the scarcity of vital personal application and the heavy tedious style.

THE CONSECRATIVE OBJECTIVE

The consecrative objective seeks to enlist Christians in God's service. This objective is also called the actional, service, and stewardship objective. The actional objective concerns itself with enlisting the total man in total kingdom causes. The objective seeks all the time, talent, and personality factors one possesses and desires that this total man serve Jesus Christ. The need for the actional objective can be seen when one observes that 30 percent or less of the church membership carries about 99 percent of the church responsibility; that the average church congregation gives to the church not a tithe or more but 1, 2, or perhaps 3 percent of its income; that the average Christian man, woman, and young person lives his life in conformity to the world rather than in conformity to Christ; that American churches retain and use 90 to 99 percent of their religious vocational workers in the United States while the vast ignorant, lost, and suffering world gets the leftovers; and that indifference on the part of the people of the congregation all but crushes the minister and his staff.

The need for a separated but not a pharisaical people confronts the twentieth century church. How the church of Jesus Christ can be all she should be and avoid pharisaism and/or fanaticism challenges each pastor and church staff in America. Pure dedication without legalism, pride, or majoring on incidentals stands before the church as a worthy goal. The actional objective points in the direction of this pure dedication and beckons the preacher to lead the way through his living and preaching.

The author's actional sermon, "The Walk of the Pharisee," describes the ancient and the contemporary Pharisee and expresses the desire that Christians walk as Jesus walked.[2] This sermon is a direct Biblical sermon with actional purpose.

---

[2]H. C. Brown, Jr. (ed.), *Southwestern Sermons* (Nashville: Broadman Press, 1960), pp. 36-42.

THE WALK OF THE PHARISEES

MATTHEW 23:1-36

1. *Explanation* by illustration: (1) direct introduction, (2) factual event, (3) a newspaper article.

Two blindfolded soldiers who were part of an experiment designed to determine directional accuracy without physical sight were led to the edge of a runway. The two men were equipped with special metal containers, filled with lime, to spray white streams to mark their routes as they marched across the field. Within a few minutes after the soldiers started walking it was evident that they were unable to walk a straight line without physical vision. When the accompanying attendants stopped them, both men were hundreds of feet from their assigned targets. Even though they both tried to walk straight courses, they both failed.

2. *Explanation* by exposition treating background of the text.

We have recorded in the Bible, and in other sources, the story of a group of people who intended to walk straight for God but whose spiritual judgment proved to be faulty. Around 200 B.C. these people separated themselves from heathenism and diluted Judaism for the purpose of doing the will of Jehovah. They were called the "separated" or the "Pharisees." Their motive was exalted: they were counted among the best people God had.

3. *Explanation* by exposition of the text.

Between the time of their noble dedication and the time that Jesus preached something happened. Matthew's Gospel, in chapter 23, verses 1-36, sets forth a graphic picture of the Pharisees in Jesus' day. This chapter shows that a dreadful change had come to the exalted purpose of the Pharisees. The origin of the pharisaical group was pleasing in God's sight, but the conclusion was abominable.

4. *Application* by showing desired action and by *explanation* using exposition.

It is important that we see the Pharisee as Christ saw him for the purpose of avoiding the walk of the Pharisee. In the New Testament the term "walk" is used as a designation for a course of action or a course of life. Thus the subject is "The Walk of the Pharisee."

5. *Application* by showing relationship.

The person most likely to be a Pharisee in the biblical sense is the person who tries to please God but fails. The title "Pharisee" will never be given to a drunkard, an atheist, or an ungodly person in revolt against the Lord. Rather, it is to be given to the person who loses his way in God's service. He it is who is most likely to be a modern Pharisee.

BODY OF THE SERMON:

The pharisee conceitedly craves personal prominence. He seeks to be seen of men as he serves God. "But all their works they do for to be seen of men: they make broad their phylacteries, and enlarge the borders of their garments" (Matt. 23:5).

6. *Explanation* by division I and by exposition.

7. *Explanation* by exposition.

Phylacteries were small leather boxes, strapped to the forehead or to the left arm near the heart, containing Scripture verses written on parchment. The size of the phylacteries gave an indication of the zeal for God's Word on the part of those wearing them. It was easy to enlarge those phylacteries and to allow that visual mechanical display of obedience to God to take the place of true obedience.

8. *Explanation* by exposition.

The borders of garments referred to in the text were the borders of prescribed clothes that the Jews wore in recognition of obedience to the laws of Jehovah. In order to demonstrate that they were wearing the proper clothes with the prescribed borders, some Pharisees deliberately enlarged those borders for all people to see.

9. *Application* by showing relationship.

Christ placed His finger upon a problem that is very real to a religious person. This delicate problem is to know the difference between service for God and service which sinfully and shamefully displays self. If an individual serves God, he must be active, and to be active means to be seen of men. The pressures that would drive a person to a sinful desire to be seen of men are insidious and terrifying. In the desire to solve this dilemma some individuals resort to sub-Christian levels of conduct. When the Pharisee does engage in service for God, he does so for the purpose of having people notice that he is serving the Lord. The person with the Pharisaical mind has an insatiable appetite for prominence, and he feels that appetite by constantly pushing self to the center of the stage.

10. *Explanation* by exposition.

The Pharisee seeks to be honored by men as a reward for his service to God. They "love the uppermost rooms at feasts, and the chief seats in the synagogues" (Matt. 23:6).

11. *Application* by showing relationship.

When does a simple desire to have one's work recognized become a sinful craving for praise and honor? The problem is in knowing the difference between serving God for the glory of God and serving God for the purpose of being honored by men. There is a dividing line between these extremes, and a dedicated individual who desires to serve God must know where the point of division is. To cross that invisible line and to court honor and glory from doting parents and admiring friends because of service for God is to walk like a Pharisee.

12. *Application* of the text showing relationship.

Christ gave a remarkable answer to this perplexing problem when He said: "But he that is greatest among you shall be your servant. And whosoever shall exalt himself shall be abased; and he that shall humble himself shall be exalted" (Matt. 23:11-12)

13. *Explanation* by division II and by exposition.

The Pharisee tragically endangers the eternal destiny of men. He refuses to enter the kingdom of God. "But woe unto you, scribes and Pharisees, hypocrites! for ye shut up the kingdom of heaven against men: for ye neither go in yourselves . . ." (Matt. 23:13).

14. *Explanation* by exposition.

Christ presented a paradox. Though the Pharisees throught that they, as religious people, were within the kingdom of God, the judgement of Jesus was that they were not. Because of their training, the Pharisees should have been the first to accept Jesus Christ as the Messiah, but because of their spiritual blindness they rejected Him. How pitiful and tragic was the example set by the Pharisees!

Within the doors of many churches there are, no doubt, individuals who are just as lost to the kingdom of God as were the Pharisees. Because these individuals are active in church affairs and are honored by fellow church members, they suppose that they are in the kingdom. As modern men who walk like Pharisees, they too stand outside the kingdom of God.

The present day Pharisee tries to prevent seeking sinners from entering the kingdom. "But woe unto you, scribes and Pharisees, hypocrites! for ye shut up the kingdom of heaven against them: . . . neither suffer ye them that are entering to go in" (Matt. 23:13).

The Pharisees tried to prevent seeking sinners from entering the kingdom by closing the door to the kingdom. They denied that the kingdom was at hand; they spread false teachings about the kingdom of God and about Jesus Christ; and seeking sinners were turned from the door of eternal life. The Pharisees tried to prevent seeking sinners from entering the kingdom by proselyting those sinners to themselves and to their cause. "Woe unto you, scribes and Pharisees, hypocrites! For ye compass sea and land to make one proselyte, and when he is made, ye make him twofold more the child of hell than yourselves" (Matt. 23:15). The tragic truth is that when the Pharisees won other individuals to their cause, the disciples were more perverted than their teachers. The Pharisees went to fantastic extremes to win individuals to their position without any regard as to the consequences to those persons.

A preacher who resorts to high pressure tactics, whether in a revival or in personal visitation, to cause a person to join a church is in danger of adding one to the church but not to the kingdom of God. The church mem-

---

15. *Application* by showing relationship.

16 *Explanation* by exposition.

17. *Explanation* by exposition.

18. *Application* by showing relationship.

ber who is more concerned with numbers on the Sunday school record book than with eternal life for the Sunday school pupils is in danger of pushing people into the church apart from conversion. It is absolutely necessary that a person be converted before he be counted.

19. *Explanation* by division III and by exposition.

The Pharisees deliberately deceived others with a double standard of speech. "Woe unto you, ye blind guides, which say, Whosoever shall swear by the temple, it is nothing; but whosoever shall swear by the gold of the temple, he is a debtor!" (Matt. 23:16).

20. *Explanation* by exposition.

The religious leaders of Jesus' day practiced trickery in speech in regard to the use of promises and oaths. The Pharisees could make vows and seal those vows with oaths to the Temple. Then if they desired to do so, they could break those vows because, they said, general oaths to the Temple did not bind them. But if they had sealed their promises with oaths to the gold on the Temple, they were obligated to keep those vows because, they said, oaths to the gold on the Temple were specific and binding. All of this was a system of duplicity and trickery which allowed religious leaders to be liars and to be honorable at the same time.

21. *Application* by showing relationship.

The modern Pharisee also uses a double standard of speech. In each situation he is able to say the correct words and to win admiration and approval for his conduct because he is a master of duplicity. He agrees verbally with the position of his church that drinking alcohol is immoral, but he sips cocktails with his friends. He loudly praises, on Sunday, integrity in business, but he sells shoddy shoes on Monday morning. He condemns unclean speech at prayer meeting, but he tells filthy yarns at the Thursday morning coffee break. There is an inconsistency here.

22. *Explanation* by exposition.

The Pharisee blindly deceives himself with his double standard of speech. "Ye fools and blind: for whether is greater, the gold, or the temple that sanctifieth the gold?" (Matt. 23: 17).

23. *Explanation* by exposition.

Christ called the Pharisees blind fools for their stupid use of oaths. The Pharisees tried to make the gold on the Temple of more importance than the Temple and used this incorrect logic as a basis for their nefarious system of vows. Christ bluntly told them that their logic was false because the Temple was more valuable than the gold which adorned it. The Pharisees thus found themselves under condemnation from the Lord because of their insincerity in speech.

24. *Application* by showing relationship.

Christ demands from His disciples not professions of orthodoxy of speech but simple, sincere speech which matches a pure and good life. Jesus taught that it is necessary to exemplify words as well as to speak them.

25. *Explanation* by division IV and by exposition.

The Pharisee proudly majors on the mechanics of religion. He is scrupulously careful about money matters. "Woe unto you, scribes and Pharisees, hypocrites! for ye pay tithe of mint and anise and cummin, and have omitted the weightier matters of the law, justice, mercy, and faith: . . . Ye blind guides, which strain at a gnat, and swallow a camel" (Matt. 23:23-24).

26. *Explanation* by exposition.

Christ was not critical of the Pharisees because of their minute attention to money matters. Rather, He commanded them to have financial fidelity to God. The point of the criticism was that the external, material, and mechanical features of religion were of more importance to the Pharisees than the internal, spiritual, and moral aspects of religion. Our Lord did not hesitate to press upon the Pharisees the importance of having a passion for justice, mercy, and faith.

27. *Application* by showing relationship.

As a person gives scrupulous attention to the material aspect of God's kingdom, he is to recognize that this physical aspect is not of paramount importance. Those distinct elements of religion commanded by Christ—justice, mercy, faith—speak of righteous conduct in relation to God and man. Because these relate to God and to man, they are the vital elements of religion.

28. *Explanation* by exposition.

Jesus pointed out that the Pharisees, who were diligent about material matters but who failed to be just, merciful, and faithful, were like the Jew who strained a gnat out of his glass of wine and then swallowed from the same glass a dusty, dirty, smelly camel. If this were not so tragic, it would be laughable, would it not?

29. *Explanation* by exposition.

The Pharisee is scrupulously careful about form in religion. "Woe unto you, scribes and Pharisees, hypocrites! for ye make clean the outside of the cup and of the platter, but within they are full of extortion and excess" (Matt. 23:25).

30. *Explanation* by exposition.

A cup and a platter—bright and beautiful on the outside, but dirty and filthy on the inside—were the object lessons Christ used as He criticized the Pharisees because they were more concerned with a formal faith than they were with an ethical faith. The Pharisees were largely concerned with proper dress, with endless rules for dealing with sinners, with hundreds of laws for sabbath conduct, and with requirements dealing with feasts, food, and fasting. These formal elements of religion surpassed their concern for ethical righteousness.

31. *Application* by showing relationship.

The descendants of the first century Pharisees live yet in the twentieth century, do they not? The modern Pharisee is primarily concerned with proper clothes, dignified personal bearing, social respectability, a stately edifice for worship, an elaborate ritual, a famous preacher, and other niceties of a formal religion. These are the supreme values to a person walking like a Pharisee.

32. *Explanation* by division V and by explanation.

The Pharisee piously practices hypocrisy. He falsely displays righteousness. "Woe unto you, scribes and Pharisees, hypocrites! for ye are like unto whited sepulchres . . ." (Matt. 23:27).

33. *Explanation* by exposition.

A revolting contrast was presented by Jesus. Outside, the tombs were clean, white-washed, and attractive, but inside the tombs were dirty and full of corruption. So, said Christ, the Pharisees had external characters which were godly and righteous, while they had internal characters which were ungodly and corrupt. The Pharisees, Jesus said, knew that they were not righteous. Their pretense of piety earned for them the name "hypocrite."

34. *Application* by showing relationship.

The graveyard simile commands attention because it is dramatic, graphic, and revolting. It strikes the conscience because it deals with a constant and critical problem. When an individual wants to be righteous before God and man, the task is difficult. It costs much to avoid sham, pretense, and hypocrisy; and it costs sacrificially to practice right action in religious affairs, family activities, business dealings, and personal matters.

35. *Explanation* by exposition.

The Pharisee falsely proclaims reverence for tradition. "Woe unto you, scribes and Pharisees, hypocrites! because ye build the tombs of the prophets, and garnish the sepulchres of the righteous" (Matt. 23:29).

36. *Explanation* by exposition.

With great earnestness the Pharisees professed reverence for the sacred heritage of their faith. Christ said they lied because they professed one thing and prepared to do another. Christ said, in effect, "You hypocrites have not listened to me, and you are preparing to murder me. You thereby demonstrate that you are exactly like your fathers."

37. *Application* by showing relationship.

How many people today profess a reverence for the noble heritage of the faith and then deny that profession by pharisaical deeds? Many, no doubt. It is commonplace to note that people piously affirm their belief in great traditions such as the freedom of the pulpit, Christlike conduct in race relations, and the

authority of the Word of God as an adequate
guide for personal living. But they pay only
lip service to these lofty ideals. The modern
Pharisee professes to honor the magnificent
principles of our faith, but he proves by his
hypocritical deeds that he is a true descendant
of the biblical Pharisee.

An embarrassing name, vicious enough to
cause the chords of terror to ring in the heart,
is the name "Pharisee." The connotations of
this name are so ugly that no one who is even
remotely acquainted with the thundering de-
nunciations of Jesus against the Pharisees
could possibly want to be a Pharisee.

Every Christian should examine his heart
critically to determine if there are evidences
of a pharisaical walk. The Pharisee conceitedly craves personal prominence; he tragically
endangers the eternal destiny of men; he
deceivingly professes sincerity of speech; he
proudly majors on the mechanics of religion;
and he piously practices hypocrisy.

The supreme purpose for this message has
been that you and I will avoid that walk of
the Pharisee by walking as Jesus walked. As
John said, "He that saith he abideth in him
ought himself also so to walk, even as he
walked" (I John 2:6).

CONCLUSION:

38. *Application* by
showing relationship.

39. *Application* by ex-
hortation and summary.

40. *Application* by challenge and *illustration:*
(1) direct introduction,
(2) factual, (3) Bib-
lical.

The "Walk of the Pharisee" is a direct Biblical sermon with actional
purpose and rhetorical form. The introduction and the conclusion are
in fairly good balance in that the introduction is developed by five
paragraphs and the conclusion by three. The body has five major divisions with two subdivisions under each major point. In matters of style,
the sermon has a degree of clarity, appeal, and force but could be improved.

In regard to improvements, style could be improved by having longer
and stronger paragraphs. While explanation and application are used
generously, illustration is missing except for those illustrations which
grow out of the text. There are too many points covered: five major
and ten subpoints. This message could have been strengthened by omit-
ting the subpoints under the five headings and by developing the five
major headings solely with the functional elements rather than by divid-

ing the major points and then developing the ten subpoints with the
functional elements. Too many ideas and sub-ideas are stressed. The
sermon's primary strength is explanation and application.

THE SUPPORTIVE OBJECTIVE

The supportive objective seeks to help people with troubles, problems,
and difficulties. This objective is also known as the enheartening, the
life situation, the pastoral, the inspirational, or the psychological objective. This purpose seeks to aid people with problems so that they will
appropriate God's grace, strength, and comfort. The persons with difficulties may be strong, mature, and resourceful Christians who are
experiencing temporary crises, or they may be individuals with a life-
time of weaknesses, fears, and frustrations. The supportive purpose seeks
to aid, encourage, and undergird all men in need of a word of grace
from the Lord.

The need for this objective can be seen as one considers death, illness,
accidents, job losses, failures, disappointments, betrayals, misunderstandings, and countless frustrations which come to people hour by hour.
There is no one in a congregation who does not need support, grace,
and strength from time to time from God and the pastor. On numerous
occasions in preaching classes the observation has been made that there
is at least one tragedy on each row in the class. One day a student
added a corrective, "Would it not be more accurate to say that there
is a tragedy in each chair?" On numerous occasions men have followed
the teacher to the office to say about the observations on tragedy, "You
were talking about me!" There is sadness and suffering in each life. An
old Spanish proverb says, "Each family has its *hush!*" Therefore, the
minister will speak to these life situations with a word from the Lord.

The twentieth century emphasis calling for a message to those burdened with tragedy reaches to the heart of a minister's work. The method
of speaking to these burdens, however, solely with an emphasis on
psychology, sociology, science, and counseling ignores the Bible. The
need for pastoral preaching strongly challenges the minister, and he
should depend upon God's Word as the main staple for feeding God's
children who are in distress.

The sermon by Harry Emerson Fosdick, "Handling Life's Second
Bests," is a supportive message with direct Biblical authority and
rhetorical form.[3]

---

[3]Harry Emerson Fosdick, *Riverside Sermons* (New York: Harper & Brothers, 1958), pp. 54-62.

HANDLING LIFE'S SECOND BESTS

INTRODUCTION:

1. *Explanation* by exposition.

2. *Explanation* by illustration: (1) formal and mechanical, (2) true and factual, (3) biography.

3. *Explanation* by exposition (the text).

4. *Explanation* by exposition, by illustrations: (1) all direct introductions, (2) all true and factual, (3)

We are concerned today about a factual personal problem so nearly universal in its application that we need not be bothered by its exceptions: namely, that very few persons have a chance to live their lives on the basis of their first choice. We all have to live upon the basis of our second and third choices. To one who reads biography this comes to be so much a matter of course that he takes it for granted.

Whistler, the artist, for example, started out to be a soldier and failed at West Point because he could not pass the chemistry. "If silicon had been a gas," he used to say, "I should have been a major-general." Instead, he failed in soldering, half-heartedly tried engineering, and then tried painting—with such remarkable results as one sees in the portraits of his own mother, Miss Alexander, and Carlyle.

Let us approach this inescapable human problem of handling life's second bests by way of one of the most impressive exhibitions of it in history. In the sixteenth chapter of the book of The Acts, in the record of Paul's journeys, we read this: "When they were come over against Mysia, they assayed to go into Bithynia; and the Spirit of Jesus suffered them not; and passing by Mysia, they came down to Troas, And a vision appeared to Paul in the night: There was a man of Macedonia standing, beseeching him, and saying, Come over into Macedonia, and help us. And when he had seen the vision, straightway we sought to go forth into Macedonia, concluding that God had called us to preach the gospel unto them."

So simple and succinct is this narrative that one would little suspect that we are dealing with one of the most significant events in human history. Here Christianity passed over all history.

5. *Explanation* by exposition and by narration.

6. *Application* by showing relationship.

from Asia into Europe. It was a momentous day when Columbus set sail from the shores of Spain or Vasco da Gama discovered the sea route to the Indies, but could even such events be more pregnant with consequence than the day when Paul carried Christianity out of Asia, in a few centuries to be overrun by Mohammedanism, through Troas into Macedonia and so to Europe, where Christianity was going to have its chance? But Paul had not planned to go to Europe. That was a second choice. Paul had planned to go to Bithynia. "They assayed," it reads, "to go into Bithynia." And no wonder, for Bithynia was one of the richest provinces of Asia Minor, and to have carried Christianity there would have been a triumph indeed.

Moreover, we may be sure that if Paul wanted to go into Bithynia he wanted to go very much and tried to go very hard, for Paul was never a half-way man. And he could not go; the way was blocked; his plan was broken. We read, "The Spirit of Jesus suffered them not," but that is only another way of saying that some circumstance blocked their course. It must have seemed to Paul lamentable at first. I picture him arriving on the shores of the Aegean, saying, I wanted to go to Bithynia and here I am in Troas! And lo! through Troas a way opened to the preeminent ministry of his career. Paul rendered his most significant service with the leftovers of a broken plan.

Wanting Bithynia and getting Troas, how familiar an experience that is! But to take Troas, the second-best, the broken plan, the leftover of a disappointed expectation, and make of it the greatest opportunity we ever had, how much less familiar that is! Yet, as one reads the story of human life, one sees that powerful living has always involved such a victory as Paul won in Troas over his own soul and his situation.

7. *Explanation* by exposition.

8. *Explanation* by illustration: (1) formal and mechanical introduction, (2) true event, (3) biography.

When a career has at last been finished and the halo of well-deserved reputation now hangs over it so that one cannot think the name without thinking of some high enterprise with which the name is indissolubly associated, then in the glamor of that retrospect we are tempted to forget that almost always the turning point of the career is the experience that Paul had—getting Troas when he wanted Bithynia.

When, for example, we think of Phillips Brooks, we think of spiritual ministry, a great personality pouring his soul out with abundant power upon the people. Of all the letters that Phillips Brooks received, it is said that he cherished most this one from a small tailor shop near Copley Square in Boston: "Dear Mr. Brooks: I am a tailor in a little shop near your Church. Whenever I have the opportunity I always go to hear you preach. Each time I hear you preach I seem to forget all about you, for you make me think of God." Nevertheless, remember that Phillips Brooks did not plan to be a preacher. He planned to be a teacher. That was his Bithynia. As soon as he graduated from college he plunged into his chosen profession of teaching and he failed. He failed completely. Listen to young Brooks writing about his scholars as he is failing: "They are the most disagreeable set of creatures without exception that I have ever met with. . . . I really am ashamed of it but I am tired, cross and almost dead, so good night." Listen to Phillips Brooks after he had failed and been dropped from his position: "I don't know what will become of me and I don't care much"; "I shall not study a profession"; "I wish I were fifteen years old again. I believe I might make a stunning man; but somehow or other I don't seem in the way to come to much now." Listen to Phillips Brooks' father, concerned about his son, so humiliated that he will not

9. Illustration continued.

talk even with his friends: "Phillips will not see anyone now, but after he is over the feeling of mortification, he will come and see you."

There is a sense in which Brooks never recovered from the disappointment. At the flower of his career he came down once from the office of President Eliot of Harvard white as a sheet and fairly trembling because he had declined what he knew to be his last opportunity to become a teacher. He wanted Bithynia and he got Troas but through Troas he found the door into a service that if he had lived a hundred lives he might never have found again.

10. *Explanation* by illustration: (1) direct introduction, (2) factual, (3) biography.

Or consider Sir Walter Scott. We think of him as the novel writer whose stories charmed our youth so that for many years some of us would have voted Ivanhoe the best tale ever told. Sir Walter, however, did not want to be a novelist; he planned to be a poet, but Byron's sun rose and dimmed his lesser light. "Byron hits the mark," he said, "where I don't even pretend to fledge my arrow." Then he turned to writing novels, so ashamed that, as you know, he published the first of them anonymously. He did not want any one to know that he was writing novels. He wanted Bithynia; he got Troas and through Troas an open door to the best work he ever did.

11. *Application* by questions and by transition to the sermon body.

Is there anybody here who has not wanted Bithynia and gotten Troas? We older people watch the youths come up, as we did, with their ambitions and plans for Bithynia and we wonder what they will do when they face the inescapable experience. When they are shut out from some Bithynia and land in Troas, will they know how to handle that? Will they have the spirit and attitude and the technique to make of it their finest chance? And since it is so inescapable a problem, we well may ask what it was in Paul that enabled his to turn his defeat into victory.

*BODY OF THE SER-
MON:*

12. *Explanation* by division and by exposition.

13. *Explanation* by four illustrations: (1) all d i r e c t introductions, (2) the first a theological creed, the second poetry, the third a Scripture, the fourth a historical allusion, (3) the first used hypothetically, the second used hypothetically, t h e third from the Bible, and the fourth from history.

For one thing, his religion entered in. Whatever else was shaken when he got to Troas, his conviction still was there that God had a purpose for his life, that if God had led him to Troas there must be something in Troas worth discovering, that God's purpose included Troas just as much as Bithynia, that God never leads any man into any place where all the doors are shut. Paul's religion entered in.

It is in just such situations as this that one can tell how much real religion a man has. We hear a man reciting a familiar creed: "I believe in God the Father Almighty, Maker of heaven and earth," but no matter how serious he may seem about it you cannot tell from that alone how real it is to him. You hear a man singing,

> He leadeth me: O blessed thought!
> O words with heavenly comfort fraught!
> Whate'er I do, where'er I be,
> Still 'tis God's hand that leadeth me.

But however much in earnest he may seem you cannot tell from that alone how deep it goes with him. When, however, you see a man who, wanting Bithynia, gets Troas and, still certain that there is a purpose for his life, takes a positive attitude toward Troas as if to say, "If God has led me here there is something worth while here to do," you know that that man's religion is practically operative. If, therefore, Paul had merely said what he did say, "To them that love God all things work together for good," we might have cocked suspicious eyebrows at him, thinking that that proposition is extraordinarily difficult to prove. What is impressive about Paul is that whenever he did land in a disappointing Troas, and he landed in a good many of them, he did so effectually love God that he *made* all things work together for good. Paul's religion meant to him a positive faith about

14. *Explanation* by illustration: (1) direct introduction, (2) factual, (3) Judson—biography; and by *application* showing relationship.

life and a positive attitude toward life so effective that watching his career is again and again like watching the Battle of Marengo—in the morning an obvious defeat, in the afternoon a resounding victory.

Consider a modern counterpart of Paul, Adoniram Judson. When Judson was a young man he gave himself to missionary service and his ambition centered on India. That was his Bithynia. When at last he reached India they would not let him in. The East India Company would not allow him to stay and the governor told him to take the first ship back to America. For a year he labored to open the doors of India and they were bolted shut. So he turned to Burma. That was his Troas, unknown, untouched Burma. Can one suppose that through all that humiliation and disappointment Judson could always see the leadership of God? Of course he could not; he was human. Can one suppose during those months that he lay in the prison of the Emperor at Ava and Oung-Pen-La he could always see evidences of the divine purpose? Of course he could not; he was human. But he did so handle the affair in Burma that the doors began to open until no well-instructed man today can think of Burma without thinking of Adoniram Judson, or think of Adoniram Judson without thinking of Burma; and when the consequence began to appear, he could look upon his life in retrospect as though it had been planned of God. To live your life through—not argue it though; that never is sufficient—to *live* your life through into the conviction that there is an eternal Purpose with which a man can ally himself is one of the finest achievements of the human spirit.

15. *Explanation* by illustration: (1) direct introduction, (2) factual, (3) Biblical.

Altogether the most thrilling story in the Old Testament is on this theme. One day in Palestine we stopped our automobile by the roadside and ate our lunch at Dothan where long ago Joseph had been sold by his brethen.

Still the camel trail goes up from across Jordan, and then runs down to the coast cities and so to Egypt. Now Joseph, stolen from his home, betrayed by his brethren, dropped into a pit, sold to Midianite slave dealers, made a man servant in a household in Egypt, lied about by his master's wife and put in prison —can one suppose that during all that humiliation and disgrace he could see where God was taking him? Of course not. But he so kept his faith and handled his life that the doors opened into the biggest business of his career, and when at last those penitent and frightened brethren stood before him, you remember what he said: "I am Joseph your brother, whom ye sold into Egypt. And now be not grieved, nor angry with yourselves, that ye sold me hither: for God did send me before you to preserve life. . . . So now it was not you that sent me hither, but God."

16. *Application* by affirmation.

Such was Paul's feeling as he looked back on the day he missed Bithynia and found Troas, and such will be ours if in Troas we will let our religion enter in.

17. *Explanation* by division II.

In the second place it was not simply Paul's religion that enabled him to win this victory but the fine fruit of his religion, his care about people.

18. *Application* by affirmation of relationship.

The trouble with so many of us when we land in Troas is that we begin to pity ourselves. Paul could have done that. He could have started the process we indulge in — "ifing."

19. *Application* by using historical imagination—a hypothetical illustration about Paul: (1) direct introduction, (2) Biblical and hypothetical, (3) the Bible and Fosdick.

If I had not missed Bithynia; if my plans had not been broken, if, if! I have given up everything for Jesus Christ. I could today be one of the great rabbis of Jerusalem saluted in the market place. I have given it all up for Christ. I spent a long time in Arabia thinking through the gospel. I have been fourteen years in a trying, difficult, unrecognized ministry in Cilicia, at odds even with my Christian brethren because once I persecuted them. And now, when I am beginning to get on a good footing with my fellow Christians, with Barnabas and a few others trusting me, I have come up through Asia Minor on a preaching mission. See what they have done to me. They stoned me and left mo for dead in Lystra. Even after that, all I asked was that I might have a chance to get into Bithynia and do some good work, and now I cannot; I am foiled; my plan is broken.

20. *Explanation* by exposition—an assertion.

How easy it would have been for Paul in Troas to feel sorry for himself!

21. *Explanation* by exposition.

Upon the contrary, he at once began thinking about other people. He wondered if there was not some one who might be better off because he had landed in Troas. He had not been there a night before he saw a man from Macedonia saying, "Come over and help us." It was Paul's unselfishness, his generosity, his magnanimity that opened the doors for him in Troas.

22. *Explanation* by illustration: (1) formal and mechanical, (2) factual, (3) biographical.

Once there was a man named William Duncan who gave himself to the missionary cause and in time was sent by his board to a little Indian island off Alaska called Metlakatla. It was an unlikely Troas for a young man to land in who had doubtless dreamed of some Bithynia, for those Indians were a poor, ignorant, miserable tribe, and their morals were vile beyond description. Dean Brown of Yale, however, who visited Metlakatla after William Duncan had been there about forty years, made this report—that you will find every Indian family in a separate house with all the decent appointments of home life, that you will find a bank, a cooperative store, a sawmill, a box factory, and a salmon cannery run by Indians in profitable industry, that you will find a school where Indian boys and girls learn to read and write and think and live, and a church where an Indian minister preaches the gospel of eternal life and an Indian musician, who once was a

23. *Application* by showing relationship and by three illustrations: (1) all three direct introductions, (2) I, a historical event, II, an opinion, and III, a hypothetical illustration, (3) h i s t o r y, George McDonald, and personal creation of the preacher.

24. *Application* by illustration: (1) direct introduction, (2) hypothetical, (3) personal to the preacher.

25. *Application* by affirmation of relationship.

medicine man playing a tom-tom, now plays a pipe organ, and a congregation of Indians sing the great hymns of the church to the praise of Almighty God—and all because a man named William Duncan, landing in Troas, cared enough about people to find there the chance of his life!

My friends, there is nothing in that spirit or consequence that cannot be transferred to our lives. We are all in Troas. Just as at Sebastopol each heart thought a different name while they all sang Annie Laurie, so when today we say "Troas" each one of us thinks of some situation we would not have planned to be in. There is only one way—love. Was it not George Macdonald who said: "Nothing makes a man strong like a cry for help?" You walk down the street utterly fatigued, so tired that you would like to lie down on the curb and go to sleep, and suddenly there is a cry; there has been an accident; a child is hurt; and you never will remember how tired you are until it is all over. Nothing makes a man so strong as a call for help.

A mother is completely fatigued. She has been telling her friends for weeks that there is nothing left of her, and then a child falls ill and needs her. Week after week, by night and day, she stands by and never thinks of being tired. Nothing makes a man strong like a call for help.

It would be strange indeed if there were not some young men and women here not altogether dull to the dangers of our civilization, not altogether blind to the possibility of losing it, thinking that perhaps there is something in them that might help build a more decent world for human children to be born in. That is their strength. Nothing makes a man so strong as a call for help. And the trouble is that when we get into Troas we pity ourselves; we miss that man from Macedonia, saying, "Come over and help us."

26 *Application* by affirmation of relationship and by illustration: (1) direct introduction, (2) fiction-poetry, (3) Edwin Markham.

Indeed, so true is this principle of life that it holds good of even small excursions into Troas. When annoyances and irritations come, when one is lied about and hated and denounced, there is only one way out—goodwill. You remember Edwin Markham's lines:

> He drew a circle that shut me out—
> Heretic, rebel, a thing to flout.
> But Love and I had the wit to win:
> We drew a circle that took him in!

If in the midst of life's harassments and irritations one has grace enough to do that, he sometimes will find in that very difficulty his choicest opportunity for usefulness.

CONCLUSION:

27. *Explanation* by exposition and by two illustrations: (1) both d i r e c t introductions, (2) one from literature and the second from hypothetical creation, (3) Coue and Fosdick. Also by *Application* showing relationship; and again by exposition.

This, then, is the conclusion of the matter: that because Paul had these two elements in his life, as soon as he landed in Troas his imagination was filled, not with defeat but with victory. Coué was right that it is the imagination which makes or unmakes us. If you put a thirty foot plank as high as a cathedral tower, hardly anybody can walk it, and it is not because the physical difficulties are greater than they would be on the ground but because one's imagination keeps picturing him falling off. So when we get into Troas we think we are defeated. I wanted Bithynia, we say; I have got Troas. So we think defeat, we say defeat, we imagine defeat, and we are defeated. But as soon as Paul landed in Troas he saw an open door, a beckoning man, a new chance, and a successful issue.

28. *Explanation* by exposition and by two illustrations: (1) both direct introduction, (2) one factual and the other poetry, (3) Biblical and hymnbook.

What helped him most, I suspect, was that his thought went back, as it so habitually did, to the cross of his Master. That was a Troas to land on! What a Bithynia it would have been if his people had accepted Jesus as Messiah! And now, shut out from that Bithynia, he came to his Troas, his Calvary, and he so clothed it with the purpose of God and the love of man that

> All the light of sacred story
> Gathers round its head sublime.

He took a very hard thing and he made of it a triumph.

This sermon is a direct Biblical sermon, supportive in purpose (treating a life situation issue), and rhetorical in form. In strength these values are evident: (1) the text shapes and controls the message throughout; (2) the purpose is consistent with the text purpose; (3) the simple form is true to Scripture and modern methods of communication; (4) the title is attractive and is properly divided and developed; (5) the introduction presents the title, text, proposition, and purpose; (6) the body is mechanically accurate and balanced; (7) the conclusion enforces the purpose and concludes the sermon; (8) and the style of the entire sermon is superb, which one would expect of Fosdick, who is one of the great stylists of the ages.

In regard to places for improvement three items stand out: (1) In the introduction there are eleven paragraphs as over against two for the conclusion. One or two less for the introduction and one or two more for the conclusion would have added better balance to the message. (2) The opening sentence is a long, run-on sentence. (3) The three functional elements are not in good balance. *Argument* is omitted without damage to this sermon, *application* and illustration are present in good balance and strength, but *explanation* could have been used more often. Two or three additional paragraphs of Biblical explanation would have been a virtue. "Handling Life's Second Best" is, nevertheless, one of the most appealing sermons in print.

THE DEVOTIONAL OBJECTIVE

The devotional objective seeks for Christians to love, worship, and adore God. This objective is also called the worship objective. The devotional objective should not be confused with "a devotional talk or a devotion," which usually represents a brief five to ten minute talk before a general program begins. The devotional objective stands on the same level of strength and importance as the doctrinal, ethical, actional, and supportive objectives.

The need for the devotional objective can be measured by the poverty of one's personal piety, the drabness of the average hour of worship, and the challenges of the concept of worship held by many Christians. The need for the worship objective can be seen by observing the New

Testament church at worship and by reading the biographies and autobiographies of the saints of God through the ages. The church needs to grow in its ability to worship God, and the minister is charged with the responsibility of leading the church in devotional growth.

Devotional themes stress the joy and beauty of faith, the glory and majesty of God, the values and benefits of Bible study and church attendance, and the need and value of personal growth in love for God. Moreover, there are numerous areas where the pastor may preach messages which show how to understand, to grow, and to mature in various devotional areas.

The following sermon by John A. Broadus, "The Lord's Prayer," is a devotional-purpose message with direct Biblical authority.[4] The structure is rhetorical.

---

[4] *Favorite Sermons of John A. Broadus,* ed. Vernon Latrelle Stanfield (New York: Harper & Brothers, 1959), pp. 66-74.

THE LORD'S PRAYER

INTRODUCTION:

1. *Explanation* by exposition (the text).

2. *Explanation* by exposition of text background.

3. *Explanation* by illustration using Luke's parallel account: (1) direct introduction, (2) factual, (3) Biblical.

Our Father which art in heaven, Hallowed be thy name.

MATTHEW 6:9

The prayer which thus begins, which for many ages has been called among Christians "the Lord's Prayer," is above all eulogium for its sweetness. No wonder this is so! For our Lord presents it as a specimen, as a model of prayer. He said, "When ye pray, use not vain repetitions, as the heathen do: for they think that they shall be heard for their much speaking," saying over the same thing a thousand times. "Be ye not therefore like unto them: for your Father knoweth what things ye have need of, before ye ask him." *Thus* then do *ye* pray—this way and not with vain repetitions, not with much speaking, *thus* do ye pray! He gives it as a sample, as a model. So on a later occasion, recorded in the 11th Chapter of Luke—probably a long time after this, most likely in quite another part of the country, certainly on a later occasion—our Lord was praying Himself, and when He ceased, the disciples asked him, "Teach us to pray," and He said "When ye pray, say" and then He gave them substantially the same prayer as the one here before us.

Now it very naturally occurs to many persons that our Lord has given this as a *form* of prayer; that when we pray we ought always to say these words. I do not object to using these words whenever anyone thinks them appropriate, that they express his sentiments; but it is very certain that our Lord did not give this as a form of prayer. If you will notice a moment, I shall prove it. On the second occasion the prayer is very different from that which we here read. Even in the common text, it is different in several expressions; but if you will take any revised text as furnished by any competent scholar of the day, you will find that the prayer on that occasion is quite different. Allow me to repeat it as it is there. You all know the words as they occur here but on that second occasion this is what he said: "Father, Hallowed be thy name. Thy kingdom come. Give us day by day our daily bread. And forgive us our sins; for we also forgive every one that is indebted to us. And bring us not into temptation."

4. *Explanation* by comparison and contrast of the parallel passage in Luke.

Now you observe that I have omitted several phrases of the familiar prayer given here in the Sermon on the Mount. If you look a little closely, you notice that nothing of essential importance, no distinctive idea, has been omitted here. Instead of "Our Father which art in heaven," you have simply "Father." You have lost some pleasing words, but you have really lost no part of the essential thought. When after the petition "Thy kingdom come," you find wanting the words "Thy will be done on earth as it is in heaven," you observe in a moment that although a pleasing expression has been expunged, it is involved in the preceding petition, "Thy kingdom come;" for when God's reign on earth is fully come, His will must of necessity be done on earth as in heaven. And so, when after the prayer "Bring us not into temptation," you miss the words "But deliver us from evil," you observe that they do, at most, but express the other side of the same truth; something that is implied in the words that remain.

5. *Explanation* by exposition.

On that second occasion then, our Lord has omitted no idea that belongs to the prayer. It is substantially the very same, but in form it is exceedingly different. Is not there the proof at once that He did not intend this as a form of prayer? If He did so intend, why in the world should He not have repeated His form correctly on the second occasion? No: He intended it not as a form of prayer, that precisely these words should be used, but as an example, "Thus do ye pray." Avoid the vain repetitions and much speaking of the heathen: Thus: thus comprehensively; thus simply. Oh, how much is included in these few, brief, simply expressed petitions! "Thus then do ye pray."

6. *Explanation* through preview and by *application* showing our conduct in prayer.

And my brethren, I venture to ask your special attention to this model in one respect. We have two good classes of petitions here, as is obvious at once, petitions with reference to God's glory, and petitions with reference to our own good. And my point is, that the petitions with reference to God's glory come first. Now you have noticed, and indeed it seems natural to us that when we pray, we pray first about ourselves, and a great deal about ourselves, and then if we do not forget, if there seems to be time left before we close the prayer, we may introduce some petitions as to God's glory. But here the class of petitions which refer to God's glory come first. That is their rightful place. I do not feel they should always come first in order, that there ought to be any formality or stiffness in it, but that they should often be put in the place of priority, and regularly in the place of preeminence. Much more important is it that God's name should be hallowed, and God's kingdom come in the world, than that you and I, as individuals, should gain the blessings we desire.

7. *Explanation* by transitional sentence.

And now I propose to you, that while of course we cannot bring out many of the thoughts involved in this comprehensive prayer, we shall try to get some practical lessons from it.

8. *Explanation* by division. *I.*

I. Observe first, the petitions which relate to God's glory.

9. *Explanation* by division *1* of *I*, by exposition, and by illustration: (1) direct introduction, (2) factual,

1. "Hallowed be thy name." The words are so simple, we have known them so well from our childhood, that it is really difficult to stop and ask what they mean. Let Thy name

(3) Biblical; and by *application* using exhortation.

be made holy. God's name represents Himself. It is a prayer that His name, and Himself as represented by His name, may be regarded as holy—spoken of as holy—treated as holy. We have a model here in the picture given by Isaiah, the adoring Seraphs covering their faces in awe before the throne. What do they cry? Not, as often we do; great, majestic, glorious—not a word about His power, nor even about His wisdom—"Holy, Holy, Holy, Lord God of Hosts." That is the central thought, that ought to be our deepest desire, that God may be regarded, and spoken of, and treated, as *Holy.*

10. *Application* showing relationship.

Oh, what a contrast between that scene of the vision, and the sights and the souls of this world in which we live. Walk the streets anywhere; listen to the talk wherever you find it, especially when men grow excited. Hear them! Hear how that high and holy name is bandied as a jest and polluted with profanity. It is enough to make a man shiver to hear the profanity that abounds everywhere. I have shivered, literally, sometimes as I listened.

11. *Application* by showing relationship, by illustration: (1) direct introduction, (2) opinion, (3) literature —Dr. Johnson; and by exhortation.

But my brethren, have we nothing to do but to look with horror at other men's profanity? There are some things important to our own life here. Have a care that while you may not use in vain the sacred name of God itself, you shall not fall into the practice of using other sacred expressions lightly and irreverently. I have heard even refined ladies use phrases in a light way, that were appropriate only in solemn prayer; and to a certain extent that was irreverence, that was profanity. Have a care about indulging wit that comes from profaning the language of Scripture, and allusions to God. Bluff old Dr. Johnson once said that "a man that has any respect for himself ought to be above that kind of wit, it is so cheap: any one can do that." Yes, anyone that has any respect for himself ought to be above that kind of wit, and a man that has any reverence for God ought to shrink from it. Have a care how you repeat the profanity of other men. You want to tell a good story and the point of it perhaps lies in a profane expression. Now is it that you should repeat that expression? Is it good for yourself to repeat it? Is it healthy? Especially is it good for that boy there that is hearing, and may not make the nice distinction that you make, when you repeat other men's profanity? I would not inculcate scrupulosity about trifles, but perchance this is not a trifle, and it seems to me that we who pray this prayer, ought to lay such things to our hearts, and shrink with horror, and cultivate ourselves into shrinking with shuddering, from anything like profanity. Oh, that God's name might always be spoken with deepest reverence. Oh, that God Himself might come to be everywhere thought of, and talked about, and obeyed, as holy. Anyhow, let us try to have it so in our hearts, on our lips, in our lives.

12. *Explanation* by division 2 of I, by exposition (word study), and by three illustrations: (1) all direct introduction, (2) all factual, (3) and all Biblical.

2. And the second petition, "Thy reign come." I am not going to explain all these simple words of course, but here is one that wants explaining. The Greek word which is rendered "kingdom" in the text requires three English words to convey its meaning. Primarily the word means "kingship," the condition of being a king, the possession of royal power. Then secondarily it means "reign," the exercise of royal power. As a final derivation it means what we call "kingdom," subjects or territory over whom or in which this royal power is exercised. Kingship, and reign, and kingdom. There are many cases of that kind in translation, where several terms have to be used in one language to convey the meaning of a single word in another. Now the leading thought here is evidently that which we express by the word "reign." And

the reference is to the Messianic reign which
the prophets had long foretold; that Messianic
reign of which David had sung; that Messianic reign which John the Baptist had declared was now near at hand, and Jesus at the
beginning of His ministry in Galilee took up
the same cry, "The kingdom of heaven is
near at hand; repent therefore and believe
the good tidings." Men had long prayed that
that reign might come, and now there was
all the more propriety in such a prayer, for
it was near at hand.

13 *Application* by ques-
tion and answer, by
illustrations: (1) all direct introduction, (2)
all factual, (3) all Bib-
lical; and by strong
exhortation.

Do you think there is no need of that prayer
still? Do you think the reign, the Messianic
reign of God in the world, has come? It has
but begun. It was beginning when Jesus
taught these teachings. It began still more
when He rose triumphant from the grave and
ascended glorious into the sky. It began still
further, on the day of Pentecost. It began in
another sense at the destruction of Jerusalem,
which He spoke of beforehand as the time
when He should come in His kingdom. It has
begun on the earth, ah! it has not come yet.
Alas, for the wide portions of the world where
the very name of the King Messiah has not
come. Alas, in the metropolis of one of the
great Christian nations of today, the great
mass of the men that surge around us, are
utterly unsanctified by the gospel, utterly
heedless of the reign of God. Stop any moment
and think, between two heartbeats, of this
great world you live in, of this great city you
live in, and then you shall address yourself
with new fervor to the prayer: "Thy reign
come, O God! thy reign!" Anyhow, let it
come in us; let it pervade our whole being; let
it control our whole life; let it sanctify our
home life; let it elevate our social life; let it
purify our business life; let men feel, as they
note our conduct, that we are subjects of the
Lord God.

14. *Explanation* by di-

3. I shall not dwell, for lack of time, upon

vision 3 of I (only hinted at), by exposition, and by *application* showing relationship using illustrations: (1) all direct introduction, (2) all factual, (3) and all Biblical.

the third petition here, which is but an expansion of the preceding. For, as I have said, whenever God's reign has fully come, then His will must be done on earth. Many things occur now that are not according to God's will. The prayer is that God's will may take place; that everything may happen on earth in accordance with God's will, as in heaven everything does happen. Many times for us, I know it is hard even to *consent* that this shall be so. When it is plainly God's will that something should happen, which to us is painful, we shrink and with difficulty we say, "Thy will be done." No wonder: it has been so with better persons than we are. Certain disciples, when they besought Paul not to go up to Jerusalem and he would not be persuaded, ceased and said: "The will of the Lord be done." The struggling Savior in Gethsemane as He strove in agony and prayer to nerve Himself up for what He had to bear, said again and again—for it would not stay said: "nevertheless, not my will, but thine be done." No wonder we find it hard sometimes to say that. The prayer teaches us not merely to submit to God's will, but to desire that God's will may take place in the world; that everything concerning us and concerning all around us may happen according to His will. And if He takes away our property, our health, our usefulness, our life, or someone we love better than our life, still we would say and we should rejoice when we say, "Thy will be done." Oh, if it could be so; if in the world, whether gaining or losing, in success or failure, it could be so, in us and about us, that God's will were done in all things—what a joy in the thought; what a springing gladness it puts into the heart, the very idea!

15. *Explanation* by division II.

II. But perhaps we shall find, not more important but more practical lessons if we turn to the second part of the prayer, which contains petitions relating to ourselves.

16. *Explanation* by division 1 of II, by exposition, and by illustrations: (1) direct introduction, (2) a hypothetical man and child observed, (3) b o t h creations by Broadus.

17. *Applications* by showing relationship.

18. *Application* by giving exhortation, by using two illustrations: (1) both direct introduction, (2) both hypothetical, (3) both by Broadus; and by exhortation again.

1. First; "Give us this day our daily bread." Now I entreat you, don't listen to the commentaries, so many of which tell you that this means spiritual bread. I am weary of that everlasting spiritualizing. Spiritual things are far above temporal things, but there are many references in the Scriptures to our temporal and material wants, and why should we lose their meaning, and sustaining power, because we go on allegorizing everything. It is plainly a prayer for temporal good, as represented by that which is most essential, and thus stated in the simplest possible form; and a prayer with reference simply to day after day. A little child sees its meaning and feels its sweetness, and the wisest man can find no higher wisdom than to cry still: "Give us this day our daily bread."

My brethren, I should be inclined to think that above all the petitions of the prayer this needs to be enforced in our time. I have known some Christians who were very unwilling to realize that there was any human exertion in obtaining spiritual good. They say, if that be true, how is it the gift of God? And if it be the gift of God, how can it be the effort of our own labor? Yet if spiritual good is the gift of God, so is temporal good the gift of God, though it is obtained only by human effort. The truth is, we see, that both are the gift of God, and both are the result of our own exertions.

Especially with reference to one of the great tendencies of thought in our time is it important that we should cherish this petition for our daily bread. "Pshaw!" men say, "that depends upon physical forces and laws, upon material things; upon your own exertion, man; upon the climate and the weather." Now in the face of these notions it becomes all the more appropriate that we should pray to God to give us daily bread. Yes, and I tell you plainly and boldly, though I have not time to develop the thought, if it is not right and wise to ask God for daily bread, if as they tell you in the newspapers so often, there is no efficacy in prayer, there is no use in praying for rain, then there is no God at all. You are driven straight to it by absolute logical necessity. If it is not proper to pray for daily bread and to pray for rain, there is no God; there is nothing in existence but matter, with its organization and its results. You cannot help it; there is no standing room, for the life of you, between those two positions. Alas, alas, how many in our time, one-sided or superficial, have gone into utter materialism. Never was there a time when it was more needful that the Christian world should realize in their experience the sentiment of this prayer. We work for daily bread, and we plan for years to come, but none the less are we to seek it as the daily gift of the daily goodness of our Father in heaven.

19. *Explanation* by division 2 of II and by exposition. This is applied exposition.

2. "And forgive us our debts, as we forgive our debtors." The simple prayer for temporal things all embraced in that one petition for what is most indispensable, and now in addition, a twofold prayer—forgiveness for past sin, and deliverance from sin in the future. That our God may be glorified; that our earthly wants may be supplied, and that we may be forgiven our sin, and delivered from evil—that is all there is to pray for.

20. *Explanation* by exposition (word study) a n d by *application* showing relationship and using exhortation.

You know that the term "debt" is used here as an Aramaic expression to denote sin—sin regarded as a debt, which we must pay to God, or in the kindred phrase of other languages, "pay the penalty." You notice that when our Lord repeats the thought a moment later He say trespasses, or transgressions. You remember that when He gives the prayer on a subsequent occasion it is: "Forgive us our sins; for we also forgive everyone that is indebted to us." "Forgive us our debts" means, forgive us our sins. My friends, does it ever occur to you that you are more anxious about the "give" than the "forgive"? Does it ever happen in your experience that you pray that God would give and forget to ask that God would forgive? And yet, is not this last as deep a need? Yea, a deeper need than the other? Ah! that a man should have all earthly things given him, and his sins not forgiven, would be a poor gift. Yet a man who should be deprived of early things and go starving into the other world, yet with his sins forgiven, would be rich and might rejoice. Let us not forget as we go on praying for what God has to give, to ask still more earnestly that He would forgive us our sins.

21. *Explanation* by exposition. This is applied exposition.

I must beg you in connection with the prayer to dwell upon the condition which our Lord here presents. It is a matter of the utmost practical importance to all of us. "Forgive us our debts, as we forgive our debtors." You have noticed surely, that after completing this simple prayer, Jesus, before going on to speak of other things, takes up again one of the thoughts of the prayer; and which one is it? Something about God's name being hallowed, or His reign coming? Something about daily bread? Something about temptation, or evil? Nay: it is this one; this one thought He repeats, repeats it positively and negatively. For if you forgive men their trespasses, your Heavenly Father will also forgive you, and if you forgive not, neither will your Heavenly Father forgive you. You know why—you know yourself but little if you do not well know why He dwells upon this. The disposition to be revengeful, or at any rate to be unforgiving, is one of the deepest rooted, one of the hardest to correct, one of the most hurtful and ruinous in its influence, of all the evil dispositions that belong to our sinful human nature. So our Lord presents forgiving as the condition of being forgiven, the condition *sine qua non*—if we do not forgive men we cannot be forgiven. He does not mean that our forgiving is the meritorious ground of our being forgiven. It is an indispensable condition. Only if we do forgive men can we be forgiven, but then we are forgiven on the ground which the gospel provides—the merit which is not our own.

Now let us make a practical distinction. We use that word "forgive" in a somewhat ambiguous fashion. In the strict and and proper sense it is not our duty to forgive a man unless he repents. God forgives in that sense no man but the penitent, and Jesus said, you remember: "If thy brother sin against thee seven times in the day and seven times in the day turn saying, 'I repent,' thou shalt forgive him." It is not right that you should restore a man to the confidence he has forfeited, unless he shows himself worthy of it. It is not right that you should forgive a man, in the full sense of the term, unless he repents; not only is it not your duty, but it is not right. "Love your enemies, that ye may be sons of your Father in heaven." God forgives only the penitent, and loves them as His friends, but even the impenitent, God loves. "He makes his sun to rise on the evil and the good, and sends rain on the just and the unjust." He wishes His enemies no harm, but does them good. We need not, and really should not, forgive a man in the full sense while he remains impenitent, but we must in the other sense forgive him. We must bear him no malice. We must do him no harm. We must be glad to do him good, in anything that will not promote his evil designs against us. Thus shall we be the sons of our Father in heaven.

I think this distinction is practically important. The idea of forgiving a man who is impenitent does seem to be impracticable, and that is not what the Scriptures teach; but that we should bear no malice and yield to

---

22. *Explanation* by exposition. This is applied exposition.
Also, *explanation* by illustration: (1) direct introduction, (2) factual, (3) Biblical.

23. *Explanation* by exposition and by *application* showing relationship giving exhortation.

no revenge, that is what the Scriptures teach. Ah me, even this is hard enough for poor human nature! Let us strive to do that; let us lay it to heart. Who is there here today among us who has not sometimes thought himself to have been cruelly wronged? Who? We all have need then to exercise this forgiveness.

3. And finally, "bring us not into temptation." For it is not simply *lead*, it is *bring*. Human agency is, for the moment, here left out of account. The thought is, of God's providence as bearing us on, and bringing us into certain situations, and the prayer is that God will not bring us into circumstances of temptation of trial. Why? Because we are afraid we cannot stand temptation. Ah, every man that knows himself will most certainly feel an echo in his heart, "I am weak, O Lord, bring me not into temptation."

A man advertised for a coachman, and when the applicants came, he asked each one, "How near would you undertake to run my carriage wheel to the edge of a precipice?" The first one said he would run within a foot of it. The second said he would run within six inches. The third was an Irishman, who said, "I would kape away as far as I could," —and he got the place. Maybe you will remember that, if you forget my solemn injunction. O my Christian friends, pray that you may be kept away from temptation, for you are weak, and let him that thinketh he standeth, take heed lest he fall.

"Bring us not into temptation, but deliver us from evil."

My brethren, this simple prayer ought as a model to control all our praying. Its spirit ought to strike into our blood, shaping our whole character, regulating our whole life. And as we pray it, oh, ought not our life's endeavor to accord with it? What folly to pray, "Thy reign come," and never a finger

---

24. *Explanation* by division 3 of II, by exposition, and by *application* showing relationship.

25. *Application* by illustration: (1) direct introduction, (2) anecdote—not sure if fact or fiction, (3) source unknown; and by exhortation.

26. *Explanation* by exposition (the text).

CONCLUSION:

27. *Application* showing desired results and presenting exhortation.

lifted to urge forward the progress of that reign; never a sacrifice made, never deed done, nor word spoken, nought but idle prayer. What folly to pray for forgiveness of sin, and pray for deliverance from evil, if along with the prayer there be not the cherished desire after holiness, and the perpetual effort to abhor—*to abhor*—that which is evil, and cleave to that which is good.

"The Lord's Prayer," by John A. Broadus, is a direct Biblical sermon with a devotional purpose and rhetorical form. The introduction is well developed with seven paragraphs. The body of the sermon contains two major divisions with three subpoints under each. The body points are balanced and well developed with the functional elements. In matters of style the message has clarity, appeal, and force.

The sermon is almost a homily in that the emphasis throughout is on successive phrases and words of the text. However, because Broadus chose to divide his discussion into two major points and then to treat the next by phrases and sentences under each heading, he has an analytical or orderly rhetorical pattern. This simple and clear procedure is really only about one-half step removed from the advanced homily which is discussed in chapter nine. In any event, Broadus treated his text and sermon quite properly.

Concerning improvement, Broadus could have strengthened his body structure by using a more appealing style of language for his subpoints, by breaking up some of his rather long paragraphs, and by lengthening and strengthening his conclusion. One paragraph for the conclusion is hardly adequate in this case.

Chapter 9

ACCEPTABLE SERMON FORM

In addition to securing Biblical authority and purpose in his sermon, the preacher should secure acceptable form. Acceptable form, a highly flexible item, shapes and molds Biblical authority and purpose without distorting either. Moreover, acceptable form pleases the hearers or readers without undue intrusion into their conscious awareness.

Sermonic form comes to us in the modern English speaking world as a legacy from the past. From the Hebrews we received a simple and informal type of structure, and from the Greeks and Romans we received a "formal" rhetoric with emphasis upon unity, emphasis, and coherence. Both the Hebraic and Greco-Roman concepts exist still in modern preaching form, and both present values to be recognized and utilized. What, then, are the basic forms available to the modern preacher?

THE HOMILY

The homily is the simple and informal pattern developed and used by the Hebraic mind. Through the centuries numerous variations of the homily have emerged, two of which remain to assist the modern preacher.

The Simple Homily

The simple homily has been from its origin a free and informal, though not unstudied or unthoughtful, presentation of truth. Usually, this informal presentation consisted of a running commentary on the various verses of the text. The simple homily appeared as the earliest form of prophetic preaching as the prophets informally delivered revelation in an oral form to Israel, continued in the preaching of Christ, the Apostles, and the Seven (Deacons), and generally shaped preaching patterns into the second and third centuries A.D. Moreover, variations of the simple homily have continued into modern days.

Variations of the simple homily. In general, three variations of the early, or simple, homily have appeared in preaching history. First, the simple homily consisted of a word-by-word, and/or a phrase-by-phrase, and/or a verse-by-verse commentary of the verses of a passage of Scripture. The preacher discussed in order the various words, phrases, and verses of a passage of Scripture, and added illustrations, arguments, and applications as needed. Second, the simple homily often presented a free-running commentary on a topic or subject. This subject homily has appeared in published sermons more often than has been generally recognized. Third, perhaps the form most often encountered in preaching literature has been a blend or mixture of the verse by verse and subject homily.

The functional elements in the simple homily. The ministers preaching simple homilies have utilized the basic functional elements in filling out or elaborating on their subjects and Scriptures. Explanation, arguments, and application have been supplied as needed according to the judgment of the preacher.

The authority in the simple homily. By virtue of the simple homily's variations in approach and use of the functional elements of preaching, all degrees of authority appear in published sermons. The simple homily has used the direct Biblical authority, indirect Biblical authority, casual Biblical authority, combination Biblical authority, and, unfortunately, corruptions of Biblical authority.

The Advanced Homily

Beginning in the third century after the death of Christ, sermons took on a more formal structure. Changes began to shape sermons when a stated or fixed text became the accepted foundation for sermons. This newer form may be called the advanced homily and, as did the simple homily, it used Scripture as text, context, support, and illustration.

The advanced form, not too elaborate at first, simply added an introduction (at times), and a conclusion (occasionally) to the same three variations which existed for the simple homily: (1) verse-by-verse comments, (2) subject homily, and (3) combination of the two. Also, all variations used the basic functional elements of preaching, and the resultant sermons indicated all types of Biblical authority: direct, indirect, casual, combination, and corrupt.

For an illustration of an advanced homily, see the message by Karl Barth, page 78.

THE RHETORICAL SERMON

The rhetorical sermon is organized (outlined and developed) according to the best current rules and principles of rhetoric. Since these rules and principles are highly flexible and current emphases change frequently, a study of contemporary books and articles on communication will assist ministers in speaking and writing.

Basically, the method of treating the sermon *body* (rather than the introduction, conclusion, and invitation) determines whether a message is a homily or a rhetorical sermon. With this in view, consider that many things have transpired in the process of sermon preparation before the body of the sermon is prepared. The total sermon process involves securing an idea to preach, locating a text which is totally harmonious with the idea, making a careful study of the text to determine the central idea of the text (the historical thesis), phrasing a contemporary statement of the central idea (the thesis or proposition), stating the specific objective for the sermon, and writing an interesting, pleasing, and divisible title. When these various items have been prepared, the preacher may begin the construction of his sermon body.

Outline Procedures for the Rhetorical Sermon

In organizing the sermon the preacher may make use of seven separate processes, or he may group these processes. With some men, the natural method is to perform these sermon body organizing processes separately, while with other men, the natural method is to eliminate, group, or change the processes according to personal preference. The seven processes in organizing the sermon body are: (1) gathering materials, (2) separating related and unrelated data, (3) identifying and classifying the natural divisions or ideas in the data, (4) grouping the major and minor elements in the natural divisions, (5) arranging the order sequence for the natural divisions, (6) phrasing the tense of the points and deciding about the application for the sermon, and (7) checking and testing the rhetorical accuracy of the outline.

Gathering materials. Throughout sermon preparation one should write down all possible ideas for body development. He should take notes on the originating idea for the sermon, Bible study, the central idea of the text, the thesis, the specific objective, and the title. He should experiment in organizing these notes, give them time to mature, and meditate and pray about them. The process of gathering materials goes on constantly for the alert preacher. Gathering material for a particular sermon goes on from the moment of the origin of the idea up to and through the writing and polishing of the manuscript.

Separating related and unrelated data. Though the process becomes so natural that it often becomes an unconscious one, care should be exercised in separating related and unrelated data. By rejecting and deleting all unrelated data, the preacher will prepare a clearer and sharper sermon. Since this unrelated material may be useful for other texts and sermons, he should file it for future use.

In separating related and unrelated data, the text (with the central idea of the text, thesis, specific objective, and title) become the best guide. By insisting that all materials actually relate to the text, Biblical unity and authority are more likely to be present.

Identifying and classifying the natural divisions. The natural divisions are called marks of cleavage or marks of division. Through a process of writing, experimenting, waiting, meditating, praying, and testing, the preacher will discover one or more natural divisions. These patterns or marks of cleavage are broad and general. They are not to be used mechanically for phrasing the body points but are to be used suggestively to discover the natural and logical divisions of the sermonic data.

Though the centuries, ministers have discovered and used many of these efficient sermon patterns. They have found that by using these patterns as general guides they can discover similar patterns in their sermon materials. There is no fixed number of these natural patterns, and they must be viewed merely as suggestions which can prompt one's mind.

One pattern is the divine-human approach. In this pattern the sermon material relates approximately equally to God and to man. Thus, it relates both to God and man not by arbitrary choice but because the text and all sermon data treat some relationship of God and man. These data will provide an excellent two-point sermon arrangement. The text, central idea of the text, thesis, specific object, and title will be divided in the body; one point will discuss God and one point will discuss man.

Other natural groups or patterns which may be used to prompt one's thinking for body division are: (1) objective-subjective, (2) earth and heaven, (3) time (now) and eternity, (4) desire and means, (5) comparison and/or contrast, (6) cause and/or effect, (7) one or more answers to such logical questions as what? why? who? when? how? which? where? whose? how many? how much?, and (8) such aspects of drama as time, place, event, and situation. When the text and sermon data *naturally* contain these or other natural patterns, the preacher may discover such patterns through analyzing his sermonic data in the light of the marks of cleavage.

Grouping the major and minor elements in the data. After the most natural and appealing approach has been selected, the minister should set out the major and minor ideas in this pattern. Some thoughts will prove to be major structural divisions while other ideas will prove to be subdivisions of the major divisions.

As a general procedure, the best sermon arrangement will utilize only major divisions or at the most major divisions and subdivisions. When *sub*-subdivisions appear, the preacher can best use them by incorporating the thoughts into the discussion of the subdivisions.

Arranging the order or sequence for points. The preacher has available two broad orders of arrangement: natural and logical. By studying the sermon material carefully, the minister will discover the most compatible order or sequence for his sermon data. The orderly arranged sermon carries great appeal.

The sermon may be arranged by a natural order which results from an arrangement of materials according to experience with *time* and *space*. The order of time (a subdivision of natural order) arranges data by sequence of time (past, present, and future) or by sequence of steps in a process (planting, watering, cultivating; or by origin, development, and consummation). The order of space arranges material by stage setting (up, center, down), by geographical reference (up and down; lower and higher; length, breadth, depth, height; north, south, east, and west); and by proximity (near and far).

Five problems should be considered in regard to natural orders: (1) the temptation to force these patterns on material not conducive to such treatment, (2) the danger of overuse, (3) the danger of triteness because another pattern should have been used, (4) the problem of undue familiarity (since the natural orders are so well known, the audience may reject them), and (5) the danger of premature exposure of the thrust of the sermon. Once the preacher indicates that he will first show the past, the audience can easily guess that he will move to the present and to the future. Even with these problems, however, the natural orders are useful occasionally.

The sermon data may be arranged by logical order. The logical order results from an orderly arrangement of the material according to the preacher's judgment. The preacher's judgment will be controlled by the text data, the thesis and purpose of the message, the title, and the type of invitation to be given.

The basic logical orders are: (1) analytical, the same order for sermon points as data in the text; (2) synthetical, a rearranged order of sermon points in relationship to the text; (3) the general view to the particular view, or vice versa; (4) the most important issue or point to the least important issue, or vice versa; (5) the human perspective to the divine perspective, or vice versa; (6) comparison to contrast, or the reverse; (7) the known to the unknown, or the reverse; (8) the acceptable to the unacceptable, or vice versa; (9) cause to effect, or the reverse; (10) problem to solution; (11) partial answer to full answer; (12) the possible to the actual, to the necessary; (13) the routine to the surprise; (14) the simple to the complex; and (15) the order of utility or need. There are numerous other logical orders, but these fifteen indicate the nature of the logical order concept.

Deciding about tense and application. The precise language of the sermon divisions normally comes into focus following the decision concerning order. With the title as a guide, as well as the basic sermon data (the text, central idea of the text, thesis, and purpose), the preacher will phrase his sermon points.

In phrasing sermon points the choice of tense (grammatical tense) influences the shape and tone of the sermon body and especially the matter of application. The reason tense and application constitute one common concept is that if the preacher phrases his divisions in the past tense, he will tend to discuss the past events and to overlook contemporary application. If, however, the preacher phrases his divisions in present tense form, he will more likely apply his material to his audience. The major burden upon the preacher in using present tense points and contemporary application is to be sure that the points and application are actually Biblical.

The factors bearing on the decision concerning tense and application are hermeneutical, theological, and grammatical. The Scripture passage must be understood (the hermeneutical), translated into contemporary meaning (the theological), and phrased in relevant terms (the grammatical). The common assumption that these processes are easy is not true. In fact, many modern sermons fail at the hermeneutical, or theological, or grammatical step.

The sermon points may be phrased in past tense in certain intances. When the past tense is employed, each point speaks about something said, thought, experienced, observed, or done in the past. Each point treats a person, place, idea, or event in past tense as befitting the description of historical data. When each point is written in past tense, the title must permit past tense points, and all the body points should be consistent with the tense used. There are two forms of past tense sermons: without stated application and with stated application.

If the choice is made to state the divisions in past tense, a second decision must be made concerning application. The preacher must decide whether to have formal application or not. If the choice is that there will *not* be formal application, the preacher should have strong faith and earnest conviction that the Holy Spirit will take the words of Scripture as they are explained and will make the proper application. Many preachers believe that when Scripture is explained, the Holy Spirit will automatically apply the explanation without formal sermonic application. Therefore, those who believe this use little or no stated application. Other preachers, with just as much faith in Scripture and the leadership of the Holy Spirit, insist on adding formal sermonic application. These men may also state the sermon points in past tense, support them with Scripture explanations, add carefully thought out applications of points and text, and depend upon the Holy Spirit for true and final application. Both views are correct, but the second is preferred.

Moreover, the sermon points may be phrased in the present tense. In order to place sermon points in present tense, the preacher simply takes forward by one pace the latter step (past tense sermon points with application). If one can determine the true application to make in past tense sermon points, he can easily phrase his points in present form. The sequence in arriving at present tense points is to place the sermon points in past tense (describe the major facets or ideas of the text), determine true application, then transpose the past tense points to the present tense by using the essence of the application.

The process of deciding whether or not to use application with present tense sermon points is unnecessary because an understanding of application is a prerequisite to the use of present tense points. If the preacher, therefore, has decided against a past tense sermon without application, and if he has moved through the process of stating his points in past tense with application, then he can proceed to phrase his points in present tense. As a rule, the present tense sermon with application is the best sermon.

Illustrations of tense and application (possible choices):

Illustration one: Past tense points with no application.

    Introduction
        The text, central idea of the text, thesis, purpose, and title used in any order.
    Body of the sermon
        I. Past tense sermon point
           Explanation of text primarily
           Argument as needed
           (No application)
        II. Past tense sermon point
           Developed as I
    Conclusion
    Invitation (s)

Illustration two: Past tense points with application.

> Introduction
>> Text, central idea of the text, thesis, purpose, and title used in any order
>
> Body of the sermon
>> I. Past tense sermon point
>>> Explanation as needed
>>> Argument as needed
>>> Application as needed
>>
>> II. Past tense sermon point
>>> Developed as I
>
> Conclusion
> Invitation(s)

Illustration three: Present tense points with application.

> Introduction
>> Text, central idea of the text, thesis, purpose, and title used in any order
>
> Body of the sermon
>> I. Present tense sermon point
>>> Explanation as needed
>>> Argument as needed
>>> Application as needed
>>
>> II. Present tense sermon point
>>> Developed as I
>
> Conclusion
> Invitations(s)

Checking the rhetorical accuracy of the outline. Checking rhetorical accuracy involves determining whether or not the sermon structure obeys basic outline procedure. Checking accuracy should not be confused with polishing rhetorical style which comes later.

The basic rules for outlining are: (1) Use roman numerals for major points (I and II). (2) Use arabic numerals and indent for subpoints (1, 2, 3. The use of A, B, C, and D for the subpoints is a valid alternate procedure. The use of I with 1 and 2 is clearer and simpler, however). (3) Use, as a general rule, only two degrees of steps for points (major points and subpoints: I, 1, 2, 3 and II, 1, 2). The preacher may use as many major and subpoints as he desires, but the best procedure confines the outlining to the first two steps. (4) If a *sub*-subpoint must be used, indent and use parenthetical points [(1) and (2)]. (5) All sermon points should be written in sentence or phrase form with the sentence form preferred (this suggestion omits the key word outline).[1] (6) Every

---

[1] H. C. Brown, Jr., H. Gordon Clinard, Jesse Northcutt, *Steps to the Sermon* (Nashville: Broadman Press, 1963), p. 106. This rule and the following nine are from this volume.

point that is divided must have two or more parts. (7) Every subtopic should explain the point of which it is a division. (8) Illustrations are not numbered as divisions in the outline. (9) Scripture references used to illustrate or support the text are not numbered as points in the outline. (10) Functional rhetorical materials, such as explanation, application, and argument which develop a point but do not divide it, should not be numbered in the outline. (11) The parts of the sermon—introduction, body, conclusion, and invitation—should not be assigned numbers in the outline. (12) No item of any rank should contain more than one concept or idea. (13) If verb tense is used in the sermon title or division, then all divisions and subtopics which follow should be consistent with that tense. (14) If persons, places, or objects are used in the title or its divisions, then all points which follow should be consistent with these persons, places, or objects.

Functional Development for the Rhetorical Sermon

In addition to following the correct outline procedures in preparation of the rhetorical sermon, the preacher must also consider the functional elements of preaching—explanation, application, and argument. A full review of chapter four is desirable at this time.

The excellent sermon "A Drama in Christian Joy" by Jesse J. Northcutt is used to demonstrate the rhetorical sermon.[2]

---

[2]H. C. Brown, Jr. (ed.), *Southwestern Sermons* (Nashville: Broadman Press, 1960), pp. 161-66.

A DRAMA IN CHRISTIAN JOY

PHILIPPIANS 1:1-2

INTRODUCTION:

1. *Explanation* by exposition (the context) and by descriptive language.

2. *Explanation* by exposition and by *application* giving an affirmation of results.

3. *Explanation* by division I and by descriptive language.

4. *Explanation* by exposition of background using two illustrations: (1) both direct introduction, (2) both factual, (3) both Biblical.

In the four brief chapters of Paul's letter to the church at Philippi the words "joy" and "rejoice" occur about sixteen or seventeen times. The pervading spirit of the epistle is that of joy. Someone has described the theme of joy in the Philippian letter as the melody of a musical composition. Another has described it as a rushing, happy mountain stream, singing its way to the plains below, now in the shadow and then out again, sometimes disappearing entirely from view and then breaking out again into the sunlight.

The amazing fact about this joy is that nothing in human circumstances can explain it. Actually, human circumstances were against it. Paul's joy was attained in spite of circumstances. Every Christian, in spite of everything, can be happy in Christ.

When the curtain rises on scene one, it is a dismal, dreary Monday morning in the city of Rome. The setting is the closely confining four walls of Paul's rented house in Rome. With him is a silent, surly Roman soldier. It is one of those days when one awakens with a sense of depression and finds it easier to count his troubles than to count his blessings. Let's suppose that the apostle experienced such a day.

Paul had long planned to visit Rome. To the Roman church he had written, "I have often intended to come to you (but thus far have been prevented)" (Rom. 1:13, RSV). He recognized Rome as the center of his world and knew of its significance for the preaching of the gospel. He had visioned its thronging streets and crowded market places. He had dreamed of the time when he would stand in the midst of its teeming crowds and preach the glorious gospel of redemption,

5. *Explanation* by exposition of the background using an illustration: (1) direct introduction, (2) factual, (3) Biblical.

6. *Explanation* by exposition of the background.

7. *Explanation* by exposition and by illustration: (1) direct introduction, (2) factual, (3) Biblical.

8. *Explanation* by exposition.

9. *Explanation* by exposition of text and context and by *application* showing relationship.

"the power of God unto salvation to every one that believeth" (Rom. 1:16).

Now in the providence of God he had come to Rome. "And so we came to Rome" (Acts 28:14, RSV). But he did not come as he had planned. He did not come as a free man to preach in the streets and marketplaces. He came to Rome as a prisoner, confined to the four walls of his own rented house, guarded day and night by Roman soldiers. It must have been a trying time for this servant of Christ so used to an active life.

This man of dynamic energy and intense dreams was confined to inactivity. It was a confinement not of his own asking or choosing. It would have been such a simple thing to have questioned, "But God, why?"

Tradition says the Paul was guarded, actually in chains, by a Roman soldier day and night. As an imperial prisoner—"I appeal to Caesar"—he was guarded by the imperial guards. They were the best of Roman soldiers. They were native born, received double pay, and were granted special privileges. Their officers had become men of significant political position. But to say that they were the best soldiers of the first century is not to say that they were understanding and sympathetic friends of the Christian apostle. If they were typical, they were surly, violent, gluttonous, drunken, and immoral.

For a man who loved Christian fellowship, as did the apostle, these were trying and vexing days. It was easy to think if not to say, "Lord, don't you think that you have made a mistake?"

Surprisingly, there were those within the Christian ranks in Rome who did not like Paul. Jealous of him and possibly fearful of their own positions of leadership, they sought to hurt him. "Some indeed preach Christ even of envy and strife . . . the one preach Christ . . . not sincerely, supposing to add affliction to my bonds" (Phil. 1:15-16). Conceiving Paul to be as small and petty as they, they supposed that they could affict him by their own successful achievements in the proclamation of the gospel while he was confined and inactive. One does not particularly expect sympathy and understanding from outsiders or possible enemies, but it comes as a particular shock when so-called Christian brethren are unkind and unloving.

10. *Explanation* of context by exposition.

In Philippians 1:20 the apostle expressed cloud.
could have hung over him like an appalling some hope for release from imprisonment. The context of the verse, however, reveals that he was uncertain. His destiny was in the hands of a Roman emperor, perhaps Nero, one of the most capricious, unpredictable, and likely most insane emperors that ever sat on the throne of the Empire.

11. *Explanation* by exposition.

There was no way of knowing what another day might bring. Every knock on the door could be an order of release, command to trial, or sentence of death. The uncertainty

12. *Explanation* by division II and by descriptive language (historical imagination).

If Paul on a dismal Monday morning ever permitted himself the doubtful pleasure of such dark thoughts, it would not have been for long. He must have shaken himself and remonstrated, "Now wait a minute. Brother Paul. You know better than all of this. God has been too good to you and the Savior too real for you to think like this." Even as he began to think of God's goodness, the sun began to break through the clouds and to shine through his small window. piercing the gloom and driving away the chill. There was growing light and warmth where once there was darkness and gloom.

13. *Explanation* by illustration: (1) direct introduction, (2) factual, (3) personal to the preacher.

Many years ago I walked in the door of a little country church where I was holding a revival. I suppose that I was as discouraged as a young preacher could ever have been. When I entered, the junior choir was singing, loudly if not well, "I am resting all my burdens on Philippians 4:19; I am resting all my burdens . . ." I am certain that I had read Philippians 4:19, but I did not then remember what it said. Quickly I turned in my Bible to read it: "But my God shall supply all your need according to his riches in glory by Christ Jesus."

14. *Explanation* of context by exposition.

The church at Philippi had remembered Paul. They had sent him a gift, "an odour of a sweet smell, a sacrifice acceptable, well pleasing to God." They had become agents of God in adequate provision for the apostle. He had seen demonstrated in his own life that God cares for his own. Paul knew and believed that God through Christ will care for and provide for his own.

15. *Application* showing results.

It is difficult to defeat or discourage one who believes in God's all-sufficient provision. When others falter and fail, the man who believes in God's care finds strength to undergird his faltering feet.

16. *Explanation* by exposition, and by illustration: (1) direct introduction, (2) hypothetical, (3) personally created by the preacher.

Paul had had his own strategic plans for evangelizing Rome. It was the strategy of a Christian statesman. Then God with sudden abruptness had taken his beautiful plans and swept them all away. In the place of proclamation of the gospel in street, marketplace, and philosopher's hall, God had substituted imprisonment, isolation, personal testimony to unlikely subjects, and the loneliness of inactivity. I think that if I had been in Paul's place I might have protested, "But God, haven't you made a mistake? My plans are the best strategy."

17. *Explanation* by exposition and by illustration: (1) direct introduction, (2) factual, (3) Biblical.

Yet, listen to him! "The things which happened unto me have fallen out rather unto the furtherance of the gospel" (Phil. 1:12). What is he saying? Simply this: God's way is the best way, although not necessarily the easiest. He was but asserting in his own experience what he had written to the Roman church. "And we know that all things work together for good to them that love God, to them who are the called according to his purpose" (Rom. 8:28).

18. *Explanation* by exposition (using context).

The gospel had reached into places and had touched people whom it would not have reached had Paul been a free man. His bonds became manifest as being in Christ throughout the imperial ground and in the imperial palace (Phil. 1:13). The saving gospel had reached into Caesar's household (Phil. 4:22). Paul had discovered that God's providential way for one's life is best. He found strength in the realization that God's way is ultimately the best way.

19. *Explanation* by exposition (using context). Also *application* showing results.

In Philippians 4:13 the apostle said, "I can do all things through Christ which strengtheneth me." The apostle had discovered in the indwelling Christ a constant and abiding source of strength. When the day grew long and the companionship intolerable, Christ was a real and infilling presence. When his heart was tempted to falter and when resolution wavered, the infilling strength of Christ sustained him. When one believes in and knows in experience the presence of Christ and quietly rests himself upon the surety of this presence, there is strength for every test and trial.

20. *Explanation* by division III and by descriptive language.

The sun, which had filtered through the small window and had begun to drive away the gloom and chill of Paul's prison, was now shining in warmth and brilliance. Possible depression fled before its brilliance. We are not surprised to discover that the apostle was happy. Joy unspeakable possessed his heart.

21. *Explanation* by exposition of text background and context, and by illustration: (1) direct introduction, (2) factual, (3) Biblical.

The church at Philippi had sent him a gift. The gift was not important, but the fellowship that it represented was. The church at Philippi had its origin during the second missionary journey in the conversion of the household of Lydia and the experience of the Philippian jailer and his household (Acts 16:14-40). From the beginning this church had loved and shared with the apostle. For a time they had not been in touch with him, mainly because they lacked opportunity, but now at last they had sent a gift of fellowship. "But I rejoice in the Lord greatly, that now at the last your care of me hath flourished again; wherein ye were also careful, but ye lacked opportunity" (Phil. 4:10). Their love, prayers, and gifts had followed him across the first century world. "I thank my God . . . for your fellowship in the gospel from the first day until now" (Phil. 1:3,5). They had sent one of their choice young men across land and sea until at last he stood before the old man as the symbol of their love and devotion. What it meant to have Christian friends and to love and be loved broke in anew upon the apostle, and as it did, it set the joy bells ringing in his heart. "I thank my God upon every remembrance of you" (Phil. 1:3).

22. *Application* by showing results.

When one has Christian friends and shares in Christian fellowship, there is a joy beyond all joys. One can be, as was the apostle Paul, a radiantly happy Christian in the midst of adverse circumstances.

23. *Explanation* by illustration: (1) direct introduction, (2) factual, (3) Biblical. Also explanation by exposition of the background and by descriptive language (historical imagination).

Paul had written to the Roman church, "For I am not ashamed of the gospel of Christ: for it is the power of God unto salvation to every one that believeth" (Rom. 1:16). He had seen the reality of this assertion demonstrated in Rome in the imperial guard and in Caesar's household. It could have happened this way: In the course of the change of the guard there came to Paul a young and dissolute Roman soldier. Knowing Paul as we do, we may be sure that, moved with compassion, he began to speak to him of the Lord Jesus Christ. The first reaction was abrupt and violent as the young man struck Paul roughly across the face, saying, "Never speak to me again of that name." And in the changing of the guard the young man returned now and again. And as you expect, the apostle spoke to him again and yet again. Then one beautiful morning in Rome the young man slipped his big hand over the frail aged one of the apostle, as he got up from his knees, and said, "I take him as my Savior." The next day orders arrived, and his cohort was transferred to the far distant outpost of Britain as representative of the Emperor's interest. At least one young man and perhaps others went as representatives of Him who is King of kings and Lord of lords.

24. *Explanation* by exposition and by illustration: (1) direct, (2) factual, (3) Biblical.

Paul had seen what the gospel could do with Roman soldiers and imperial servants. He knew its power to save demonstrated in the most difficult situations in the imperial city. "But thanks be to God, which giveth us the victory through our Lord Jesus Christ" (I Cor. 15:57).

CONCLUSION:

25. *Application* by affirmation of relationship and by exhortation.

"Rejoice in the Lord alway: and again I say, Rejoice." Impossible? No. Through strength from God in Christ it is possible in spite of every human circumstance. You can be happy in Christ regardless of your situation. If you are not happy in Christ, you are living below your privilege as His child. The joy of God is yours for the claiming. Reach out and appropriate what He wants to give. "Rejoice in the Lord alway."

"A Drama in Christian Joy" is a direct Biblical sermon with a supportive objective and a rhetorical structure. The introduction is well developed with five paragraphs. The body of the sermon, with three major points and four subpoints under I, two subpoints under II, and two subpoints under III, is well developed. By keeping in mind that it is explanation of text and context which basically determines whether a sermon is Biblical or not, one can appreciate the large amount of explanation used in this message. In style the elements of clarity, appeal, and force stand out.

In regard to improvements, the conclusion needs lengthening and strengthening, and the paragraphs throughout would benefit from lengthening and strengthening. Explanation is exceptionally strong, but illustration and application are deficient.

Chapter 10

PRACTICAL PROCEDURES

On no point in homiletics is there a greater diversity of opinion than on practical procedures for preparing sermons. Actually, there are as many methods of preparing sermons as there are preachers. When the views of individual preachers, professors of homiletics, and authors of books on sermon preparation are considered, the number of ideas on preparing sermons is quite impressive.

No one can claim to have the only technique for preparing a sermon, any more than he can claim to have the only technique for throwing a football, hitting a baseball, or striking a golf ball. Many variables influence sports and preaching performances: personality factors, personal ability, and practice. Techniques for preparing sermons, throwing a football, hitting a baseball, and striking a golf ball vary considerably. Some techniques are obviously more desirable in certain areas than others.

In order that the suggestions of this chapter relate to Biblical preaching as much as possible, they have been drawn from the great preachers of preaching history, from the observations found in basic textbooks on techniques, and from numerous experiments with both graduate and undergraduate students in preaching classes. All ideas presented are designed to help the minister do one tremendous work: to prepare and preach Biblical messages.

No claim is made that these suggestions are the only workable procedures for preparing sermons, or that they will work for every preacher. or that they will work each time even for those who like them and use them on a regular basis. Rather, a simple claim is made that these suggestions will work. Very likely, they will work for most men who thoughtfully study them and diligently practice them. They are worthy of investigation. They will prove to be simple and natural to some men and perhaps complex and unnatural to others. They are worthy of your trying and testing because they will enable you to prepare and preach Biblical messages.

Donald MacLeod, in *Here Is My Method*, C. S. Roddy, in *We Prepare and Preach*, and the author, in *Southern Baptist Preaching* and in *More Southern Baptist Preaching*, have set out a picture of wide variety in sermon methodology. All four books, however, are general and non-specific as to sermon types. Because this volume treats of Biblical preaching as the way to have reformation in preaching, all suggested procedures point in one specific direction: toward the preparation and delivery of Biblical messages. Because of this specificity, therefore, definite methods best compatible with obtaining Biblical sermons are suggested.

MATTERS TO BE DECIDED EARLY IN PREPARATION

The most logical and natural place for a Biblical sermon to begin is in the Bible. This statement is so obviously true that many sermonizers constantly overlook it. While it is true that a sermon may begin in any number of places, it is still true that a straight path from the Bible to a Biblical sermon represents the shortest and most direct route to authentic Biblical preaching.

Locating the Sermon Idea in Scripture

The minister who desires to preach Biblical sermons will devise a procedure which enables him to do so. It would be an act of folly for the preacher who seriously wishes to preach Biblical sermons to allow chance procedures to guide him.

The most direct procedure in preparing Biblical messages is to begin the sermon with a text. The preacher can learn to originate his messages in Scripture by maintaining a regular program of Bible study, by constantly seeking for choice preaching texts, and by carefully planning to preach through the great books of the Bible. In more specific terms, the preacher may achieve a procedure which enables him to secure texts for preaching by three methods: (1) by keeping a text "seed file," or by planning his preaching around the Bible, (2) by purposefully securing variety in the choice of texts, and (3) by purposefully obtaining texts for preaching through fresh homiletic approaches.

First, the minister may purposefully secure texts for preaching by keeping a text "seed file," or by planning his preaching around the Bible. Beneficial results come to the minister who plans his pulpit work in a systematic way by the use of a one, three, six, or twelve-month preaching plan. Mature and experienced pastors find a six or twelve-month plan helpful while younger and more inexperienced men find a one or three-month plan more useful.

In a preaching plan which embraces a procedure for locating usable texts, the minister needs calendars of various types (secular, denominational, church, and personal), an understanding of the various needs of the congregation (needs as understood in terms of the major objectives for preaching), and a systematic Bible and prayer hour procedure (the mid-week service).

In preparing this preaching plan one should follow a few mechanical steps: (1) the preparation of a monthly chart of services for each month in the plan whether one, three, six, or twelve; (2) the preparation of individual folders for each Sunday service for the duration of the plan; and (3) the preparation of at least one folder for the Bible and prayer hour.

By having an entire month's plan on one page in monthly charts, the preacher can see clearly his full plan for the days ahead. If, for example, the plan embraces six months, the minister may spread his six sheets before him and examine in a few minutes one-half of a year's work. A comprehensive view often yields rich returns in pointing out errors, omissions, contradictions, and useless items. Through this comprehensive view the preacher can determine whether or not he has included a sufficient emphasis on Biblical preaching.

By putting into the individual folders all data which becomes available, the preacher has a constant flow of ideas and texts accessible. Into these folders the preacher will channel each text suggestion, and all other thoughts, ideas, illustrations, references in books, notes from lectures, sermon seeds, and notes on personal experience. Everything which the preacher sees, hears, reads, and observes becomes data for preaching. In due time this data will mature and come forth in appropriate places in creative Biblical sermons.

By planning to use Bible course teaching in the midweek service, the preacher will grow in Bible knowledge, will impart much Scriptural truth to his people, and will lay the foundation for future Biblical sermons.[1] Moreover, the preacher will break the sterile pattern, if he is in it, which traps so many men of having "three points and a poem" three times a week. If, for example, in these midweek services the minister teaches through a Bible book every three or four months, he will

---

[1]Course teaching (and course preaching) involves the consecutive use of texts from one book from the Bible from chapter one, verse one through the last verse of the last chapter. Course preaching differs from series preaching in that the former follows the Biblical text and the latter unfolds a theme such as faith in a series of messages. Each is valuable according to the needs of minister and people.

cover fifteen to twenty books over the span of five years. By using course teaching, the minister will store up unlimited Bible data which will later produce Biblical sermons. At all times in this preaching plan, keep the focus on securing texts for preaching.

The procedure of using course teaching has been criticized as being dry, boring, and barren. This accusation is true only when the preacher has been shoddy in study and dull in presentation. Depth study and creative imagination, coupled with an effective teaching method, will revolutionize the Bible and prayer hour.

Second, the minister may purposefully secure texts for preaching by deliberately selecting a wide variety of types of texts. He may begin by securing variety in text location. By making use of texts from the Pentateuch, the historical books, the prophets, the writings, the Synoptic Gospels, Acts and the general epistles, the Pauline epistles, and the Johannine materials, the preacher uses all of the Bible and thereby enriches his sermons. Moreover, the minister may select variety in text length. By purposefully selecting texts consisting of "golden words," key phrases and clauses, powerful sentences, beloved verses, attractive paragraphs, great chapters, cohesive sections of beloved books, as well as entire books, testaments, or the whole Bible, the minister will add freshness and variety of approach.

In addition to these two ways of selecting texts of varied nature, the preacher may select texts by focus of the passage. From Chalmer E. Faw comes a threefold suggestion which may be used for many texts.[2] Faw suggests using focus from three perspectives: (1) the focus on the dominant idea of the text, (2) the focus on the action or event of the text, and (3) the focus on the key person or persons of the passage. The concept of focus may be expanded to include the objective-subjective perspectives of the key character or characters of the text. Moreover, the focus may call attention to one or more basic personality factors of those prominent in the passage: spiritual, mental, moral, emotional, and physical characteristics. Again, the focus may center on motivational issues of the people involved in the text. When the preacher shifts the focus from the dominant idea of the central idea of the text, he should be careful to see that the text actually supplies the data for the changed emphasis. Unless exegetical skill be exercised in these matters, the sermon will depart quickly and easily from the Biblical path.

The preacher may secure variety in text selection by meeting the need inherent in each of the six basic objectives. By examining the text carefully for inherent purpose the preacher may find the exact

---

[2]Faw, *op. cit.*, pp. 24-33.

objective he seeks. The preacher may also use special occasions for securing variety in text choice. The various special days, weeks, occasions, times, seasons, denominational emphases, national weeks, and church events should be allowed to point out needed texts. By speaking to some of the multitudinous occasions, rich variety in the choice of texts is secured.

Third, the minister may purposefully secure texts for preaching through fresh homiletic approaches. A constant plague on the pulpit practices of certain men is to use the same form and same approach over and over with the same people. These men seemingly read the New Testament admonition to "preach the gospel" as to "use the same homiletical procedure." It is a disadvantage to be known as "Brother Obvious."

The minister can secure pleasing variety in his homiletic procedure by using course preaching on a systematic basis for his regular Sunday sermons. By preaching systematically and carefully through a great book of the Bible the minister will have his next text always available. The preacher will select his text from Amos or Matthew (or whatever book is being used) according to the need of the week. He is free to skip passages or to combine them as he desires. His purpose is to preach consecutively on the dominant ideas of his Biblical book. Invariably course preaching will be richer and more profitable if the preacher has previously taught through his book at the Bible and prayer hour.

Normally, the preacher will desire to alternate his course preaching between the Sunday morning and Sunday evening services. For six months of the year the minister may desire to have course preaching on Sunday morning and for six months to have it on Sunday evening. By so doing the minister will always speak to the most faithful members of his church, and he will also reach other groups who attend only one Sunday service.

Moreover, the preacher can secure pleasing variety in his homiletic procedure by using variations in sermon form. By using simple Biblical homilies, advanced Biblical homilies, and rhetorical Biblical sermons of various types, all with direct Biblical authority, the minister will constantly refresh himself and his people. At times, the preacher will desire to use these basic sermon forms with indirect Biblical authority, casual Biblical authority, and combination Biblical authority. When direct Biblical authority is the staple of the preaching diet, variations may be used periodically with pleasing results.

Finally, the minister can secure pleasing variety in his homiletic procedure by writing sermon manuscripts once a week. The teaching lesson at the midweek hour, as well as many sermons, will be delivered from outline notes. Though speaking from outlines allows the preacher freedom to soar oratorically, he will also benefit from the discipline of producing sermon manuscripts on a regular basis. Only by examining carefully each line of his manuscript can a preacher know whether or not he has prepared a Biblical sermon. A minister cannot be sure that an outline will produce a Biblical sermon until that outline has been developed in a fairly full manner. By forcing himself to write out sermon manuscripts, the preacher can assure himself that he has used Scripture properly.

For many preachers, no work is more difficult than that of writing a sermon manuscript. Often this difficulty results from one of several problems: a lack of time, an inadequate grammatical foundation, a lack of practice in writing, a refusal to be disciplined, a lack of incentive, an overuse of the materials of others, a preoccupation with counseling, administrative work, or visitation to the neglect of homiletic work, and laziness. Writing sermon manuscripts is difficult and demanding, but it is not impossible. Perhaps one or more of the following suggestions will aid someone in his desire to write sermon manuscripts. (1) The minister may begin the process of writing sermon manuscripts by writing the introduction and conclusion for as many of his sermons as he can. From this point, the preacher can move to writing full sermons. (2) The minister may speak the sermon aloud sentence by sentence and then write down his words. (3) He may speak the entire message aloud, record it, and have it transcribed. (4) He may record his message as it is preached, have it transcribed, and then edit it carefully. (5) The minister may write about 50 percent of one sermon each week and then gradually increase this percentage. (6) The minister may write out a full manuscript once a month and then increase his work rate until he produces an average of one sermon manuscript per week. (7) The minister may begin the task by writing out one sermon each week. By whatever process the preacher uses for learning to write sermon manuscripts, he should gain victory in this area.

Relating All Sermon Ideas to Texts

Beginning sermons with texts obviously is desirable, acceptable, and workable methodology. What does a preacher do, however, with an idea for a sermon which does not begin in Scripture and which he cannot ignore? Ideas possess wonderful and fearful power, almost as if endowed with human tenacity to catch and to hold captive a minister's mind. Spurgeon talked of ideas which capture and hold the preacher until they were preached. What does a minister do with this type of idea? The wise minister preaches it! He does more, however.

Each sermon begins with an idea. This idea is the originating thought which ultimately produces a sermon. The idea may come from one or more of five possible sources. First, the original idea may emerge from a Biblical idea (from a general Biblical concept or from a specific passage of Scripture) ; second, the idea may come from an observation of congregational needs; third, the idea may come from a planned program of preaching; fourth, the idea may come from a flash of inspiration; and fifth, the idea may come from the preacher's personal experiences.

When the idea for a sermon first comes, the minister should record it, identify the source (one of the five), and examine it for its possible Biblical relationship (general or specific). Those ideas which come from Biblical perspectives should lead more easily to Biblical sermons. Occasionally, when the sermon thought starts with a source other than the primary one (a general or specific Biblical source), the idea may also have a proper Biblical relationship at the same time. The preacher may discover a congregational need and simultaneously or immediately associate a Biblical thought with it. Or, the preacher may plan his preaching program around Biblical course preaching and around Bible teaching. Moreover, those vague but real flashes of inspiration will often come clothed in Biblical form. Finally, the preacher's personal experiences will often yield ideas which, while personal, are also Biblically based. When the original thought for the sermon comes from one of these four non-Biblical sources and the idea is at the same time Biblically related, then these ideas should also lead to Biblical sermons.

There are occasions, however, when the original idea comes from one of the four sources other than Scripture but is without a valid Biblical relationship. When the idea is not Biblically related, the preacher must take immediate steps to give the thought either a general or specific Biblical foundation. In order to be a Biblical preacher, a minister should form the habit of immediately relating his non-Biblical original ideas to Biblical ideas. The original non-Biblical idea should be given a Biblical foundation by relating it to a general Biblical concept or to a specific text. By avoiding the temptation in preparation to jump immediately from the original non-Biblical idea to body construction, as many preachers commonly do, the minister can train himself to be a Biblical preacher.

The process by which a preacher connects a non-Biblical idea to a Scriptural basis is a highly individual and personal one. Usually the process moves from a general non-Biblical thought to a general Biblical thought and then to a specific text. For example, the popular slogan "Crime does not pay" may suggest the general Scriptural thought that God punishes sin. From this broad Biblical thought, the preacher may move to Romans 6:23, ASV: "For the wages of sin is death; but the free gift of God is eternal life in Christ Jesus our Lord." As to how quickly and efficiently a preacher can move from non-Biblical to Biblical ideas and texts will depend upon his general knowledge of Scripture, his program of Bible study, and the nature of his devotional and prayer life. Obviously, the minister who has a ready grasp of great sections of the Bible, who studies his Bible constantly, and who "prays without ceasing" will be most efficient in moving from the original non-Biblical idea for the sermon to a relevant and compatible text. *Further sermon preparation should not proceed until the original idea and a text are matched.*

Recording a Tentative Thesis and Purpose

The combination of original idea and compatible text may say something definite and interesting to the preacher. When they do, the combination has rich preaching potential. The minister who is excited with his original idea and compatible text will discover that an affirmation (a proposition *or* a thesis) may be produced by the combination of the two. When the preacher brings the original idea and text together, sparks of inspiration, which can be expressed as a thesis and which will call for action on the part of the congregation, may be ignited. The thesis is a declaration of the essence of the sermon while the purpose is a call for action. Even at this early stage of preparation, the minister may get his first thoughts on the essence of the sermon when he brings together the original idea and the compatible text. Later, the thesis and purpose must be refined to bring them into perfect harmony with the text.

The preacher should determine at all cost to keep the thesis and purpose tentative for a time. Unless both remain flexible and tentative, the preacher faces the possibility of allowing a non-Biblical thesis and purpose to control the sermon. The thesis and purpose must remain tentative until the preacher interprets the text and writes out a statement concerning the central idea of the text. When the process of interpretation has been completed and the central idea stated, the text as interpreted should control the remainder of the sermon process. The text as interpreted should point backward to control and purify the original idea, the thesis, and the purpose. Often the thesis and purpose must be rewritten in order to insure their Biblical nature and structure. Moreover, the text data should point forward and control the title, body, conclusion, introduction, and invitation.

Suspending All Work Until Exegesis Has Been Completed

For the minister who earnestly desires to be a Biblical preacher, grave homiletical perils exist in that he is tempted to begin the construction of his message immediately after the location of a text. Sometimes he does not wait on a text. He will discover an idea and then begin sermon preparation, or he will discover an idea, relate it to a text, and then begin sermon preparation. Not one of these methods represents the true point of departure for authentic Biblical sermons. If a preacher begins the construction immediately after any one of these three, he will produce a Biblical sermon only by luck, accident, or strong determination. On rare occasions the preacher may be inspired to write out a tentative thesis and purpose. If both are kept tentative until Scripture study has been completed, they may be useful to the careful preacher.

Because the text data must control the sermon, all homiletical work must be held in suspension following the discovery of a text. To exercise a waiting discipline upon the discovery of an exciting text taxes the resources of a preacher. Who has not heard a text cry, as did Spurgeon, "Preach me or I will not let you go"? The wise preacher knows that he must first study his text.

Using the Critical Method to Study the Text

Several guides are available to assist the preacher in studying the Bible. First, he may begin the study of the text by making a thorough personal investigation of the total text. Personal investigation means to discover as much data as possible about the passage before turning to research resources outside the Bible. Personal investigation of the text should begin by reading it many times in a favorite version of Scripture. There is no substitute for an intimate knowledge of the words and thoughts of the text. After mastery of the plain meaning of the text has been secured, one should make an analytical outline of the passage. This outline need not be a polished or refined one but may consist of personal summary statements about the meaning of each verse. The preacher should then list in simple consecutive order the ideas presented in the text. Again, he should keep the simple analytical outline available and read the text numerous times in several additional versions. He should stop and compare the various words used to translate the same thoughts in the various versions. Each preacher would benefit by possessing the King James Version, the 1901 American Standard Version, the 1946-52 Revised Standard Version, the New English Bible, and several modern translations such as those of Moffatt, Williams, Goodspeed, and Phillips. A meditative, thoughtful examination of a text in six or seven of these translations will often give a minister a substantial grasp of his text before he does additional study. Again, he should read and study the passage in Hebrew or Greek if possible. A command of the Biblical languages is a valuable tool to possess. Furthermore, he should think intently about the text. He should carry the text in his active consciousness and give frequent attention to mental efforts to probe the depths of the selected passage of Scripture. In addition, it is helpful to revive the old-fashioned custom of discussing texts with fellow preachers or fellow Christians. Perhaps a friend will be surprised to be asked the meaning of Genesis 1-3 rather than to be asked the latest batting average of baseball's most recent hero or the latest news from the stock market, but he will survive and enjoy the experience. Finally, pray and meditate about the text. God has promised to instruct His children in all truth, and He will illumine the mind of the inquiring disciple.

Obviously, this type of personal investigation cannot be accomplished between Saturday and Sunday. If a minister takes seriously the task of coming to grips with a text which will shape and mold his sermon, he must begin early in the week or weeks in advance. No one really knows how early this procedure should begin since no one really knows what early means in this connection. Each minister should determine for himself how soon he should begin this process of personal involvement with a selected text.

Second, in addition to making a personal investigation of the text, the minister should make a careful scholarly investigation of the passage. A scholarly investigation involves the effective use of such research tools as commentaries, dictionaries, atlases, grammars, historical works, theological volumes, and any and all other tools demanded by the text. A full investigation of a text involves discovering the grammatical, historical, lexical, syntactical, rhetorical, practical, spiritual, and theological facts of the passage. Each of these will not necessarily be needed for each text, but each one that is needed should be investigated.

In addition to using technical works for Scripture study, the preacher may also desire to use practical volumes. Practical volumes consist of light or popular commentaries, books of sermons, and devotional writings. More benefit will accrue to the preacher if he reserves practical study until he has completed technical study. By using solid technical data as a foundation, the preacher will be more likely to receive Biblical sermonic benefit from his practical readings than if the process be reversed. Following technical and devotional study, the minister should rewrite his first simple analytical outline. By this time in text study, the preacher will be able to prepare an accurate and technical outline of the text. This revised technical outline, when translated into contemporary sermonic terms, can serve as the essence of the authentic Biblical sermon.

Stating the Central Idea of the Text

Following a careful critical study of the text, the minister should move to a prayerful condensation and synthesizing of the heart of the passage. This condensation and synthesizing of the heart of the text will enable him to draw out or simply to state the central idea of the text. In addition to securing the central idea of the text, the minister will examine his Scripture for possible subdivisions, minor or secondary ideas, and for formal as well as informal ways of developing the text. All valid ideas should be recorded. The central idea of the text is the bridge, the springboard, or the launching pad for moving the sermon data from the Biblical world to the contemporary world. Without the historical thesis to guide the sermon process the minister will experience grave difficulty in preparing Biblical sermons.

Translating the Historical Thesis into a Contemporary Thesis

The contemporary thesis for a direct Biblical sermon is a present tense statement of the central idea of the text. The thesis, also known as the proposition and affirmation, represents the thought which the minister believes God wishes to speak to a modern congregation from a specific text on a particular occasion. To the degree that the thesis moves away from the central idea of the text, to that degree the thesis is non-Biblical. There are, therefore, affirmations which point toward indirect Biblical sermons, casual Biblical sermons, and combination Biblical sermons. Obviously, then, the minister seeking to prepare a Biblical message will write his thesis so that it is a present tense state-ment of the central idea of the text.

Establishing the Purpose of the Text

By the time the minister has completed his investigation of his text, has stated the central idea of the text, and has written his affirmation, he will know the intent and purpose of his Scripture passage. Often the knowledge of purpose come early in critical study, and often it becomes clear only after the contemporary thesis has been written. When purpose is known, the minister will identify which broad area is involved and then write out the specific objective. The specific objective always completes the proposition by pointing to the specific

248 A QUEST FOR REFORMATION IN PREACHING

results desired from the sermon under construction. The more precise the language which can be used, the better the specific objective will be.

MATTERS TO BE DECIDED INTERMEDIATELY IN PREPARATION

Following the preparation of the early matters in sermon preparation, two intermediate procedures are involved. First, the minister should read as widely as he can about his text and related materials in order to secure other materials from theology, ethics, philosophy, history, church history, and a host of related disciplines. Second, the preacher should add a dimension of maturity to his homiletic work by a continuing spiritual relationship with the Lord, by the careful use of time, and by the creative use of his subconscious mind. Because of limitations of space, these two intermediate processes must be merely indicated. However, numerous works in basic homiletics treat both matters of securing enriching data and dimensions of maturity for the message.

MATTERS TO BE DECIDED LATE IN PREPARATION

Following the preliminary stage of sermon preparation—which involves securing a text, determing the central idea of the text, translating the central idea into a proposition, and determining the purpose of the text and sermon—and following the intermediate matters of securing additional materials and achieving sermon maturity, the minister will engage in the final construction work for his message. Six items are involved: title, body, conclusion, introduction, invitation(s), and style. Considerations concerning space forbid more than a brief mention of these sermon items. Basic works on general homiletics abound in details on each of these six.

Preparing an Attractive Title

The title, or the name of the sermon, is created from the unity of five items: the original idea and text, central idea of the text, thesis, and purpose. The title should be fresh, appealing, contemporary, and divisible most of the time.

In order to insure a divisible element in the title, one should use either a sentence or phrase. If the sentence form is chosen, one should use a question, imperative, or assertive sentence. If the phrase form is chosen, the preacher should use a phrase with an emphatic word or a phrase with a modifying word. Examples of these five types of titles (the divisible words *underlined* are) :

Why Do Men Believe in Prayer?
Crown Christ Your King
Jesus Is the Lord of Life
The *Power* of Faith ..
The *Second Coming* of Christ

Preparing an Authentic Biblical Body

In brief, the sermon body of an authentic Biblical sermon is constructed through the framing of an acceptable outline and then is completed through an adequate development of that outline.[3]

Preparing a Purposeful Conclusion

The target of the sermon is the specific purpose on the specific objective. The time and place to press the purpose on the hearers is the
conclusion. By relating the entire conclusion to the specific objective,
the conclusion will have a high degree of unity and vitality. Apply and
illustrate the specific objective and move directly to the public invitation.

Preparing an Appealing and Informative Introduction

In writing the introduction, give careful attention to two matters.
The key places or sections of a good introduction are the opening
sentence or sentences and the bridge or transition sentence. By giving
attention to see that the introduction has rich, fresh, vital, and relevant
material in these places, the preacher will assure strength in interest
and continuity.

In writing the introduction, one should also give careful attention
to five important items. In the introduction the text (and context if
needed), the central idea of the text, the thesis, purpose (some men do
not present the purpose in the introduction lest too much data be given
too early), and title should be presented to the audience. The presentation of these items may take many direct or indirect forms, but these
five items should be delineated. One or more of the five may be used
as the core material for the opening sentences, may be used to present
the issue or thrust of the sermon, may be used for the bridge sentence,
or may be the focus of the overall content of the introduction.

Preparing Moving Invitations

The invitation may take the form of a challenge for action in the

---

[3]See Chapter nine for a full treatment of this procedure.

heart, a call for a counseling session with the pastor, a call for a public committal of some type, a challenge for overt conduct in everyday life to reveal decision in the heart, or a call for some combination of these. The invitation should be based on the specific objective for the sermon. Responses may be varied as indicated in the first part of this paragraph. Moreover, more than one invitation may be given. After the minister gives an invitation compatible with his sermon purpose, he may wish to add a second, a third, or even a fourth invitation. His desire and the needs of the people will determine the procedure.

Polishing the Style of the Sermon

When the minister completes his sermon outline and his plans for functional development, he is ready to write the sermon and then to polish it. He should write out the sermon in manuscript form by following the outline, point by point. He should write rapidly with feeling and conviction, not stopping to correct errors, to check spelling, or investigate additional data. He should write as if he were preaching, putting life, meaning, and feeling into the manuscript. He should write vigorously but not carelessly. Following the first writing, which will be a rough draft, the minister should check the entire manuscript for errors of all types. He should correct spelling errors, eliminate punctuation mistakes, rephrase grammatical blunders, and eliminate all possible errors.

Following the writing and checking steps, one should polish the manuscript carefully. By now the sermon appears somewhat as it will be preached, but work remains to be done. He should polish the entire manuscript with loving care. He should be careful to see that the basic elements of style (clarity, appeal, and force) are present to a large degree. The minister should rewrite as much of the material as necessary. He should not hesitate to pull out choice passages, favorite illustration, and basic convictions and recast them in order to secure the exact phrasing desired. No effort is too strenuous for the production of an excellent sermon.

He should test the manuscript on one or more objective readers. He should not fear their questions, doubts, misunderstandings, and outright criticisms. Invaluable assistance can be secured from objective readers.

As a final process of testing the sermon, the minister may profitably ask himself the following seven questions:

One: "Am I spiritually prepared and qualified to preach this sermon?"

Two: "Did my sermon begin in Scripture? If it did not, has it been related to a Scriptural text?"

Three: "Have I exhausted the meaning of the text by drawing out the central idea of the text and other related ideas?"

Four: "Have I enriched the text with related materials?"

Five: "Have I matured the entire sermonic process?"

Six: "Have I properly related my original idea and text, central idea of the text, thesis, and purpose, and then from all these built the title, body, conclusion, introduction, and invitation?"

Seven: "Have I reworked, correlated, and polished all parts of the sermon?"

If a preacher can answer "yes" to each of these tests, he is ready to preach his sermon. And his sermon will be Biblical!

Through the preaching of authentic Biblical sermons reformation can come to preaching.

May God grant to each one the joy of sharing in the reformation of preaching!

> God of grace and God of glory,
> On Thy people pour Thy power;
> Crown Thine ancient church's story,
> Bring her bud to glorious flower.
> Grant us wisdom, Grant us courage,
> For the facing of this hour,
> For the facing of this hour.
>
> Set our feet on lofty places;
> Gird our lives that they may be
> Armored with all Christ-like graces
> In the fight to set men free.
> Grant us wisdom, Grant us courage,
> That we fail not man nor Thee!
> That we fail not man nor Thee![4]

---

[4]Used by permission of Harry Emerson Fosdick